THE SELF-MANAGEMENT PSYCHOLOGY SERIES
Carl E. Thoresen, Ph.D., *General Editor*
Stanford University

This series of self-help books presents techniques that really work based on scientifically sound research.

Designed with the layman in mind, each book presents a step-by-step method you can readily apply to solve real problems you confront in everyday life. Each is written by a respected behavioral scientist who has achieved success in applying these same techniques.

THOMAS J. COATES is a post-doctoral research associate at the Center for Educational Research, Stanford University.

CARL E. THORESEN is a professor of education and psychology at Stanford University.

BOOKS IN THE SERIES

How to Control Your Drinking, by William R. Miller and Ricardo F. Muñoz

Becoming Orgasmic: A Sexual Growth Program for Women, by Julia Heiman, Leslie LoPiccolo, and Joseph LoPiccolo

How to Sleep Better: A Drug-Free Program for Overcoming Insomnia, by Thomas Coates and Carl E. Thoresen

How to Become an Ex-Smoker, by Carl E. Thoresen

Take It Off and Keep It Off: A Behavioral Program for Weight Loss and Exercise, by D. Balfour Jeffrey and Roger C. Katz

Don't Be Afraid: A Program for Overcoming Fears and Phobias, by Gerald Rosen

PRENTICE-HALL, INC., *Englewood Cliffs, New Jersey 07632*

HOW TO SLEEP BETTER

A Drug-Free Program For Overcoming Insomnia

A SPECTRUM BOOK

Thomas J. Coates / Carl E. Thoresen

Library of Congress Cataloging in Publication Data

Coates, Thomas J   Date
How to sleep better.

(Self-management psychology series) (A Spectrum Book)
Bibliography: p.
Includes index.
1. Insomnia.   I. Thoresen, Carl E., joint author.   II. Title.
RC548.C6   6168949   77-5646
ISBN 0-13-433862-6
ISBN 0-13-433854-5 pbk.

To my brothers and sisters—
Ray, Rita, Terry, and Joe.

T.J.C.

To Kay,
whose patience and love
help make my nights
(and our days)

C.E.T.

A Spectrum Book

10 9 8 7 6 5 4 3 2 1

Printed in the United States of America

PRENTICE-HALL INTERNATIONAL, INC., *London*
PRENTICE-HALL OF AUSTRALIA PTY. Limited, *Sydney*
PRENTICE-HALL OF CANADA, LTD., *Toronto*
PRENTICE-HALL OF INDIA PRIVATE LIMITED, *New Delhi*
PRENTICE-HALL OF JAPAN, INC., *Tokyo*
PRENTICE-HALL OF SOUTHEAST ASIA PTE. LTD., *Singapore*

Contents

Preface

This book has a single purpose: to teach persons suffering from unsatisfactory sleep certain skills so that they can sleep better without having to use drugs.

Insomnia, in one form or another, affects at least 20 million Americans most of the time (and almost all of us some of the time). Until now, persons bothered by insomnia had only one alternative: sleeping pills. But this is really no solution at all; in fact, almost all medications ("over-the-counter" or prescribed) make the problem worse rather than better. In the past few years, we and other investigators have been searching and experimenting with ways to help persons to improve their sleep without medications. The results of that research are presented here for you to follow and use to improve your sleep. We also wanted to inform physicians and mental health counselors about these procedures so that they might know that there are alternatives to drugs. We hope this book will help them in their professional practice.

The approach we use is termed *behavioral self-management.* Briefly stated, these procedures are designed to teach persons the skills necessary for them to reach personally meaningful and important goals. We begin by presenting an overview of current sleep research. Readers are then invited to watch their sleep closely and monitor conditions associated with good as well as poor sleep. Next, basic physical and mental relaxation procedures are presented, followed by procedures for returning to sleep when awakened in the night. Special attention is given to designing a good sleep environment. Individual problem-solving techniques are then presented, followed by strategies for reducing daytime stress and improving mood during the day. Some suggestions for maintaining progress and preventing backsliding finish the treatment procedures.

In the appendices, resource materials for the professional and the interested non-professional include an overview of the technical literature on the procedures presented along with suggestions for further reading.

One important theme runs through our approach. We call it *personal science.* We don't pretend to have the answer for everyone, nor do we want our readers to apply what we offer blindly and without critical reflection. We do propose specific strategies, to be sure. But more than that, we propose a *process* of *personal problem solving* that teaches you how to look at your problem, how to analyze it from various perspectives, how to propose creative solutions, and how to test them out to see if they work.

In the long run, only you know what you need and what really works. If you can learn to be a personal scientist, you will have taken the most important step in conquering poor sleep and, perhaps, solving other problems as well.

We have confidence in these strategies. They have been tested experimentally. We have also evaluated the effects of this book with groups of persons complaining of poor sleep. The results have been encouraging. We believe you will find these procedures useful in overcoming your own sleep difficulties or in working with clients who need help in learning how to sleep better.

Acknowledgements

Many persons have contributed to the development of these techniques and to this book. We would like to express our gratitude to them.

Bob Phillips encouraged us a great deal in the early stages of our research, offering valuable technical assistance at critical points. We thank him for his continued support. He read versions of the manuscript carefully and offered many helpful comments and reactions.

The continuing interest and collaboration of Drs. William Dement, Vincent Zarcone, Christian Guilleminault, and Joanna Van den Hoed of the Stanford University Sleep Disorders Clinic (School of Medicine) have been important and encouraging. We could not have pursued our research without their continuing support. The help of Dave Raynal and Mary Carskadon is also appreciated.

Leah Friedman, Kathy Gray, Mark Rosekind, and Olga Grinstead have been stimulating colleagues and collaborators. Many of their ideas have been incorporated into these procedures, and their critical comments on the text proved to be invaluable. Olga Grinstead and Julie Isaacs conducted the initial evaluation of the text with a group of poor sleepers; we thank them for their efforts. Rita Coates read the manuscript and offered several useful suggestions. Ann Gladstone, Ruth Bergman, and Elizabeth Gong-Guy did a masterful job of typing and retyping, making suggestions along the way.

We also acknowledge the research support of the Clinical Research Branch of the National Institute of Mental Health, the Spencer Foundation, and the Boys Town Center for Youth Development at Stanford. Their support permitted the experimental evaluation of the basic treatment procedures, many of which have been assembled in this book.

Gratitude is extended to Dr. William C. Dement, President of the American Association of Sleep Disorders Centers, and Ms. Lynne Hassler for compiling the listing of Sleep Disorders Centers in the Appedix.

We are grateful to Ann Dunham Ewart for her fine work in preparing the illustrations for this book.

Finally, the contributions of our clients cannot be overlooked. They have been patient when we stumbled, willing to chronicle their sleep endlessly, and willing to spend many a night sleeping in the laboratory complete with electrodes and other devices. They shared with us their successes failures, frustrations, and insights. We thank Lois, Suzanne, Jack, Raul, Fred, Willie, Candace, Wanda, Eric, Martha, Pauline, and others who have taught us so much of what we know.

Part One

INTRODUCTION

1

An Invitation

ROY. *Roy, a 35-year-old electrician, was unable to fall to sleep easily for 10 years due to extreme physical tension. Physical relaxation exercises helped him learn to relax his body so that he could fall asleep easily and quickly.*

ELAINE. *Elaine complained because she constantly awakened at night, and would sometimes lie in bed for hours worrying about her problems. The problem persisted until she mastered mental focusing skills.*

STEPHANIE. *Stephanie had fallen into the habit over the years of using sleeping pills quite regularly. She preferred the morning hangover to the torment of lying awake. By learning to relax physically and mentally, and* *by practicing different ways of thinking about herself and her actions, she was able to stop using drugs and get restful sleep.*

We wrote this book for persons (like Roy, Elaine, Stephanie, and perhaps you) who get less sleep than they would like, and consequently feel poorly during the day. During the past few years, we and other investigators have been developing methods for helping persons with insomnia obtain more restful sleep without using drugs. A number of people have learned to sleep better. The techniques we present here may also be helpful to you if:

- you suffer from chronic insomnia: difficulty in falling asleep at night, waking in the middle of the night and being unable to fall back to sleep easily, or waking up too early in the morning;
- you suffer from occasional insomnia either for no apparent reason or due to normal pressures;
- you are taking sleep medications regularly and want to stop using them.

WHAT IS THERE BESIDES DRUGS?

If you feel that sleeping pills are not the answer to your problem (we discuss in Chapter 2 why they're a poor answer for most sleeping problems), then the alternatives offered here may help you overcome your sleep problem. "But if I can't take drugs, what else is there? What magic does this book offer that is going to help me sleep better?"

We don't have any magic up our sleeves. Rather, we offer you some useful ways, termed behavioral self-management, for changing your actions. These procedures have proven extremely useful in helping people overcome a variety of personal and medical problems. We want to put the tools for change into your own hands, to give you the skills to direct your actions in ways that are important to you.

Change is never easy and this is especially true of long-standing habits. Witness the countless persons who struggle with the routine habit only to succumb to temptation again. How many people can you name who let their weight "yo-yo" up and down? They work hard for awhile and diet carefully, but then tire of watching every bite (or perhaps the holidays arrive) and put it all back on again. How many New Years' resolutions make it past the Rose Bowl?

We might be inclined to believe that people fail to change for a variety of reasons: laziness or maybe lack of motivation. Perhaps it could be that they are deficient in that mysterious energy we all want more of, "will power." Examined closely, however, "laziness," "lack of motivation," or "lack of will power" don't really tell us very much. These terms merely describe something without giving us any reason why it is happening, and the terms don't tell us what needs to be done to change. They give us no direction for action.

We believe that people have difficulty changing because *they don't know how to change or how to behave differently.* People fail to quit smoking or to control their eating not because they are morally weak, but because they don't know how to change themselves.

People continue to have sleep difficulties for the same reason. We believe that poor sleep results for many from some bad habits developed over the years. Telling you to change (to use your will power to stop thinking so much at night, to turn down the motor, and to relax) accomplishes nothing. You probably know that all too well. Statements like that may make you angry or depressed or frustrated, but not much else is likely to happen. Those bad habit patterns are doomed to continue until you *learn* better habits.

Learning and practicing new habits is what behavioral self-management is all about. We will help you identify what habits you need to learn, and will show you how to master new habits.

Most important, use them at critical times every day. Both pieces are important. We can't change the way we behave without learning new actions. But it's also important to put what we know into practice, and that can also be difficult. Behavioral self-management recognizes that what we do every day is influenced by our mental state, our physical surrounding, and our social interactions. Changing a habit requires that we do more than grit our teeth and tell ourselves to "shape up." Changing a habit requires that we analyze carefully our mental, physical, and social surroundings, determine what may be causing our problem, and try to make changes where needed. Cutting down on your alcohol intake may require that you give away that favorite fifth, and losing weight may mean putting the fattening foods where you won't be tempted to eat them. Learning to sleep well may mean doing things differently, setting up your physical, social, and mental "environment" in advance so that you can be sure to follow through on your plans. Most important, *behavioral self-management is designed to help you use and practice new behaviors until they come naturally.*

WHAT ARE WE GOING TO DO?

Writing a book to meet everyone's needs is difficult. In assembling this self-help book, we attempted: (1) to include information and techniques which we believe are important for everyone with a sleep problem to know and practice; and (2) to offer you the option of learning a variety of other skills, depending on your sleep problem and those things maintaining it.

Chapters 1 and 2 are for everyone. Chapter 1 presents an overview of the program and a rationale for the procedures to follow. Chapter 2 introduces you to current scientific knowledge about sleep. Sleep is a fascinating topic, but one sur-

Behavioral Self-Management

- Is designed to help persons like yourself learn and practice new ways of behaving.
- Recognizes that changing a habit pattern requires that we
  - learn new behaviors
  - put what we have learned into practice
- Changing a habit means
  - analyzing our mental, physical, and social surroundings
  - determining what may be causing our problem
  - working to make changes where needed

rounded by a lot of myths. Anyone struggling with insomnia should be aware of the most up-to-date scientific information available so that false beliefs and wrong information will not make you believe that your problem is worse than it is or stand in the way of your progress.

Chapters 3 through 13 offer you methods for learning to sleep better. Some chapters present basic skills, important for everyone with a sleep problem to learn and use. The techniques presented in these chapters are to be used *systematically and consistently*. Other chapters are designed to be read and used by you only if you feel that the problems we address therein will help you overcome your particular sleep problem. The resource materials include a brief technical review of the scientific research on insomnia for readers concerned with clinical research studies and related areas.

Table 1-1 presents the sequence of activities we have planned for you to follow. Each chapter is designed to achieve a particular objective through specific exercises. By accomplishing these objectives and mastering these skills, we believe that you will learn two important things. First, you will become aware of the things you do or that happen to you that may lead to unsatisfactory sleep. Becoming aware is an important first step because this process may reveal important clues about things that, if changed, could help you improve your sleep. Second, you will learn ways to improve your sleep.

Table 1-1 also gives our estimation of the time needed to accomplish each objective. These times represent the *minimum* amount probably needed to learn each skill. *Be patient with yourself as you proceed through the book.* (Above all, don't lose any sleep worrying about not sleeping!) Learn each procedure well before moving on to the next so that you can achieve the greatest benefit from the strategies offered. Most important, once a technique has been mastered, continue to use it even as you begin the next exercise. Maximum improvement in your sleep will result from the combined procedures. Check off your progress on Table 1-1 as you go along.

Part II lays the foundation for the entire program. Everyone with any kind of a sleep problem needs to learn and practice the skills. Chapter 3 teaches you to observe your sleep carefully and measure your progress as you go along. Also, you will learn some important ways to help you stick to the program, even after your initial enthusiasm may falter. Chapter 4 teaches you some methods for building and maintaining your commitment to change by modifying your "mental ecology," what you think and believe about your sleep and sleep problems. Learning to think about your sleep differently can take you a long way in solving your problems.

Part III teaches basic physical and mental relaxation skills. Everyone with a sleep problem needs to master these skills because everything else that follows assumes thay you know how to relax mentally and physically. Disturbed sleep is often associated with high levels of physical and mental arousal at bedtime. Systematically relaxing at bedtime prepares both your body and your mind for sleep. Chapter 5 teaches you to relax your body and Chapter 6 teaches you how to stop all that mental chatter. Both are important, and work hand in hand to provide total personal relaxation.

Parts IV and V teach a variety of techniques. You need not master all of them because they are designed to help overcome specific sleep-related problems. Many persons suffering from insomnia have no trouble falling asleep initially. In fact, they may find themselves collapsing when they hit the pillow at night. But once awakened during the night, they find it impossible to fall back to sleep. They find themselves awake because of some outside noise, the need to go to the bathroom, or no identifiable reason. Once awake, the "motor" starts running and sleep flees in the distance. If you are lucky, it may return in an hour or two. You may find yourself thinking until it is time to get up and start your day. Chapter 7 presents strategies for helping you learn: (1) to make sure that the "motor" does not get turned on in the first place; or (2) to shut it off once it gets started.

Chapter 8 presents methods for looking at your "sleep environment" to see what might be interfering with your sleep. We show you how to use that information systematically to design an environment to help you sleep better.

Chapter 9 represents a critical transition in this program. Everyone's sleep problems are unique and can be related to different causes. In this chapter, you learn to analyze your own

sleep. Your good and poor sleep may be related to your personal actions, and to your social and physical surroundings. Most important, you will find out how to use this information to design conditions so that you can sleep better most of the time. Learning self-analysis and problem-solving skills form the foundation for continued trouble-shooting once you are ready to begin your maintenance program (Chapter 13).

Part V teaches skills for managing what you do *during the day* as it relates to your nightime sleep. Because insomnia is often associated with high levels of physical tension and mental arousal at bedtime, systematic relaxation at bedtime prepares both body and mind for sleep. But it is unrealistic to expect to be tense and anxious throughout the day and then relax totally when it is time to sleep. Overall improvements in sleep will

TABLE 1-1
Learning to Sleep Well

Chapter	*Exercise*	*Objective*	*Time Needed*	*Objective Reached (check when completed)*
	Becoming Aware			
3.	Initial diagnosis	Determine if your poor sleep is possibly related to a physical disorder	7-14 days	________
	Watching your sleep	Assess your sleeping problem and events associated with good and poor sleep	4 days	________
	Self-contracting	Encourage you to continue program and maintain progress	1 day	________
4.	Building commitment	Change your thoughts and perceptions that may interfere with good sleep	7 days	________

TABLE 1-1 Continued
Learning to Sleep Well

Chapter	Exercise	Objective	Time Needed	Objective Reached (check when completed)
	Basic Relaxation Skills			
5.	Deep muscle relaxation	Learn to relax the body	14 days	________
6.	Mental relaxation	Learn to relax the mind	7 days	________
	Managing Your Special Problems			
7.	Mental focusing	Learn to relax in the middle of the night when you awaken so that you can get back to sleep	7 days	________
8.	Changing your sleep environment	Analyze your sleep environment and change those things preventing good sleep	7 days	________
9.	Problem solving	Learn to analyze factors related to good and poor sleep. Devise solution for your particular needs.	7 days	________
	Relaxing during the Day			
10.	Instant relaxation	Learn to relax during the day in stressful situations	10 days	________
11.	Thinking about yourself	Learn to think differently about yourself	14 days	________
12.	Thinking about your world	Learn to think differently about your daytime activities	11 days	________
	Maintaining Progress			
13.	Continued application	Continue to use the skills you have learned	Depends on how you're doing	________

result when you learn to remain relaxed more during the day as well.

Chapter 10 teaches you some extremely useful ways to relax in those situations where stress is being experienced. Rather than waiting until it is possible to stretch out and go through the entire relaxation process, you can learn to relax "instantly" in the midst of an ongoing activity. Learning to do this, however, assumes that you already know how to relax physically and mentally.

Chapters 11 and 12 help you analyze and change other factors often associated with poor sleep. Changing some of your perceptions about yourself and the world may improve your daytime mood and reduce tension by helping you view events more positively. These techniques may also help by preventing events that often interfere with good sleep.

Finally, in Chapter 13 we discuss some steps for you to take to insure that your progress will be maintained. This is the "proof of the pudding." Can you learn to apply these skills over time and keep up your progress?

PLANNING FOR CHANGE

Changing your actions—what you do and think both during the day and at night—will not come easily and automatically. It is necessary to practice these skills until they become second nature, part of who you are. This takes persistence and sometimes requires that you keep plugging away even when it seems that very little progress is being made. Some people have found that they are much more likely to stick to the program if someone else works with them to offer support and encouragement. You, too, may want to ask a close friend or someone in your family to serve as your helper.

There is another possibility open to you as well. You might prefer to work with another individual (or even small group of persons) also bothered by poor sleep. Collaborating with someone else can help if you set aside regular times to discuss and work on the program and give yourselves specific assignments to complete in the meantime. Checking with someone every few days can also help you to remember to use and practice the skills in between your regularly scheduled meetings.

If you really prefer to work by yourself or are unable to find a collaborator, don't worry. You can still follow and use the program. But you are going to have to be especially careful and conscientious so as not to begin and then let your progress slip by the wayside in the rush of ongoing events.

YOUR FIRST TASK

Reading about these strategies isn't going to be enough. *This book will help you only if you put what we say into practice.* If you need help, as many of us do, in translating intentions into actions, we have included a series of "self-improvement tasks" throughout the book. These represent decision points for action, and help you commit yourself to the completion of a specific objective. We recommend strongly that you follow the self-change exercises. Some persons, however, have found them "legalistic," and prefer to read the book and do the exercises on their own. Follow your own preferences, but be ready to get help if you find yourself slipping (remember those New Year's resolutions!).

The first self-improvement task asks you to decide if you care to nominate a helper. If you decide to work by yourself, think of some specific aids to make sure that you follow the program. You might, for example, establish a definite reading and practice schedule to follow, setting aside some time every day to work on the program.

If you do want to work with a helper, you and your helper should decide on a specific meeting time. No other commitments need to be made right how.

Recognize, of course, that these decisions can be changed; they are not chisled in granite. Feel free to change your arrangement at any time if it seems like the right thing to do.

Recognize, too, that you may not be ready to begin. You may prefer to leaf through the book to see if it is something you want to do and can work into your schedule at the present time.

With these thoughts in mind, you are about ready to begin your change program.

BEFORE YOU BEGIN

A caution seems appropriate. You need to be prepared to spend effort and to change some of the things you currently do if you want to learn how to sleep better. The strategies presented cannot be expected to improve your sleep if you approach them half-heartedly, use them only occasionally, or view them skeptically. We'd actually prefer that you not use them at all rather than apply them infrequently and experience failure.

Why? Because we do not want to reinforce the belief that you really can't do anything about your sleeping problems. We would like to get you away from the all too common notion that there is (or should be) some kind of super pill (". . . just give me a prescription, doctor. You know, something I can take to. . . .") that will instantly and effortlessly solve the problem. *We want to build your self-esteem by helping you learn to solve your own problems.*

Self-Improvement Task I: Deciding About a Helper

I am ready to begin the program and agree that I need some help to stick with it.

I have decided that I can work alone on my change program to learn to sleep better.
But in order to help me stay with the program, I am going to do the following: ______________________________

____

Signed

____

____
(datc)

- -

I have decided that I prefer to work with someone else on my program for change.
That person will be: ______________________________
We will meet ________ per week to work on the program.
(how many times)
We have decided that we will meet on ____________________.
(day)

at ____________________.
(time)

Signed

____

____
(helper/collaborator)

____
(date)

2

These Activities Called Sleep

We know very little about sleep, and this is surprising considering that it is something we all do every day. Consider the effort and expense put into sleep. Bedrooms, bed clothes, bedroom furnishings, and the thousands of motels and hotels across the country attest to the importance of sleep in our lives. Drugs to help people sleep, called hypnotics in the professional literature, comprise a multimillion dollar industry. And what about the value we place on a good night's sleep? Most of us agree that there is nothing better than waking up feeling refreshed and ready to tackle the day after a peaceful slumber. As you probably well know, there is nothing worse than feeling washed out and fatigued after one or several nights of restless and fitful sleep.

Most of us spend more than one-third of our lives sleeping

(24 years out of 70). Considering the investment in time and energy, it is reasonable to expect that we would know quite a bit about this extensive and seemingly all-important human activity. Ironically, until most recently, sleep was not considered a suitable topic for scientific study. The scientific pioneers—most of them working in the twentieth century—relied on crude and sometimes obtrusive methods to study what happened when people entered this mysterious slumber state. A few adventurous medical researchers tried experimenting on themselves. (Of course, it was a bit difficult to sleep and study one's own sleep at the same time. Try it sometime!) Others watched people while they slept, sometimes taking their blood pressure, measuring their heart rate or body movements, and poking and prodding them in various ways and places to see what would happen to their sleep.

Dreams, of course, have fascinated man since history began and may comprise the earliest form of sleep research. The ancients regarded dreams in a special way: they served as a vehicle for revelations of the deity and provided visions of future events. The Bible used dreams to prophesy impending doom and provide tantalizing glimpses of the wonderful world to come. In the Old Testament, for example, Joseph (that gentleman with the coat of many colors) got into trouble with his brothers because of his dreams, but also found favor with the Pharoah when his dreams allowed Egypt to prepare for the famine. The Egyptians believed that the person ventured into the nether world during the dream state and the future was revealed to the dreamer. The oracles interpreted dreams for the Greeks, and priestesses at selected temples used dreams for healing. Patients were drugged, suggestions that healing was occurring were made during the induced dream state, and the "visions" were interpreted by the priestesses as messages from the gods.

William Shakespeare captured well the Elizabethans' views of dreams. Dreams were unreal, the product of fantasy, a pale reflection of what was possible in the real world. Dreams also expressed the hidden conflicts of troubled minds (Sigmund Freud used this same idea much later).

> Merciful powers,
> Restrain in me the cursed thoughts that
> Nature
> Gives way to in repose!
>
> (Macbeth, ii,1,7).

In modern times, the Senoi, a primitive Malasian tribe, use dream material to learn about life and the best way to carry out daytime activities. To the Senoi, dreams are just as real as what we experience when we are awake. Incomplete dreams need to be resolved so that the dreamer and fellow tribesmen can learn something useful from them. Each morning the tribe gathers to share the previous night's dreams and to resolve incomplete or unhappy dreams. Members reporting dreams of pleasure and happiness are urged to continue having and telling them. Unhappy or incomplete dreams are either interpreted positively or the person is urged to continue the dream the next night so that a resolution can be found. For example, if someone dreams of having an argument with a friend, the dreamer is urged to continue the dream until the disagreement is resolved. A person still flying when he awakens is urged to dream some more so that he can land at his distination, broken objects are put back together, and someone who experiences fear of something or someone is urged to continue the dream until the fear is conquered.

Sigmund Freud made dream analysis central to therapy and established it as our cultural pastime. He viewed dreams as the carrier of conflicts occurring deep within the subterranean caverns of the unconscious. He theorized that all of us "repress" (push into the unconscious) feelings and thoughts that we are afraid of experiencing, such as sexual fantasies or thoughts of hatred toward another person. Our defense mechanisms prevent repressed experiences from slipping into consciousness and causing us undue anxiety when we are awake. During sleep, however, our ego (the gatekeeper) relaxes and the material in the unconscious emerges in dreams. When properly interpreted, dreams are the key to the mysterious sides of ourselves, the doorway to understanding the little understood reasons for our waking actions.

The significance and importance of dreams still remains unresolved and perplexing. Modern sleep researchers have revealed some astounding characteristics of the dream state (which we discuss below) and we know that nightmares can cause people so much discomfort that therapy is sometimes required. One common side effect of sleeping pills is that they reduce the amount of time we spend dreaming. Whether or not this is harmful remains to be determined.

Fortunately, however, we no longer have to rely only on introspection and other such observation procedures to study some of these phenomena. This century has witnessed some giant steps in the techniques available for studying sleep. As a result, our knowledge, although still primitive, has advanced in some important ways.

THE SCIENTIFIC STUDY OF SLEEP

Sleep research took a giant step forward when it became possible to record the electrical currents of the brain of sleeping subjects. The discovery that the brain emits electrical charges was made in the late 1800s in experiments with monkeys. In the 1920s, it was discovered that these electrical charges could be detected through electrodes (small flat metal discs) taped on the scalp. An important advance took place in 1935 when it was found that the brainwaves occurring during sleep followed a regular progression throughout the night and could be reliably classified into different types. It finally had become possible to study more precisely what went on in the brain and the body while people were sleeping.

REM AND NON-REM

A dramatic example of the importance of recording brainwaves is highlighted in an important discovery in the 1950s by Jacob Azerinsky and Nathaniel Kleitman at the University of Chicago. They found that there was not one, but *two different kinds of sleep. Rapid Eye Movement,* or *REM,* is perhaps the better known of the two. Most of the dreams we experience, especially the vivid ones, occur during REM sleep.

During REM sleep, the eyes move rapidly back and forth (hence the name), many of our muscles are immobilized (in fact, we are virtually paralyzed in the sense that they may twitch but we are unable to get up and walk around), and our heart beat increases to its daytime level. Perhaps you have noticed some of these things occurring in family pets. (Don't wake them up; they are merely experiencing something that all mammals do and they are in no danger.) Most amazing, during REM sleep, the brain is more active than it is when we are awake. And, as William Dement and his colleagues discovered in the late 1950s, we dream during REM sleep. Because of the intense activity taking place, some have speculated that we are not asleep at all during REM sleep. It might be accurate to describe REM sleep as an active brain in a paralyzed body.

MEASURING SLEEP

Before going further, you might be interested in knowing more about how sleep is actually studied and measured. Several laboratories around the country, usually associated with major universities, are devoted to the study of sleep. Stanford, Baylor, Tufts, Dartmouth, the University of Pennsylvania, and the University of Florida are notable examples. College students or other persons experiencing various sleep disorders are recruited to sleep in the laboratory for one or several nights.

Electrodes are attached with a special glue and tape to the surface of the skin to record the electrical impulses given off. The electrodes cause no pain and only minimal discomfort. The impulses they pick up are basically electricity given off by the body cells; that is how the brain communicates with the body and vice versa. Electrodes are attached to the head to record brainwaves (electroencephalogram), to the temples to record

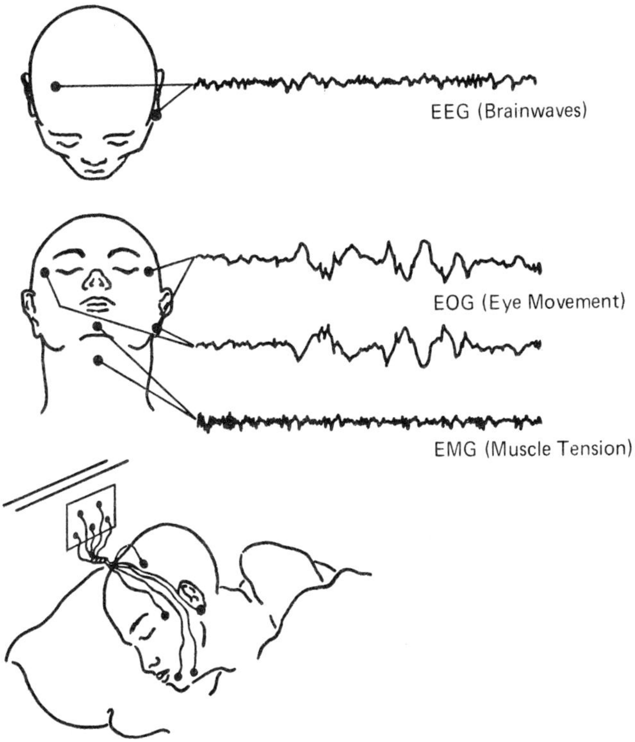

Electrode placement and standard tracings for an all-night sleep recording. Electrodes placed on the (1) head record brainwaves (EEG); (2) eyes record eye movement (EOG); and (3) chin record muscle tension (EMG). The electrodes are plugged into the circuit board at the head of the bed. From there, the terminals lead to the polygraph machine in another room. The person who is being recorded has complete freedom of movement while sleeping and can be unhooked easily if he or she needs to get up in the night.

eye movements (electro-oculogram), and to the chin to record muscle tension (electro-myogram). These three comprise the basic measures, but other things can be measured as well. Body movements can be measured through electrodes in the mattress, and breathing rates, heartbeat, leg movements, and body temperature have all been recorded continuously in certain research studies.

These electrodes are hooked up to a polygraph machine, where they are amplified and then converted into squiggly pen movements. Paper is fed under the moving pens, yielding a continuous measure of what is happening while the person sleeps. The result, at the end of the night, is a stack of paper several inches thick that must then be scrutinized inch by inch by a technician to score and interpret all of the measures taken.

NON-REM SLEEP

Back to the sleep story. In contrast to REM sleep (the active dreaming mind in an immobilized body), we also experience a completely different kind of sleep. This is called, for lack of a better term, *Non-Rapid-Eye-Movement* or *Non-REM* sleep. This is so different from REM sleep that modern sleep researchers report that we exist in three different *states*: awake, REM sleep, and Non-REM sleep. ("States", in this context, refers to completely different modes of being and experience.)

Non-REM sleep is further divided into four *stages* of sleep, reflecting the different kinds of brainwaves that are seen. ("Stages" is used to denote somewhat arbitrary divisions within a state.) These were only defined and standardized as late as 1968 after is was discovered that various sleep researchers were scoring their sleep records differently. These four stages (called Stages 1, 2, 3, and 4) represent progressively quieter body conditions and diminished brain activity. Regular breathing, slower heartbeat, increased muscle relaxation, and diminished sensory sensitivity occur as we descend through the four sleep stages. It also becomes more difficult to awaken or arouse someone as the individual progresses to Stage 4 sleep.

Brain-wave patterns are basically electrical and the EEG recordings are scored using two criteria:

1. *Cycles per second:* How many times is a specific brain-wave pattern seen during a one-second interval? (How many times does the pen move up and down in one second?)

   (Example: Alpha waves are observed when 8 to 12 cycles per second waves are seen—when the pen moves up and 8 to 12 times per second; delta waves occur when the pen moves up and down ½ to 2 times per second.)

2. *Amplitude:* A measure of voltage: how high does the pen move up and down? Most machines are set so that a brain-wave discharge of 50 microvolts moves the pen up or down by a distance of 10 millimeters.

   (Example: Delta waves are usually required to be greater than 75 microvolts in amplitude.)

Stage 1 sleep is basically a transition from wakefulness, when we are mentally and physically alert, to the deeper stages of sleep. Stage 2 sleep is defined by the presence of sleep spindles and K-complexes (surges of brain activity in the midst of relative quiet). Stages 3 and 4 ("deep sleep") are marked by the presence of delta waves, slow synchronous brain waves indicating a quiet, less active brain. Stage 4 sleep is different from Stage 3 sleep only in the amount of delta waves found. Stage 3 sleep is scored when less than 50% of the brainwaves in a 30-second period are delta, while Stage 4 sleep is scored when 50% or more of the brain waves are delta.

States and Stages of Sleep and Wakefulness

State	*Brain-wave Patterns*	*Other Characteristics*
Awake	Alpha (precedes sleep) 8–12 cycles per second; Symmetrical and rapid brainwave pattern	Relaxed wakefulness; Person is not thinking about or attending to anything specific; Free association or "non-thinking"
Rapid-Eye-Movement Sleep	Saw-tooth waves : Blood flow to brain increases and brain becomes active	Eyes move rapidly back and forth; Large muscles of body (arms, legs, trunk) are paralyzed; Small muscles (face, fingers, toes) twitch; Heartbeat increases to normal waking pace, males have an erection, breathing becomes irregular, brain becomes active; Vivid dreams
Non-Rapid-Eye-Movement Sleep	*Stage 1:* Low amplitude, fast frequency	Slow regular breathing; Slow regular brain activity,
	Stage 2: Sleep spindles: Brief bursts (½ to 2 seconds) of 13–16 cycles-per-second waves; *K-complexes:* Sharp rise and fall in brain-wave pattern	Five senses shut down, Memory processes stop; Heart and breathing rates decrease, blood pressure declines
	Stage 3: 20–50% of the record contains delta waves (rhythmic high amplitude slow waves that occur about every 1 to 2 seconds)	Body and brain become "quieter" and less responsive to environment as person goes from Stage 1 to Stage 4 sleep.
	Stage 4: More than 50% of the record contains delta waves	

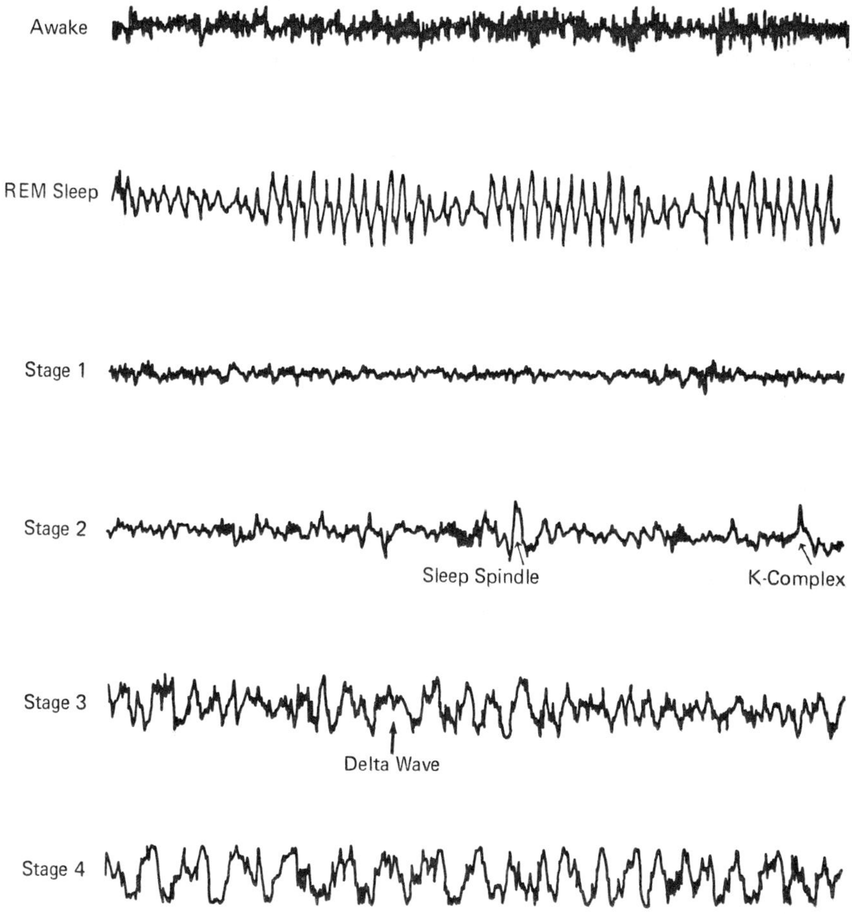

Brainwave patterns typical of various states and stages of sleep and wakefulness.

SLEEP CYCLES

Sleep cycles are the sequence of stages and states we experience while sleeping. During the night, we go through several sleep cycles, each containing some REM and NREM sleep. Figure 2-3 shows the progress of sleep for a child, a young adult, and a 60-year-old on a particular night.

As you can see, the young adult goes from wakefulness into deep sleep (Stage 4) quite rapidly. After 60 to 90 minutes, the person experiences Stage 2 sleep, immediately followed by the first REM period of the night. Several things happen as the night progresses. Sleep in the first part of the night is characterized by relatively short sleep cycles, around 70 to 80 minutes in length. As the night progresses, these become progressively longer, lasting as long as 100 minutes. Stage 3 and 4 sleep predominate during the first part of the night. This is often considered the deepest sleep because people are hardest to awaken and are least sensitive to outside noises at this time. As the night progresses, the REM-sleep periods become longer and Stages 3 and 4 sleep disappear. Notice also the brief awakenings that occur as morning arrives.

It should be remembered that this represents one night for one young adult. This is clearly an average. Your sleep can vary quite a bit from night to night, and your sleep can be quite different from your neighbor's.

Our sleep undergoes some interesting changes as we grow and develop. The human embryo and infant experience just two kinds of sleep, REM and non-REM (without the sleep stages) sleep. The fetus, at seven months along in pregnancy, spends 84 percent of his time in REM sleep. This goes down to 36% shortly after birth. At one year of age, the four stages of sleep can be differentiated, and REM sleep accounts for 20 to 25 per cent of the total sleep time (top diagram in Figure 2-3). The various stages including REM remain fairly constant throughout life. However, older persons tend to experience less Stages 3 and 4 sleep (sometimes this disappears completely), sleep time may be reduced to six or seven hours per night, and may experience more frequent and longer nighttime awakenings (bottom diagram in Figure 2-3). A natural kind of insomnia seems to set in with age.

It should be remembered, of course, that all this information is based on averages. Individuals often differ considerably

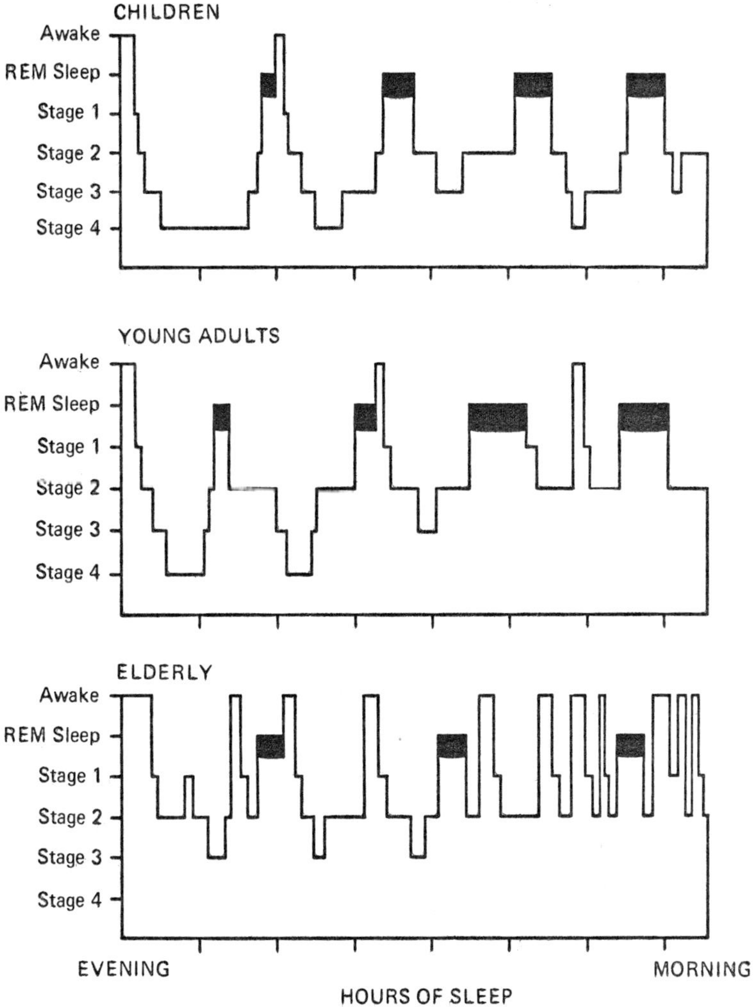

Sleep cycles for children, for young adults, and for the elderly. Notice the changes that occur in Stage 3 and Non-REM sleep and in REM sleep with aging. Notice also that the elderly awaken more frequently toward morning than children and young adults.

in the amount of sleep they require and in the structure of their sleep throughout the night. It is very important to remember this, especially in understanding your own sleep.

WHY SLEEP?

One of the problems that continues to perplex researchers is understanding why we sleep at all. *Why do we need to spend at least one-third of our lives unconscious and unable to pursue important activities?* Common sense suggests we all need a good eight hours' sleep! You probably wouldn't be reading this book if you didn't think sleep was important. But do we really need to sleep? What does sleep do for us?

There seems to be a biological "need" for some kinds of sleep. When persons participating in experiments in sleep laboratories are deprived of REM and Stage 4 sleep, for example, they show a "rebound" effect. Their sleep during the next few nights will show larger amounts of REM or Stage 4 sleep, almost as if they are making up for what they lost. Most of us value sleep because it seems to refresh our minds and restore energy to our bodies. We've all grown up with the notion that we'll get sick if we don't get an adequate amount of sleep. Our own experience tells us that if we get less than enough sleep or if our sleep is restless, the following day will be miserable. Perhaps you feel sluggish and tired or irritable and depressed. We know that we will not be able to think as clearly as we would like. These complaints can become much worse if the condition persists for a number of days, as it often does with people bothered by insomnia.*

But modern sleep researchers are not prepared to accept the theory that we sleep only to eliminate fatigue. Several lines of research come together to question the idea that we need to

*Be careful, though! We can blame our feelings of daytime fatigue on our sleep when, in reality, the cause is often something else. Depression, irritability, and fatigue can be caused by physical problems (e.g., anemia or thyroid disorders) and life-style difficulties (e.g., boredom, interpersonal problems, or job dissatisfaction). Be sure that you are not blaming your sleep when the cause may lie elsewhere.

sleep in order to refresh body and mind. There are some rare individuals who require very little sleep. Thomas Edison worked very productively with very few hours' sleep during the night and occasional catnaps during the day. Dr. Raymond Meddis and his colleagues in England are currently using modern electroencephalographic techniques to study persons who sleep for an hour or less at night. One man sleeps for only 15 to 60 minutes per night! He leads an active and full life, and is really happy to be accomplishing twice as much as the rest of us who need to sleep the night away. His wife sleeps a normal amount of time, but their baby daughter seems to have inherited his need to sleep very little. As many parents would realize, some shifting in child-care tasks was needed in order to permit his wife to keep from experiencing total fatigue and ultimate collapse!

There is no question that these individuals who sleep very little are rare. Most of us cannot get along with less than six or seven hours of sleep.

Under unusual circumstances persons can stay awake for long periods of time and even alter their sleeping patterns. Perhaps the most famous nonsleeper during recent years was a 17-year-old high school student named Randy Gardner. Randy was able to maintain a 264-hour vigil (that's 11 days) without sleep, and this was confirmed by Dr. William Dement and his colleagues at Stanford University. To stay awake that long, Randy had to exercise his muscles continually and work hard to keep his mind active. He did several things during this vigil to make sure he would not fall asleep: played games, walked, and talked to the researchers. Movement and some physical activity seemed essential in order for him to stay awake. Most amazingly, he recovered with very little sleep.* On the first "normal" night afterwards, he slept 14 hours, awakening at 10:00 the next

*It seems that we don't need to "make up" sleep in a one-for-one fashion. Loss of four hours sleep in one night does not need to be compensated by sleeping four extra hours the next night. A normal night's sleep can usually take care of any fatigue experienced because of one or several poor nights' sleep.

evening. He stayed awake until the following evening almost 24 hours later, and then slept a normal 8 hours.

Since Randy kept his vigil, however, researchers have documented the existence of *microsleeps*, brief flashes lasting no more than one to two seconds in duration in which the brainwaves reveal that sleep is occurring. These may add up to substantial amounts of sleep during periods of prolonged wakefulness. This phenomenon also suggests that there are other ways to reverse fatigue besides climbing into bed and reposing there for extended periods of time.

Other more controlled experiments have studied what happens to people when they are placed in strange environments, cut off from everyday sensory stimulation. Under these conditions, people tend to cut their sleep down to half of what it is under normal conditions and feel no fatigue as a result.

Finally, animals vary greatly in the amounts of time they sleep during the day. Table 2-1 presents some representative examples. The sloth, topping the list with 20 hours, appears to deserve his name. Humans share 8 hours with the mole (an interesting bed partner), while one species of porpoise apparently does not sleep at all! Based on this information, some have suggested that sleep exists as part of a mechanism to regulate behavior. We are awake when we are most able to cope with the environment. For humans, this occurs during the daylight hours. Our food gathering and other activities can take place when we are ready to see what is happening around us and respond to danger if necessary. Animals who sleep less time may have greater food gathering needs (elephants do require a fair amount of food), while those who sleep more can accomplish these tasks in relatively short periods of time. Once these necessary activities have been completed, the animal can then retire to the shelter of a cave and hide from its enemies. Sleep prevents it from venturing out and encountering harm when the animal is least able to cope with it. This kind of social biological explanation, based on an evolutionary viewpoint, seems reasonable. It will be interesting to see how human sleep evolves with more years of electric lights and technology.

TABLE 2-1

Where Do We Fit?

Mammal	*Hours of Sleep*
Sloth	20
Armadillo, bat	19
Lemur	16
Hamster	14
Rat, cat	13
Chinchilla	12
Jaguar	11
Hedgehog	10
Human beings, mole	8
Cow, guinea pig	7
Tapir, sheep	6
Horse, pilot whale	5
Giraffe, elephant	4
Dall's porpoise, shrew	0

CIRCADIAN RHYTHMS

But don't jump to the conclusion that sleep is totally unnecessary and something that you can do away with altogether. Some vital functions may occur during specific sleep stages and staying awake for prolonged periods of time does require special and concerted effort. Our bodies are still programmed to sleep; even if we try to cut down gradually and systematically on the amount of time we sleep, we will reach a point from which we can no longer function normally. In experiments where this was tried, most people found that they could not go much below six hours per night. Even then, most of them returned to former sleep patterns once the experiment was over.

Sleep appears to be part of a total cycle of sleeping and waking termed *circadian rhythm* (*circa* meaning "around"; *die* meaning "day"; hence "around the day"). In man and other mammals, over one hundred physical functions (heartbeat, respiration rate, body temperature, and production of crucial hormones) fluctuate on a daily rhythm. Mood and mental performance also follow this course. If you have ever traveled from San Francisco to New York, you will recognize the phenomenon. After arriving on the east coast, it may take several days for body time to adjust to clock time so that you can rise and retire easily at accustomed times. This rhythm is internally generated and is independent of environmental events. Sleep, of course, coincides with the low points in this rhythm.

DO WE NEED TO SLEEP OR DON'T WE?

It must be apparent by now that we are answering the question, "Do we need to sleep?" with some complex, if not evasive answers. Let's summarize what we know so far:

- There seems to be a biological need for some kinds of sleep.
- If we don't sleep well, we will not function at our peak during the day.
- Some people require very little sleep; and loss of sleep or even disturbed sleep is not harmful physically or psychologically.
- We may blame depression, irritability, and fatigue on poor sleep, but these conditions may be caused by other factors, such as boredom or stress.

It seems reasonable to conclude that sleep is an important part of what we do. We know that we cannot stay awake for long periods of time without special effort and staying awake indefinitely is impossible. Most important, we know that our bodies go through daily fluctuations with high and low points, and sleep usually coincides with the low points in this cycle. But the precise purpose, if any, of both this cycle and sleep remains to be determined by further research. And, most important, we still need to find out why disturbances in sleep like those experienced by the insomniac cause so much discomfort.

SLEEP DISORDERS

This view gives us some perspective in beginning to understand sleep disorders such as insomnia. Disorders may be experienced if we are "out of rhythm," when the various physical functions that occur together are desynchronized. *This rhythm view suggests that although we may feel poorly and function less effectively when we experience something like insomnia, we will continue to live and our health is not likely to be impaired.* Before talking more about insomnia, perhaps the most common sleep disorder, let's discuss some other disturbances related to sleep that have been discovered and identified.*

SLEEPWALKING AND SLEEPTALKING

These disorders occur most commonly in children, but continue into adulthood for some persons. It is estimated that 20 per cent of the general population has talked in their sleep.

Sleepwalking and sleeptalking occur primarily in Stage 4, or deep sleep. Interestingly, almost any child can be made to walk while asleep if someone stands the child upright during Stage 4 sleep. Thus contrary to popular belief, scientists do not believe that sleepwalking episodes have a purpose or represent the acting out of a dream. Usually sleepwalking and sleeptalking do not indicate an emotional or psychological problem.

*Our discussion of these sleep disorders is brief and is provided only to give you a sampling of the kinds of sleep problems people experience. It may help you realize that you are not alone if you have a sleep disturbance. If you want more information on any of these disorders, we suggest that you consult some of the people and technical books listed in the resource materials in the back of this book.

Sleepwalkers need to be protected during their nighttime forays. Thus, sharp objects or other things that might hurt them should be out of the room. A person discovered sleepwalking should be helped gently back to bed. Even if awakened immediately, the individual will have little or no awareness of being out of bed. If sleepwalking persists beyond childhood, drugs are sometimes prescribed to suppress Stage 4 sleep. As in all cases, however, these should *not* be given unless absolutely necessary and then only with the consultation of a sleep specialist. We are always eager to find the right pill, but there's no reason to compound the sleepwalker's problem with unnecessary drugs.*

Sleeptalking presents no major problems either to the individual or to those around him. (It may, of course, be irritating to bed partners who are awakened by the prattle. Insomnia might result as the bed partner tries very hard to figure out what was said or the significance of these nocturnal mutterings!)

NIGHT TERRORS

This is another condition that occurs with surprising frequency among young children, and occasionally adults. Modern sleep researchers have divided frightening dreams into two categories. *Nightmares*, probably more common, are less intense than night terrors and are usually associated with a rather elaborate dream sequence. These occur during REM sleep. *Night terrors*, occurring during Stage 4 sleep, are accompanied by intense physical arousal and usually a sudden scream. Neither experience indicates emotional or

*As you might suspect, we believe that all too many problems are classified as medical "diseases" and treated with drugs. Many problems such as nightmares, bedwetting, and disturbed sleep might be treated better by other means. Refferals to other professionals (such as psychologists or social workers), competent to handle such problems, can be made by a family physician, by local universities, or by local professional associations.

psychological problems; comfort and reassurance are usually sufficient to handle the problem. If either continues to recur, however, some professional consultation might be helpful. In recent years, some techniques have been developed to help children and adults become "desensitized" to the frightening content of their dreams. Once the person overcomes fear of dream content, the dreams themselves stop occurring and other problems seem to go away as well.

BEDWETTING

Bedwetting (called enuresis) also affects a large proportion of the population and should not be viewed with undue alarm. Our culture expects children by the age of three to remain dry through the night. But this standard should not be applied too stringently. Children vary widely in the age they are able to control their bladder sufficiently to stay dry through the night. Popular opinion has it that bedwetting is often related to dreams of urinating, but this is generally not the case. Children who go into a REM period (i.e., a dream period) after wetting their bed may incorporate the wetness into their dreams, giving the mistaken impression that they probably dreamed of urinating and then did so. Bedwetting can occur during any stage of sleep, but is commonly associated with deep sleep (Stage 4) in the first third of the night. When put together with other facts, this finding is very reasonable. Remember, in our discussion of sleep cycles and the changes that occur in sleep with age, we mentioned that young children experience large amounts of Stage 3 and 4 sleep in the first third of the night. One characteristic of this sleep is that the person is not easily aroused. Thus, if bladder capacity is exceeded, it is not unreasonable that the child will fail to awaken before urinating. Often simply getting the child up and to the bathroom about an hour after going to bed will solve the problem.

Unless caused by physical problems (and this should always be checked out), bedwetting probably indicates a limited bladder capacity but rarely anything else. There's usually no reason to get too excited or worried about it and thus raise the child's anxiety level or make the child believe that there's a serious emotional problem. Despite the culturally encouraged "solutions," drugs should be avoided if at all possible. The person needs to learn how to control the bladder. Drugs can interfere with learning the self-control needed. In recent years, procedures for helping people learn this kind of control have been developed, and professionals in the mental health disciplines may be able to help if the problem becomes severe.

NARCOLEPSY

Narcolepsy is a less common sleep disorder. In order to avoid any misunderstanding and so that you don't misdiagnose a somewhat rare condition, we want to be very precise in our description of this disorder. Narcolepsy is characterized by:

- *Cataplexy:* an unusual condition in which the person is fully aware and yet completely paralyzed (the person is fully aware of what is going on, but unable to move a muscle for as long as one minute or more).
- *Sleep attacks*: an irresistible and unavoidable onset of sleep accompanied by vivid and often frightening hallucinations and paralysis. These conditions are characteristic of REM sleep and when the narcoleptic's sleep is studied, one of the diagnostic signs is the immediate appearance of REM sleep. Thus, the person goes from paralysis to REM sleep and back to wakefulness. This condition can be extremely dangerous. Persons have been known to have these attacks while driving a car or under other equally precarious conditions.

The cataplexy is usually precipitated only by an intense emotional reaction such as happiness or anger. Anyone who has this condition should be under the care of a physician, preferably someone expert in sleep disorders. A stimulant like one of the amphetamines is often prescribed, but these should be avoided at all costs. They are dangerous drugs and are easily abused. If the problem is not severely disabling, occasional naps may help. If drugs are unavoidable, other safer drugs can be used.

HYPERSOMNIA

Hypersomnia is a condition referring to excessive sleep and daytime sleepiness and fatigue. (Remember, however, that there are wide individual variations in the amount of sleep that people require.) Hypersomniacs may find themselves sleeping for long periods at night and feeling fatigued enough during the day to take extended naps. In contrast to the narcoleptic, *sleep is normal and is not irresistible.* The hypersomniac also does not fall directly into REM sleep like the narcoleptic. There are no established treatments for hypersomnia, but occasionally sleeping continually for a few days may stave off the need for excessive napping for months. Sometimes amphetamines are used, but again these should be avoided. Some of the procedures we teach in this book may be helpful in overcoming hypersomnia.

Finally, there are those events we all experience that are somewhat unusual but should not cause undue alarm. Many people report experiencing *hallucinations* when they are falling asleep. They can hear or see objects or persons in the bedroom. Others experience *sleep paralysis*; they will wake up and be unable to move. Sometimes you may have experienced a sensation of falling while going to sleep. None of these should be cause for alarm; many people have the same feeling and sensations. Folklore has it that if you hit bottom when falling (either when going to sleep or in your dreams), you will die. Fortunately, those of us who did get all the way down have managed to survive the experience and tell about it!

INSOMNIA: SOME BASIC FACTS

If you experience insomnia, you are not alone because it is probably the most common sleep disorder. Most of us have at one time or another suffered from occasional bouts of sleeplessness lasting one night or even extending to a few weeks. The best current estimates indicate that from 25 to 30 million Americans suffer from chronic insomnia. Included in this group are people who, night after night and day after day, suffer from inadequate sleep. Certainly, the dramatic increase in the sale of tranquilizers and other sleep inducing drugs attest to the prevalence of sleep disturbance in our society.

One of the difficulties in discussing insomnia derives from the fact that it is not a disease like measles or the mumps (that's why drugs are not necessarily the best solution). It includes a variety of sleep disorders all called by the same name. Complicating the picture still further is the fact that people vary considerably in the amount of sleep they "need" in order to feel rested and function effectively. One individual may not be able to get along on less than ten hours per night, while four hours is quite adequate for another. We may even sleep different amounts of time from day to day and feel just fine each day.

CRITERIA FOR INSOMNIA

Insomnia affects people in one or a combination of three ways. A person may have *difficulty initially getting to sleep; difficulty staying asleep during the night* (bothered by long awakenings or many short arousals) or *may wake up very early in the morning and not be able to fall back to sleep.* For scientific purposes, sleep researchers have settled upon some arbitrary criteria any of which define insomnia: (1) a person does not fall asleep within thirty minutes after turning the lights

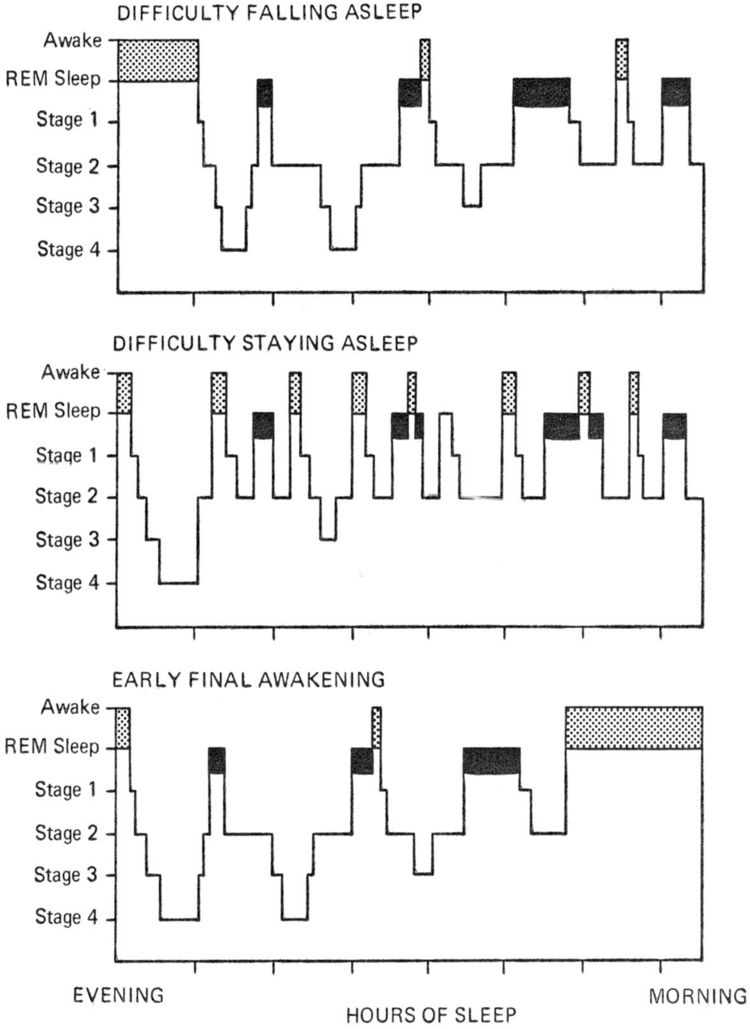

"Insomnia" is a term used to describe these three types of sleep patterns. Persons complaining of insomnia can experience one, two, or three of the complaints in any combination.

out; (2) a person is awake for longer than 30 minutes during the night; and/or (3) a person's total sleep time is less than 6½ hours.

In addition to reporting that sleep is disturbed, a second important criterion must be included: because of the disturbed sleep, *daytime fatigue results*. Thus a person whose sleep is fitful and restless but functions well during the day would not be considered an insomniac. Most important, if you sleep short amounts of time or wake up early, but feel fine all day, you are not an "insomniac." *Your sleep is normal and there's nothing to worry about.* You have a sleep problem if you feel physically tired during the day and generally feel washed out most of the time and *know* that your sleep is disturbed.

Later in this book we provide some methods for you to use to evaluate how well you sleep and how well you feel during the day. But even if you don't seem to fall within the criteria discussed, don't worry. You may find some of the techniques presented in this book helpful in making your sleep less

---

Poor Sleep		*Daytime Fatigue*
Fail to fall asleep within 30 minutes after going to bed and/or Awake for longer than 30 minutes when awakened during the night and/or Bothered by many short awakenings throughout the night and/or Total sleep time is less than 6½ hours	AND	You experience daytime fatigue • physically tired • unable to concentrate • depressed • irritable • lethargic

- Don't consider yourself an insomniac unless you experience poor sleep *and* daytime fatigue.
- Be sure your daytime fatigue is caused by poor sleep and not something else (e.g., boredom or personal problems).
- If your sleep is not normal (short, disturbed) but it does not bother you during the day, you do not have a sleep problem.

---

disturbed or in combating those occasional bouts of sleeplessness. Our purpose is to help people with a wide variety of sleep problems, from the person with chronic and severe insomnia to the individual who occasionally has difficulty sleeping to those who would like to make their normal sleep even better.

IS INSOMNIA DANGEROUS?

Generally speaking, there is no reason to be worried or concerned about your psychological or physical health if you experience occasional or even frequent insomnia. Insomnia rarely results in any physical problems. But it can lead us to feel down in the dumps, irritable, depressed, lethargic, or anxious. These are its unpleasant effects (and maybe its causes for some people) and are the things we hope to remedy by helping you learn how to sleep better.

WHAT ABOUT DRUGS AND ALCOHOL?

Over $100 million was spent in 1967 on drugs to alleviate sleeping problems. By now the amount may have doubled. Because it has been viewed as a medical problem, insomnia is most commonly treated by the variety of prescription and nonprescription drugs. A recent survey of insomniacs in the San Francisco Bay area revealed that 40% used sleeping drugs—almost every night. Another 26% used them only occasionally, while 33% used alcohol to achieve the same purpose. A full 14% used a combination of drugs and alcohol to get to sleep.

Let's start with the group that uses both drugs and alcohol. This combination may result in people thinking they are sleeping better, but the combination can be dangerous. Too much of one or the other may result in death. It might be preferable, if you find that you are using both rather often, to try to use only drugs. At least that way you are less likely to be endangering your life and your health.

Drugs are not without their problems either. In recent years, sleep researchers have devoted much of their energies to studying the effects of these drugs on sleep. All-night sleep recordings have been used to determine the precise effects of these drugs on sleep. And the Federal Drug Administration now requires that all sleeping drugs be evaluated in this way before they are put on the market. And it is a good thing, too. This flurry of research has led to some important discoveries. *Almost all drugs currently available actually make sleep worse rather than better.* One effect is shown in Figure 2-5.

Sleep-inducing drugs typically suppress both REM and Stage 3 and 4 sleep. When the person attempts to sleep without them, Stage 4 sleep gradually returns to normal levels. REM sleep, however, shows a "rebound" effect. For a while, the person experiences large amounts of REM sleep, and the dream content is often nightmarish and fearful. The person thinks that sleep is getting worse (rightly so) and thus returns, understandably, to taking drugs.

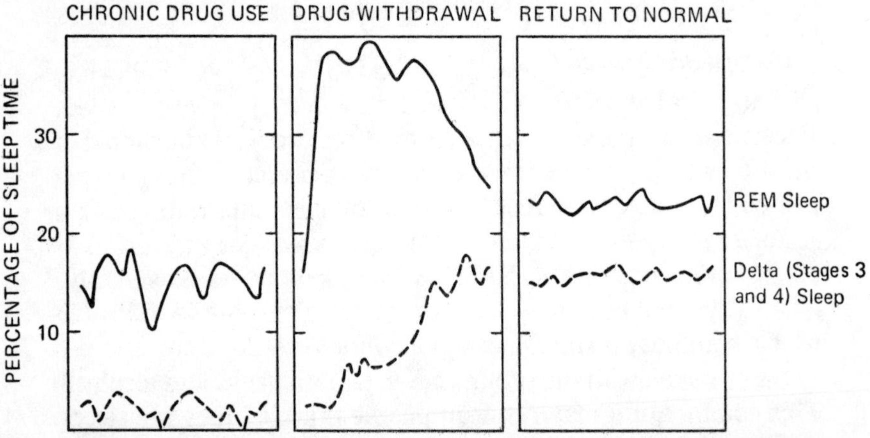

Sleep patterns during chronic drug use, during withdrawal of drugs, and when returned to normal. During chronic drug use, Stage 3 and 4 non-REM sleep and REM sleep are suppressed. During withdrawal, REM sleep increases sharply and this can be associated with increased dreams and nightmares (REM rebound). Stages 3 and 4 sleep increase gradually. Following withdrawal, REM sleep levels out at 20 to 25 percent of total sleep, whereas Stages 3 and 4 sleep account for 15 to 20 percent of total sleep.

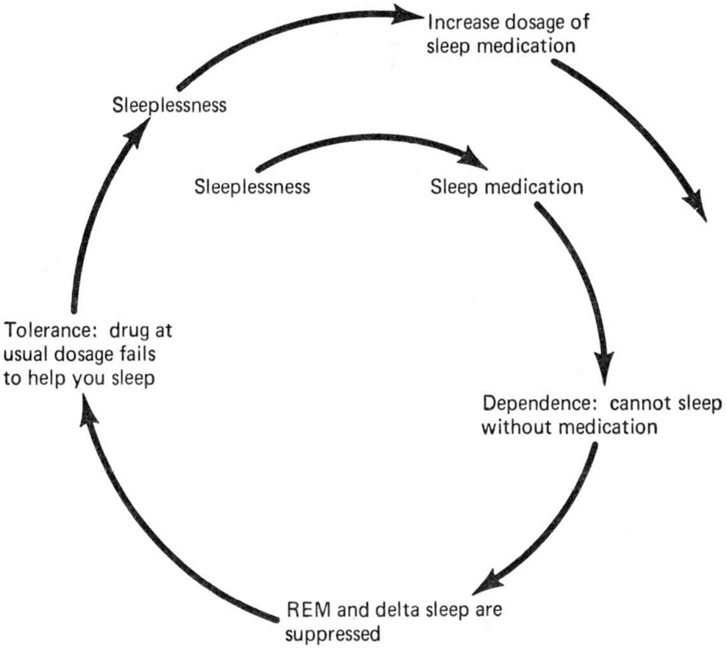

Sleeping pills: be careful.

Other problems also occur. The most common one is tolerance. The person's body adjusts to a drug dosage and it begins to need larger and larger amounts of the drug to achieve an effect. Thus, a terrible cycle is established: sleeplessness leads to drug taking which in turn leads to dependency and more drug taking. Getting out of this cycle can be very difficult. Certainly it should never be attempted abruptly, and not without the consultation of a sleep specialist or at least a physician. With the professional, you can establish a schedule to reduce your drug intake *gradually* so that your sleep will be less disturbed in the process. Some of the techniques we present in this book can also help by teaching you procedures to use as you are getting off the drug and helping you maintain normal sleep as you become completely free of them.

The problems cited above occur with the vast majority of

drugs currently available when they are used chronically*, and these same results can happen with alcohol and antihistamines (the ingredient often found in nonprescription sleep medications).

WHAT WILL I LEARN IN THIS BOOK?

We have adopted the view that sleep is one part of a total daily body rhythm. Insomnia, rather than being a "disease" in any traditional sense, may be the result of some behavior patterns that have thrown some of our body rhythms out of phase with the others. Sleeping pills somehow seem to disrupt this rhythm, throwing the body out of kilter and causing more problems than they solve.

The procedures we present are designed to achieve a different objective. When insomniacs retire, they commonly report higher states of physical tension and mental activity than normal, or good, sleepers. Research has shown that poor sleepers are more physically aroused at night. Their body temperature, heart rate, and muscle tension, for example, tend to be high in comparison to good sleepers.

A number of strategies, *which work in harmony with body rhythms,* can be used to help reduce this arousal at night and thus prepare the body and mind for restful and normal sleep. These include techniques to help you:

- relax physically and mentally before retiring;
- reduce your tension level during the day;
- manage your time, activities, and thoughts to prepare for a good night's sleep.

These are the procedures we are attempting to teach in this book. We sincerely hope they are useful in enabling you to learn to sleep better.

*Hypnotic medications commonly producing tolerance and dependence include sodium seconal, sodium amytal, sodium pentobarbital, barbital, sodium amobarbital, sodium secobarbital, glutethidimide, methypyrlon, and ethochlorynol.

Part Two

BECOMING AWARE

3

Becoming a Personal Scientist

We can't guarantee that the program offered in this book will work for you automatically without any hitches or setbacks. This doesn't mean that we think the techniques are not effective. To the contrary, our clinical and research experience suggests they can really help. What the statement does mean is this: *The effectiveness of the techniques depends on what you do with them.* Many self-help books promise overnight success and instant miracles—"Just follow these ten easy steps and your problems will disappear." *We refuse to make these kinds of claims* because we would feel dishonest in doing so and worse yet, we would be setting you up for failure. *You will not experience improvement instantly and without effort.* It's this failure cycle that we want to prevent. There's nothing more discouraging than believing that you can do something, trying hard, and then failing badly. We want to help you succeed and to realize that *you* can do things to sleep better. But it takes a slow, step-at-a-time, "trial-*until*-success" approach.

Effort is required in two ways. First, it is important that you be *systematic* in trying out and applying the strategies presented. It is unreasonable to expect to change a habit, any habit which has had a long history and is part of who you are, without concerted and consistent effort.

Second, adapting and using the strategies for greatest personal benefit will require that you become *skilled at watching yourself*. Many people love to go to various public places such as an outdoor cafe, a park, or the airport to do "people watching". Sitting and watching others can be very enjoyable, especially because you can take the time to notice and observe people's many little mannerisms and habits, the sum of which adds up to their personalities. This is sometimes interesting to do with friends as well. Studying someone's habits and mannerisms may reveal new diminsions that before we may have overlooked completely.

The same holds true for ourselves. By focusing on some small aspect of our behavior, we may discover clues about ourselves that can be quite revealing if we are trying to change something we do.

Observing yourself is the first step in becoming a *personal scientist*. Science tries to proceed in a very careful manner. Results of the scientific method have made important contributions to our modern society. All of the information presented in Chapter 2, for example, was discovered through scientific methods. Science, of course, has also contributed to modern problems. But it is the discovery process of science, with its careful step-by-step exploration and its spirit of searching and trying things out tentatively, that we want to stress.

The scientist, after staking out an area for investigation, first observes the phenomenon for the simple purpose of trying to derive some clues about what is happening. ("What's really going on here" exemplifies this point.) After some initial assessment, the experimenter develops some hunches about what may be causing things to happen the way they do. These hunches are tested out in the real world and more observations are gathered to find out more about the hunches. This process may lead to some important discoveries. For example, perhaps a theory suggested that a certain new medication would improve sleep but, when carefully observed, failed to do so. More often, hunches don't hold up. But the scientist learns from either outcome and continues to observe and refine hypotheses and theories until arriving at ones that seem to make a difference. A theory helps the scientist to better understand things by suggesting hypotheses and providing predictions about what is likely to happen. ("If I do this, then that will probably occur.")

We believe that you, acting as a personal scientist, will be able to take some strides in gaining control over your sleeping problems by applying these same discovery methods to yourself.

> ***ELEANOR.*** *Eleanor, now 40 years old, suffered from chronic insomnia for 20 years before seeking assistance. Over the years she had experimented with a wide variety of sleeping pills, with and without the advice of her physician. These brought her some relief, but she was never very satisfied with them. After learning of their bad effects, she gradually stopped using them and decided to suffer with her poor sleep.*
>
> *She experienced two sleep difficulties when we first met her. It took her a long time to get to sleep at night, and she would awaken once or twice and lie awake for a long time around 2:00 or 3:00 in the morning. The first two strategies we tried, progressive relaxation (Chapter 5) and cognitive focusing (Chapter 7) eliminated these problems most of the time. But she experienced one or the other sleep difficulty about once or twice per week.*
>
> *We were all stumped. Eleanor began to keep detailed records of her pre-bedtime activities and only then did the*

reason become clear to everyone! She was teaching two summer session classes at a nearby community college. The preparation was quite extensive because the classes met everyday. Eleanor sometimes put off doing her preparation, and would work very late in the evening in an effort to be ready for the next day's classes. She closed the books around 11:00 p. m., and knowing that she would want to be rested, immediately went to bed and tried to go to sleep. These were the nights she had difficulty sleeping. The solution was simple. By rearranging her preparation time and overcoming her procrastination, she was able to find time to wind down before retiring and thus prepare for a good night's sleep.

Becoming a personal scientist led Eleanor to discover what was preventing her from sleeping well and helped her design a strategy to handle this problem. The same approach will help you accomplish the same objective. Additionally, two other benefits will come your way. First, the information you collect should give you some hunches about which of the strategies presented will result in the greatest benefit to you. Second, that same information will tell you how to modify the techniques to meet your particular needs and problems.

Observing and recording your sleep and some factors associated with your sleep (collecting data) are the first steps in becoming a personal scientist. These are important things to do, but science also has another key ingredient that we think forms the heart and soul of the discovery process. *Scientists are never satisfied with their view of the world.* They are keenly aware that the basic assumptions they make about their approach to reality could be completely wrong and that their hunches might be totally misguided because of these assumptions. Prior to Columbus, people rarely questioned the notion that the world was flat, and who would have suspected that everything is composed of little particles of buzzing energy called atoms let alone smaller ones called quarks. Even as we write this book, we are painfully aware that our point of

Using the Scientific Method

The Scientist	*Eleanor*
Decide on area of study using theory and previous experience.	Insomnia once or twice per week; "Theory" about why she can't sleep well
↓	↓
Observe: gather clues about what might be happening	Keep Daily Sleep Diary
↓	↓
Develop hypotheses: generate some hunches about why things happen the way they do	Hypotheses: working late in the evening to prepare lectures leads to poor sleep
↓	↓
Experiment: test hunches and gather more data	Try preparing lectures at another time; still keep Daily Sleep Diary
↓	↓
Develop more hypotheses: continue to observe and refine hypotheses	Look at results, make other hypotheses until sleep is really good

view is limited. Hopefully it will be replaced at some future point by a more complete picture as more scientific findings become available.

The most striking scientific discoveries have occurred when investigators have been able to stand back and examine critically their personal beliefs and world views. Albert Einstein's famous equation of mass and energy astounded the world; Watson and Crick's discovery of the structure of DNA shows how they had to question their most cherished beliefs about the makeup of organisms in order to discover the structure of the core of life and reproduction.*

You can make the same advances in improving poor sleep when you are able to challenge your basic beliefs about your sleep difficulties, develop alternative hunches, and test them out to see if your sleep improves. This is exciting and creative living, and you can gain immeasurably in venturing forth on this kind of journey.

We suggest that you complete the *sleep diaries* for specified periods of time and use the information in a systematic way to improve your sleep. These are not trivial or unimportant exercises. *They form the heart of conquering any problem and especially insomnia.* Only by systematically observing and testing can you become aware of the progress you are making and the further changes that need to be made to achieve your objective of restful and satisfying sleep.

SOME INITIAL ASSESSMENTS

Insomnia is a catch-all category encompassing a wide variety of sleep disorders related to many causes. Insomnia might be compared to headaches, which can be related to

**The Double Helix* by Watson and Crick provides a fascinating account of the process of challenge and discovery that is the heart of the scientific method. Another excellent book on the same theme is *Zen and the Art of Motorcycle Maintenance* by Robert Pirsig.

everything from simple nervous tension to brain tumors. The procedures we are recommending in this book may not be appropriate for everyone because insomnia can be caused by some not fully understood physical disorders. Remember, we still know relatively little about sleep, and most of these causes have been discovered only recently.

Before going further, we think it is essential to pause briefly and discuss some of these disorders and the symptoms associated with them. We would like you to take some time to determine if you notice any of these symptoms, and want to suggest some steps for you to take if you do.

Table 3-2 presents the symptoms for which you should be on the lookout. Some of these can be detected by you, while others may be noticeable only to a bed partner or roomate. Let's discuss each of these briefly, and then we will give you some ideas about what to do if you notice any of these symptoms.

POSSIBLE PHYSICAL SYMPTOMS

1. Snoring, Not Breathing, and Gasping for Air. Some people, and fortunately they are few in number, are unable to sleep and breathe at the same time. This condition is called *sleep apnea.* For reasons not fully understood, the diaphragm (the large muscle at the base of the lungs) and intercostal (chest) muscles fail to operate and become immobile when the person falls asleep. The oxygen level in the blood is then reduced to very low levels signaling the brain that trouble is at hand. After 20 to 100 seconds, the person wakes up briefly (usually unaware of awakening), gasps for air, and falls back to sleep for another 20 to 100 seconds. This cycle may be repeated at various times throughout the night. As you can imagine, the person never has the opportunity to obtain any extended amounts of deep sleep.

The person bothered by sleep apnea feels very tired in the morning and naps frequently during the day. Because the individual is usually not sure of the problem, it's usually necessary to engage someone else's assistance to detect it.

TABLE 3–2
Symptom Checklist*

Symptom	*Noticed by me*							*Noticed by bed partner/roommate*						
	Mon	*Tues*	*Wed*	*Thur*	*Fri*	*Sat*	*Sun*	*Mon*	*Tues*	*Wed*	*Thur*	*Fri*	*Sat*	*Sun*
1. Snoring followed by a pause in which no breathing occurs and gasping for air														
2. Leg twitches periodically throughout the night and/or achy feelings in the legs.														
3. Higher body temperature in the late evening and at bedtime														
4. Excessive daytime sleepiness or fatigue and frequent naps (as well as nighttime insomnia)														
5. Constant use of sleeping pills or tranquilizers														
6. Pregnancy and postpartum period														
7. Chronic and excessive use of alcohol														
8. Consistent feelings of depression "down in the dumps," lack of interest in doing anything														

It may be important to distinguish two types of apnea in case you look for it. *Obstructive* apnea refers to a blockage in the upper airway passage. The diaphragm continues to move up and down, but no air is being inhaled or exhaled. In *central* apnea, the diaphragm stops completely. If you are observing someone who may have apnea, the first indicator is *snoring, followed by a period of nonbreathing (20 to 100 seconds), followed by a gasp for air.* (Snoring, in itself, is not harmful. Don't be alarmed if that's all you see or hear.) If you suspect that the person has apnea, the next step might involve holding a mirror in front of the mouth and nose to see if any air exchange is occurring. If you sleep alone, you may be able to detect the possible occurrence of apnea by recording your sleep. Timers to turn recorders on and off are available in many hardware, variety, and department stores.

2. Leg Twitches. Have you ever experienced your body suddenly jerking and waking you up just as you are first falling to sleep. Many persons, both normal and poor sleepers, have this experience occasionally or even every night. But persons with *nocturnal myoclonus* experience these jerks and leg twitches almost *continually* throughout the night. Bed partners will often complain of being kicked or nudged frequently. Again, if you suspect this is your problem, ask your bed partner to remain awake for a while on two or three nights to see if your legs kick and twitch constantly. If you sleep alone, it may not be possible to detect the possibility of nocturnal myoclonus without assistance. For example, if the bed clothes are in disarray in the morning, you might ask a good friend to come in and watch you sleep to see if continued leg jerks are noticeable. It's important, however, that the person watching you realize the difference between myoclonus and REM sleep. In REM sleep, your entire body twitches, and this is perfectly normal. In myoclonus, by contrast, just your leg muscles twitch more or less continuously throughout the night.

3. High Temperature at Bedtime. As mentioned in the second chapter, sleep is part of a total daily cycle of body functions.

One function that varies regularly throughout the day and night is the maintenance of body temperature. It is generally higher in the middle of the day and reaches its low points at sometime during the night.

Some people's circadian rhythm or body time gets out of phase with clock time, despite the fact that they are not traveling long distances in brief time periods (as is the case with "jet lag"). You can easily detect if this is your problem by taking your temperature about four times per day for four or five days: when you arise and retire, and at two times during the middle of the day. Be sure that you haven't had anything to eat and drink just beforehand and leave the thermometer in your mouth for a full five minutes. Read the thermometer very accurately as your temperature may vary by no more than one degree. Avoid doing this before and during menstruation since ovulation does affect body temperature dramatically.

Figure 3-1 shows two contrasting body temperature patterns. The upper diagram represents a normal sleeper, someone whose body time is harmonized with clock time. The low points in the morning and evening correspond to the sleep cycle, and the high points during the day are in harmony with times that the person expects to be awake and alert. By contrast, the pattern represented in the bottom diagram shows the body-temperature pattern of one person with whom we worked. She experienced a low point in the middle of the day, and a high point around the time most people are ready to retire. If your temperature is highest at bedtime or in the late evening and reaches its low point during the day, some disruption in your circadian rhythm may be partly responsible for your insomnia. Fortunately, some of the procedures in this book, especially relaxation (Part III) and environmental planning (Chapter 8) can be used in normalizing your rhythm.

4. Excessive Daytime Sleepiness and Frequent Napping. Excessive daytime sleepiness and fatigue can be one characteristic of narcolepsy and hypersomnia. As we mentioned before, persons with narcolepsy experience *cataplexy*

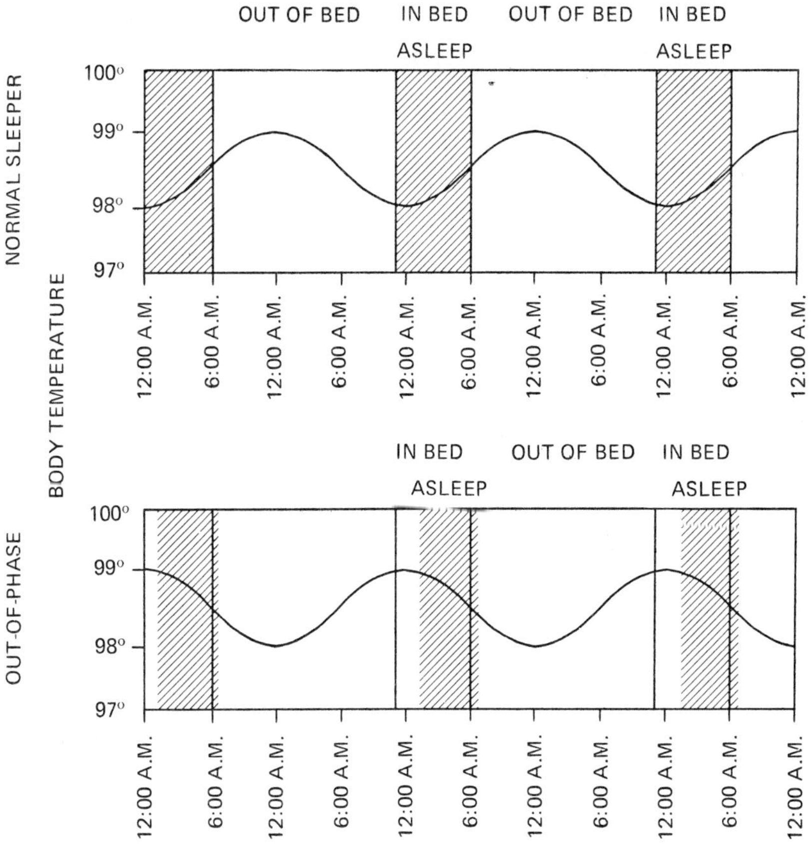

Body temperature fluctuations and sleep-waking cycles (the shaded portion represents the times when the person is sleeping). The person whose sleep-waking cycle is in harmony with his surroundings sleeps at low points in his cycle and is awake at high points. The out-of-phase person is in bed at the same time, but his sleep is delayed (and he complains of insomnia) because he is trying to sleep at the high points in his daily cycle. He feels fatigued at his low points when he is trying to pursue important activities during the day.

(awake accompanied by paralysis) and *irresistible sleep attacks* of relatively short duration accompanied by paralysis and vivid halluncinations. People with hypersomnia take longer naps on a fairly continual basis. The sufferer may feel very fatigued and tired, and will usually sleep as a result. But the hypersomniac's sleep is not irresistible. This individual can stave off sleep although it may take considerable effort to do so. The narcoleptic has no choice but to fall asleep. Both conditions can be accompanied by insomnia.

5. Drug Dependence. Almost any sleeping pill, if taken continually, will *cause* insomnia. If you are among the thousands of persons who have fallen victim to these medications, *don't do anything yet.* Sudden withdrawal could cause more serious problems. Just note that this is your problem and keep an accurate record of your drug intake for the time being.

STEPS TO TAKE

Observe your sleep and daytime behavior for four to seven days to determine if you experience any of the symptoms listed. If none are noticed, then feel comfortable in proceeding with the strategies recommended in this book. Also, be on the lookout for the medical student syndrome, reading about a disorder and then jumping to the conclusion that you have it. Read our descriptions thoughtfully and study your sleep carefully before jumping to any conclusions.

If you think that you may be bothered by one or the other of the disorders noted, take steps to consult someone who specializes in sleep disorders or some other knowledgeable medical person. Most physicians are not equipped to treat the disorders because much of the information presented here is not widely known, not even among members of the medical community. But perhaps your family physician, the local chapter of the American Medical Association, or a county medical association maybe able to recommend a sleep specialist. If you live near a major university with a medical school, you might also contact it regarding possible resources. If all else fails, a phone call or letter to one of the sleep laboratories and clinics mentioned in Chapter 2 may provide some helpful directions.

Your self-diagnosis is an important first step but recognize that it may be misleading. Exact diagnostic procedures have been established to determine the occurrence of these disorders. If you come through them with a clean bill of health but still suffer from insomnia, then it is worthwhile to continue with this book.

PREGNANCY, ALCOHOLISM, AND DEPRESSION

During the first three months of pregnancy, total sleep time usually increases. The second three months, however, are often marked by more frequent awakenings, and REM sleep may increase while Stage 4 sleep may decrease. During the final three months, sleep becomes more disturbed. It may take longer to get to sleep initially, awakenings during the night may be extended and more frequent, and Stage 4 and REM sleep may both decline. This pattern often occurs until about three to six months after birth. These symptoms will generally clear up with normal medical treatment during this time. If sleep disturbance continues, it might be worthwhile to consult a sleep specialist. (Items 6, 7, and 8 on Table 3-2 are included because they often are accompanied by disturbed sleep and insomnia.)

Disturbed sleep is also characteristic of persons who regularly drink large quantities of alcohol and for persons experiencing chronic depression. If either of these problems fit you, consult someone who specializes in their treatment.

A FINAL NOTE

We felt it important to include this brief discussion of some of the various physical disorders that can result in insomnia. We do not want to alarm you, but only to alert you to their possibility and give you some steps to take if you are sure you are bothered by them. If you have noticed none of these symptoms, then your insomnia can probably be conquered by the techniques presented here. We urge you to move forward with growing confidence that you can learn to sleep more normally. Indeed, it is our intention to help you build and maintain a high level of confidence that *you* can learn to sleep much better.

WATCHING YOUR SLEEP

The time has come to take action! The first step in finding out what to do about your sleep is to determine *how* and *to what extent* you are sleeping poorly and some factors possibly associated with your insomnia. Carefully looking at reality represents the first and most important step in using the scientific method in learning to sleep better. An accurate picture of your sleep and the kinds of disturbances you experience will help you decide which change strategies to use and will serve as a benchmark for evaluating your progress. Systematically gathering data on your sleep may also help build your commitment to change. By observing and assessing in a precise way, you will draw an accurate picture of your sleep problem and perhaps realize that it does have limits. When we view something without taking a close and careful look at it, it often appears large, diffuse, and unmanageable. By determining exactly what the problem involves, you may realize that you can overcome your sleep yourself because it does have boundaries. Your sleep may also start to get better as you begin to watch it closely. Simply observing can sometimes bring improvement, and you may begin to make small but important changes that result in better sleep.

THE SLEEP DIARY

The sleep diary is presented on the following page. Patrick Thomas (his name, of course, has been changed to protect his anonymity) was one of our first successful clients. Notice some important features of his diary and the way he completed it. Items 1, 2, 3, and 4 ask for basic information about the previous night's sleep. In completing these items, try to be as accurate as possible without becoming a clock watcher. Becoming overconcerned may make your sleep even worse, and none of us want that! We realize, of course, that there is going to be some error in your estimates, but that's okay. Just estimate your answers as well as you can. Realize, too, that the actual amount of sleep you are getting may not be as important as how you feel in the morning and during the day.

In completing Item 5, estimate the level of your physical tension and also try to notice where you are feeling the tension. Is it in your face, shoulders, neck, arms, or legs? Around your eyes and mouth, or in the stomach area?

Finally, in completing items 6, 7, and 8, be as specific and as complete as possible. Notice, for example, that Patrick indicated in item 8 the content of his pre-bedtime conversation with his wife about the *New Yorker* article he was reading.

PROMISES, PROMISES

Earlier we talked briefly of the need to be systematic. Drawing an accurate picture of sleep (getting maximum benefit from the techniques we present), means that these procedures must become a regular part of your daily routine. If the procedures are used only occasionally, they will not have their maximum impact and they are likely to drop from your schedule very rapidly. Change does not always come easily. But

Sleep Diary

Name *Patrick Thomas* Date *July 21*

1. Bedtime *10:30* Sleep time *12:00 p.m.*
2. It took me *90* minutes to fall asleep last night.
3. I awakened *2* times last night.

   Indicate *times* and *how long* it took to fall back asleep each time:

   2:30 — *40* minutes
   3:45 — *10* minutes
   ____ — ____ minutes
4. I woke up for the last time at *7:00* and slept a total of *6 1/10* hours.
5. Rate your level of physical arousal when you went to bed.

   Extremely calm/relaxed — Extremely tense/aroused

   1 2 3 4 5 6 (7) 8
6. Write down what you were thinking about as you were in bed:

   Bills and finances, trip to Los Angeles nept week, children; disagreement with boss last week, whether or not I was going to get a good night's sleep
7. Write down your activities from dinner time to bedtime:

   Washed dinner dishes — *Conversed with wife about work*
   Fifed lamp cord
   Skimmed Time magazine — *Watched 10:00 news*
8. Write down your activities once you got into bed:

   Talked with wife about trip — *Read New Yorker article on education*
   Talked about bills

we can increase our changes of success if we provide ourselves with some assistance.

THE SELF-CONTRACT

One excellent method for integrating new procedures into our daily routine is provided on the following page. Look it over for a minute and notice some of its features.

Using a self-contract to accomplish something important is one effective way to insure that we will complete what we set out to do. Its strength is based on some simple realities of being human. By specifying exactly *what we agree to do* and *under what circumstances it will be done* (Specific Behavioral Objectives), we can determine exactly what we want to accomplish and can more easily evaluate our fulfillment of the contract. It is really important to be specific here. If your agreement reads "to see how well I am sleeping," how are you going to know whether or not you have done it? If instead we say, "I agree to complete the sleep diary before leaving home in the morning for a period of three days," it becomes immediately possible for you and anyone else to evaluate your efforts. Reduce ambiguity so that you can determine if you have reached your goals.

Environmental planning is arranging our surroundings to help us to remember to get the job done, and is based on the fact that we often forget to do even important things in the press of our daily activities. This is especially true for new routines we are trying to put into our life. The self-contract calls for two kinds of reminders: physical and social (for example, notes on the wash basin, or your spouse helping by encouragement) and mental (thinking about the task at a specific time).

Finally, in providing *consequences,* we make something we want dependent upon completing the agreed upon activity. If we keep our bargain with ourselves, we agree to provide ourselves with a reward, with some "goodie," or some pleasant

Self-Contract

GOAL: help myself by learning about my sleep; keep good records of sleep-related activities

Specific Behavioral Objectives

I agree to complete the sleep diary
(specify behavior)

under the following circumstances: each morning upon
(specify where, when,
arising & before leaving the house for 3
how much, etc.)
days

Environmental Planning

In order to help me do this, I am going to: (1) arrange my physical and social environment by (1) placing the diary next to the coffee pot; and

(2) completing it before I allow myself a cup of coffee in the morning

and; (2) control my internal environment (thoughts, images) by:

(1) telling myself how important it is to complete the sleep diary; and

(2) saying to myself that I can keep accurate records for 3 days

CONSEQUENCES

Provided by me:
(If contract is kept) new record album (limit of $4.98)
(If contract is broken) no record album, no dessert for 2 days

Provided by others:
(If contract is kept) special favorite dinner
(If contract is broken) no special dinner

July 24
(Renewal Date)

Signed Patrick Thomas
Helper Melissa Thomas
Date July 20

experience we enjoy. But if we don't keep the agreement, we relinquish or "give up" the goodie. We must also provide some negative consequences as well. One client promised herself a new belt if she self-observed for three days, but decided to also forego dessert for two days if she failed (and of course not buy the belt).

It is often helpful to involve someone else in the contract. Change is almost always more enjoyable and more easily accomplished if we can work with someone else. A helper can provide the needed encouragement when our motivation or spirits might wane. Being responsible to someone else also helps us to stick to the task. Anyone can be involved in your contract—a spouse, a friend, or coworker. The only requirement is that your helper support and encourage you in your efforts to change, and to help you abide by the terms of the contract. (Critics you don't need!)

Notice also that the contract has a *renewal date.* Renew the contract every three or four days at first. The contract may lose its impact if it extends for a longer period of time. The contract is signed and dated, adding a note of formality to the entire proceedings.

OTHER STRATEGIES FOR BEING SYSTEMATIC

The self-contract may not appeal to you, and may not be the strategy you want to use to help you be systematic and consistent. That's okay. It is only one method—a very good one—to help you maintain your progress. If you decide not to use a written self-contract, then you really should plan to use some alternative strategy for being systematic. You may want to make a simple verbal agreement with your helper. Or, you may decide to "go it alone" and work by yourself. Remember, you can make a written contract with yourself without involving a helper.

Self-Improvement Task II

Watching My Sleep

I will begin helping myself learn to sleep better by:

1. Keeping the Sleep Diary for at least 3 days.
2. a. Completing a self-contract to insure that I complete the Sleep Diary;
   or
   b. Developing some other personally meaningful technique to help me be consistent and systematic.

When finished, I will:

1. Reward myself according to contract;
2. Move to Chapter Four; and
3. Congratulate myself.

If I do not succeed, I will:

1. Renegotiate the contract for shorter periods of time, for example, one or two days;
2. Do this until I complete three days' observations; and then
3. Move on to Chapter Four.

The self-contract does have the advantage of putting down in black (or blue or red) and white exactly what you agree to do. So if you and your helper decide to use verbal agreements, make sure there are no misunderstandings. If you decide to work by yourself, build in other devices to assist. It is simply too easy to drop an activity, especially a new one, when life gets a bit full. As we suggested before, you might set up a definite schedule to follow or establish specific times to devote to the program. Reminders and prompters placed in critical places at home or at work may also help. Remember, however, to change them often in terms of content and location; if a reminder becomes too familiar it has a way of "fading into the woodwork."

TOOLS FOR CHANGE

The Sleep Diary and the Self-Contract (or any other strategy you choose to use) are your basic tools for change.

Begin using them right away and continue using them all the way through this book to help you be accurate and systematic. Feel free to get copies of your own forms if you don't like to write in books.

Your first task involves completing the Sleep Diary for a period of three days. Use the forms provided to monitor your sleep, and the self-contract to draw up an agreement with yourself to complete this task.

When you have finished three days' observations (and, of course, have rewarded yourself for completing your contract), proceed with the next chapter. And, most important, offer yourself some congratulations! You have just taken the first and perhaps the most important step to improve your sleep. Don't be reluctant or resistant to encouraging yourself. Many of us have very high standards and feel that we simply do not deserve anything unless we're completely perfect. These high barriers prevent self-change. Take heart and pleasure in making progress—small step-by-step change. Be good to yourself! You deserve encouragement.

Self-Contract

Goal:

Specific Behavioral Objectives

I agree to ____
(specify behavior)

____

under the following circumstances: ______________________
(specify where, when,

____

how much, etc.)

____

Environmental Planning

In order to help me do this, I am going to: (1) arrange my physical and social environment by ______________________________

____

and; (2) control my internal environment (thoughts, images) by: ______

____

____

Consequences

Provided by me:
(If contract is kept) ______________________________
(If contract is broken) ______________________________

Provided by others:
(If contract is kept) ______________________________
(If contract is broken) ______________________________

____

______________ (Renewal Date)

Signed ______________________

Witness ______________________

Date ______________________

Sleep Diary

Name ______________________ Date ______________________

1. Bedtime __________________ Sleep time __________________

2. It took me _____ minutes to fall asleep last night.

3. I awakened _____ times last night.

   Indicate *time* and how long it took to fall back asleep each time.

   _______ _______ minutes

   _______ _______ minutes

   _______ _______ minutes

4. I woke up for the last time at _____ and slept a total of _____ hours.

5. Rate your level of physical arousal when you went to bed.

Extremely calm/relaxed							Extremely tense/aroused
1	2	3	4	5	6	7	8

6. Write down what you were thinking about as you were in bed:

   ____

   ____

   ____

7. Write down your activities from dinner time to bedtime:

   ______________________ ______________________

   ______________________ ______________________

   ______________________ ______________________

8. Write down your activities once you got into bed:

   ______________________ ______________________

   ______________________ ______________________

   ______________________ ______________________

4

Building Commitment

You've had your first experience in taking a close look at your prebedtime activities. If you did this successfully, congratulations! Be sure to reward yourself and collect your reward from your helper if you made an agreement about it.

If you weren't able to complete the three days' observations, don't worry. Sometimes it takes longer to do new things. Go back and renegotiate your contract and try again. We strongly recommend that you do this *before* attempting to take the first steps outlined in this chapter.

THE ABCs: ATTITUDES, BELIEFS, AND COMMITMENT

Being successful usually requires commitment. Especially difficult tasks demand that we really be committed; without commitment it's too easy to give up before reaching our goal.

It's unfortunate that our language has taught us to look at commitment as something we either *have* or do not have, much like a table or a car, or something we *are* or are not, much like being a male or a female, an adult or a child.

Rather than viewing commitment as something we are or have, *we think that it's more useful to see commitment as something we do.* (Remember, being scientific requires that we break away from our old ways of looking at the world.)

> *Commitment:*
>
> - *actions we perform;*
> - *individual thoughts we have about our problem;*
> - *the steps we take to solve our problem.*

Rather than seeing commitment as global and vague, as something we either do or do not have, it's more useful to see commitment as *specific thoughts.* This viewpoint allows us to examine carefully the exact nature of our commitment and *do something to change it and help it grow.* Specific thoughts and beliefs can be described and changed much more readily than a vague "all-or-nothing" concept. Certainly, changing a small piece of something is much more likely to be successful than attempting to change it all at once. Further, viewing commitment as specific thoughts and beliefs liberates us from either being completely turned on or off to a program of change. Our thoughts at various times may run the full spectrum from grave doubt to strong expectation of success. We can *assess* and we can *change* our thoughts to help us maintain our commitment to change.

Our willingness to expend effort to start and continue a plan of action can be described as specific thoughts we have about our actions.

This chapter helps you learn to take a close look at your own self-talk and change it so that you can continually improve your own commitment to change.

TALKING TO OURSELVES

Our internal monologues are endless. We constantly talk to ourselves, muttering directions, instructions and evaluating our actions as we go through the day. For example, we might engage in the following monologue in planning our day:

> Okay! What do I have to accomplish today? Let's see, I need to run some errands—the store and the dry cleaners—and then I should do some reading, and perhaps exercise a bit.

Or we might use the following self-instructions in making a decision:

> Should I go away for the weekend or not? It sure would be nice to get away, and I haven't been out of town for a couple of months. But I do have a lot of work to do, and I did promise to have that report ready by Monday. I think I could get that stuff done on Friday and get away Friday evening. Why not? I'll do it!

Consider what we might say to ourselves to cause a problem in a stressful situation: "Boy, am I losing my cool! I must look like the village idiot." Worse, we may not have an effective self-instruction ready to use in problem situations. Think back to your first job interview or a recent one that seemed especially crucial to you. What did you say to yourself as you were driving to the interview? What did you think about as you were sitting in the waiting room about to be questioned? Did recurring thoughts about how difficult the interview would be keep popping into your mind? Were you worried about your appearance and whether you would impress the interviewer?

Maybe you were already anticipating problems with others on the job before you even had it.

Many of us have had similar experiences. When it was all over, we may have felt relief and realized that it was foolish to be tense. The interview may have gone better if we could have remained calm and relaxed. Our tension may have been decreased considerably if those worrisome thoughts could have been kept under control.* *The principle is clear:* we create our reality in part by how we anticipate events and how we perceive our experiences.

Consider how your reactions might differ, given the same situation, if you are feeling happy and energetic or if you are feeling tense or depressed. Perhaps you come home from work and plan to spend some time with your children. They are probably glad to see you and feel like playing and being active. If you are feeling happy, you might view their activity as pleasant and may even want to join in their game. But if you've had a difficult day (or if you slept poorly last night), their energy and noise may be the last straw. The same event is easily viewed from two different perspectives and becomes two different experiences or realities for you.

THOUGHTS ABOUT SLEEP

The thoughts we have about sleep are really not very different. Our thoughts may be influenced by how we choose to view our experiences. "No matter what I do, I never can get a good night's sleep," is a common complaint. But there must have been times when your sleep was better. Beware of thoughts that stress "never" or "always." Such talk is a clue to "selective perception." It may seem as if we never can sleep, *but,* in fact, there are better nights and there are worse nights. Most important, *what we say to ourselves might actually make*

*Some of you may not think in sentences but rather in images. If so, try to keep track of your images and analyze what they say about your sleep. Follow the directions in this chapter and try to substitute more helpful images.

our sleep worse: "I've been lying here for hours, and I'm still awake. I'll bet this is going to be a really bad night." These kinds of thoughts may prevent us from sleeping and can sabotage our efforts to change.

We can change our view of reality by changing *what we say to ourselves*. Have you ever met someone for the first time and noticed that you really didn't like that person very well? But after a few more encounters, our thoughts about the person change; this individual might not only be tolerable, but even the kind of person we might enjoy for a close friend. The person hasn't changed. We have changed our views, our perceptions, and our thoughts about the individual.

We're not used to modifying our thoughts about anything, and certainly not about sleep. After all, we sleep poorly and our thoughts simply reflect that reality (or do they?). Maybe our thoughts get in the way of good sleep, or maybe we don't remember all the times we have slept well? Maybe it might be worthwhile to take a close look at our own thoughts and decide if they shouldn't be changed.*

WHAT DO YOU SAY TO YOURSELF ABOUT YOUR SLEEP?

The first step involves identifying exactly (in words) what you say to yourself about your sleeping problem. Most of us go through the entire day without ever really listening to what we say to ourselves. That doesn't mean our thoughts are unconscious, only that we have not taken time to tune into them.

Listed in the table on page 75 are some common "poor sleeper" thoughts. Look them over and see if any apply to you. Try to add at least on of your own in the spaces provided. If you don't experience unhelpful thoughts, don't feel that you

*Note that what we think and say to ourselves influences strongly how we *feel* about ourselves. Positive self-thoughts and monologues can make us feel better physically.

should. Just recognize that you're one step ahead of the program.

Thoughts About:	*Examples:*
Capabilities to change; motivation	"This stuff sounds very involved. I'm not sure I have the will power to stick with it." "I think I am just plagued. I'll never be a good sleeper." "I don't know why this should work. Nothing else has." My self-talk: ____________________ ______________________________
Expectations about not sleeping	"I've been lying here for an hour already. I'll bet it is going to be a miserable night." "Oh, brother. Here it is 3:30 a.m. and I'm awake. I bet I don't get back asleep." "That trip next week is going to be miserable. I can't sleep a wink being in a strange place." My self-talk: ____________________ ______________________________
Excessive worry about not sleeping	"I need to get to sleep. I'll be no good tomorrow if I don't." "I just can't go on like this!" My self-talk: ____________________ ______________________________
Excuses about the program	"I can't do these exercises now. I'm just too busy. Maybe next month when things slow down a bit." "I'm just high-strung, I guess. Nothing is going to change my sleeping patterns." My self-talk: ____________________ ______________________________

Do any of these sound familiar? Were you able to add any of your own? We think that getting a handle on these self-defeating thoughts can lay the foundation for you to benefit from the rest of the book. Indeed, with more encouraging perceptions, more positive expectations, and more helpful self-talk, you can change and maintain progress.

In addition to keeping your Sleep Diary, you should write down at least three thoughts you have about your sleep. Do it for the next two days. Put them right on your Sleep Diary, perhaps on the blank side. Try to write them down *verbatim*. (And don't worry if they are not grammatically correct!) By keeping a word-by-word account, you will know exactly what you are saying to yourself and can then take the first steps in changing them.

Self-Improvement Task III

Identifying Thoughts and Self-Talk About Sleep

I will help myself to improve my sleep by:

1. Keeping a "word-by-word" diary of my thoughts regarding my sleep.
2. Keeping my Daily Sleep Diary.
3. a. Negotiating a self-contract to insure that I complete the task.
   or
   b. Making some other arrangements to help me by systematic and consistent.

It may seem that these contracts don't cover very much time and don't require you to do very much. But that's exactly the point. We want you to be successful, and it's much easier to accomplish a little bit in a short amount of time.

Continue with the rest of this chapter after you have collected this information for two days. Remember, getting detailed information is at the heart of your developing a personally tailored way to sleep better. As a personal scientist, you need good data to make good decisions.

Self-Contract

Goal: Identify Thoughts About Sleep

Specific Behavioral Objectives

I agree to: ______________________________
(specify behavior)

____

under the following circumstances: ______________________________
(specify where, when,

____
how much, etc.)

____

Environmental Planning

In order to help me do this, I am going to: (1) arrange my physical and social environment by ______________________________

____

and; (2) control my internal environment (thoughts, images) by: ______

____

____

Consequences

Provided by me:
(If contract is kept) ______________________________

(If contract is broken) ______________________________

Provided by others:
(If contract is kept) ______________________________

(If contract is broken) ______________________________

____

______________ Signed ______________
(Renewal Date)

Witness ______________

Date ______________

SEEING REALITY DIFFERENTLY

If you found that you don't engage in unhelpful thoughts about your sleep, congratulations. You're way ahead of the game. But read the rest of this chapter so that you are aware of what can be done should negative self-talk begin to occur.

If you noticed that you have a number of thoughts that should be changed, we urge you to continue with the exercises that follow.

CHANGING THOUGHTS ABOUT SLEEP

It's time to do something to change your thoughts about sleep. You may be inclined at this point to say, "Sure, but my thoughts are real. That's the way my sleep really is!" Recall our previous discussion about *selective perception.* What we think is true is often a matter of what we choose to tune into. "Do you see the glass as half empty or half full?" is an example familiar to many of us. Events about sleep can be interpreted in many ways. You may believe that you have been lying awake for about an hour, and at least two possible interpretations are possible. You might say:

> I've been lying here for one full hour. This is miserable. If I don't get to sleep soon, I'm going to be totally wiped out tomorrow! I'll never make it through the day.

Someone else could look at the same event quite differently:

> I guess I've been lying here for an hour. But that's okay. I'm getting rest and it's very peaceful. If I continue to relax I should fall asleep soon.

Which statement do you think would be better in helping someone actually get to sleep? "Cleaning up" what you say to yourself may take you a long way in helping you to overcome your difficulty in sleeping. Think of it as your efforts to help with your "cognitive ecology."

You may not really believe what you are saying at first. But that's all right. New thoughts may seem awkward, unnatural, even artificial at first. Remember how clumsy you felt that first time you swung a No. 2 wood, or stepped on to a tennis court for your first try at doubles? Consistent practice can change what feels awkward into something that is smooth. We believe that learning to think differently about your sleep problems is probably one of the most important steps in learning to overcome them.

THINKING HELPFUL THOUGHTS

The first task involves identifying some helpful alternatives. These alternatives should be a realistic but positive appraisal of the situation. Let's look at some of the examples of unhelpful thoughts we provided earlier and see if we can generate some realistic but positive alternatives. Try your hand at generating some alternatives as you go along. It really isn't that difficult. Simply take a slightly different view of the situation.

GENERATING YOUR OWN ALTERNATIVES

It is time to generate some alternatives to your sleep-related thoughts. Using the worksheet, write your thoughts in the categories provided. Try to put down the exact words you spoke to yourself. If they don't fit exactly, you may want to make up some categories that fit your thoughts.

Next, generate some alternatives for yourself. Again, try to make them *realistic but positive.* Write down exactly what you want to say to yourself.

Some Helpful Alternatives

Category	*Unhelpful Thought*	*Possible Helpful Thought*
Capabilities to change; motivation	"This stuff sounds very involved; I'm not sure that I have the willpower to stick with it."	"Willpower doesn't count. If I just make a few changes here and there, my sleep will gradually be improved."
	"I think I am just plagued. I'll never be a good sleeper."	"If I am willing to make some consistent effort, I can learn to sleep better."
	"I don't know why this should work. Nothing else has."	______
Expectations about not sleeping	"I've been lying here for an hour already. I'll bet this is going to be a miserable night."	"That's okay. The house is peaceful and I am resting. I'll be to sleep soon."
	"Oh brother. Here it is 3:30 a.m. and I'm awake. I bet I'll never get back to sleep."	"I'll get back to sleep if I just stay calm and don't worry about it."
	"That trip next week is going to be miserable. I won't sleep a wink, being in a strange place and all."	______
Excessive worry about not sleeping	"I need to get to sleep. I'll be no good tomorrow if I don't."	"I'll get to sleep. A half hour's sleep is not going to make *that* much difference."
	"I just can't go on like this."	______
Excuses about the program	"I can't do these exercises now. I'm just too busy. Maybe next month when things slow down a bit."	"I'm always busy, and I'm no busier than anyone else. If I want to improve, I will make the time."
	"I'm just high strung, I guess. Nothing is going to change my sleeping patterns."	______

"Thoughtful" Worksheet

Category	*Thought*	*Alternative*

Self-Improvement Task IV

Substituting Helpful Thoughts

I will help myself improve my sleep by:

1. Substituting a helpful alternative thought whenever I notice myself thinking an unhelpful thought. I will *try* to do this *at least* once a day.
2. Practicing helpful alternatives at least two times per day (once shortly before going to bed).
3. Completing a self-contract to help me accomplish these goals. (If I prefer, I will substitute some other method to help me be systematic.)
4. Continuing to keep my daily Sleep Diary.
5. When I have done this for four days, I will move to the next exercise.

CHANGING TAKES PRACTICE

The next step is the most critical. Conscious and consistent effort is needed so that you begin to think and believe your new, helpful thoughts.

We suggest that you do this in two ways:

1. Whenever you notice yourself engaging in a thought that is not helpful, substitute one of your helpful alternatives.
2. Set aside *at least two times per day* to consciously think about your helpful thoughts. Practice saying each thought to yourself at least five times. This could be in the car, at lunch, or while shopping. One of your times should probably be just before you go to bed.

MAKE A SELF-CONTRACT

Your former self-contract has probably expired by now, and it's time to draw up a new one. But this time you're going to have two tasks to complete. In addition to continuing to

Self-Contract

Goal: Monitor Sleep and Think Helpful Thoughts
Specific Behavioral Objectives I agree to: ________________________________ (specify behavior) under the following circumstances ____________________ (specify where, when ____________________________________ how much, etc.) ____________________________________ *Environmental Planning* In order to help me do this, I am going to: (1) arrange my physical and social environment by ____________________________ ____________________________________ and; (2) control my internal environment (thoughts, images) by: ______ ____________________________________ ____________________________________ *Consequences* Provided by me: (If contract is kept) ____________________________ (If contract is broken) ___________________________ Provided by others: (If contract is kept) ____________________________ (If contract is broken) ___________________________ ____________________________________ ______________ Signed ____________________ (Renewal Date) Witness ____________________ Date ____________________

monitor your sleep, also include in your contract your agreement to think helpful thoughts. As part of the contract, you might provide yourself with cues and reminders so that your change efforst will be systematic. And, most important, plan to reward your efforts. You're making great strides in taking control of your sleep problem.

HOW SUCCESSFUL DO YOU EXPECT TO BE?

Expectations about the future can influence both how much effort we are willing to expend in doing something and how successful we actually are. "I'll probably really fail miserably" usually means just that. Some one who says, "I don't really expect to do very well. I'm not going to try very hard" will not put forth much effort. They'll probably perform poorly as a result.

While it's important to be realistic about our capabilities, it's also critical that we don't defeat ourselves from the outset by expecting the worst and thus insuring that it occurs. Another form of self-talk may be important to your commitment and success. We call them *behavior-outcome rules.* These rules are nothing more than "if . . . then . . ." statements about relationships between your own actions (behavior) and what you expect to happen as a result (outcome).

Behavior-Outcome Rules

Self-Perception:	"I'm the kind of person who, once awakened at night, cannot fall back to sleep."
Behavior-Outcome Rule:	"*If* I wake up at night, *Then* I will not fall back to sleep."

WAKING UP IN THE MIDDLE OF THE NIGHT

JENNIFER. *Jennifer was a 35-year-old woman, extremely active in civic affairs, who had suffered from in-*

somnia since early in her twenties. Especially stimulating activities caused her to have difficulty in falling asleep at night. Attending an evening lecture or participating in a city council or school board meeting usually aroused her so much that it would take her several hours to unwind before she could fall asleep. She minimized these late evening activities reluctantly. When she did decide to attend an evening meeting, she planned relaxing activities to follow and arranged her schedule so she could sleep longer the next morning if necessary.

She was, however, extremely fearful of waking up in the middle of the night. She believed that she would not be able to fall back to sleep if she woke up. A first step in learning about this problem involved writing it down in the form of a self-perception, and then expressing it as a behavior outcome rule. Notice that the behavior outcome rule is put down as an "if . . . then . . ." statement, and, for purposes of emphasis, is expressed as though it must always happen that way.*

It doesn't matter at this point if the rule seems true or not. The only thing that is important is that Jennifer believed that it was true and acted as though it was. It was part of her reality.

LEARNING A NEW RULE

Jennifer's is a common unhelpful behavior–outcome rule. You can imagine what her thoughts were like when she woke up in the middle of the night because of this rule. She thought immediately and automatically: "I'm awake. I'm not going to fall back to sleep."

Just as you learned to change thoughts by practicing dif-

*Most of us are not used to thinking that we can use our mental abilities to overcome emotional problems. Sometimes it's not possible to do this, but in many cases our emotional reaction is fed by our irrational self-talk. By talking to ourselves in a more helpful way, it may be possible to prevent those irrational emotions from flaring up in the first place.

ferent ones, you can also change your behavior–outcome rules by practicing different ones. This involves three separate steps:

1. Identifying an alternative behavior outcome rule;
2. Identifying an alternative self-perception based on your new rule;
3. Practicing your new rule and self-perception *and* looking for evidence to support it.

Jennifer's change program is presented below. Notice that she generated a helpful alternative behavior–outcome rule and self-perception, decided when to practice it, and looked for evidence that it was true. Once she began to *look* for evidence, she found that her new rule was more true than her former one.

Jennifer's Behavior Outcome Rules

Self-Perception:	"I'm the kind of person who, once awakened at night, cannot fall back to sleep."
Behavior–Outcome Rule:	"*If* I wake up at night, *Then* I will not be able to fall back to sleep again."
Helpful Behavior–Outcome Rule:	"*If* I wake up at night, *Then,* I will be able to fall back to sleep in a short while."
Helpful Self-Perception:	"I'm the kind of person who, once awakened at night, can fall back to sleep again."
I will practice this thought at night before retiring.	
Evidence:	Three nights this week I was awakened, and was able to fall back to sleep on two of them in less than 15 minutes.

WHAT ABOUT YOU?

Jennifer's case is not unusual. Many people generate beliefs about the world and the consequences of their behavior and then follow them without putting them to the test, without seeing if they really are true. We think it would be helpful to take a look at your own behavior-outcome rules in three areas.

1. *Examine what you believe to be true about the relationships between your behavior and how you sleep.* Like Jennifer, do you have some fixed and firm

Thoughts and reality

- are not the same;
- can be influenced by many things such as mood;
- influence bad habits such as always thinking negatively about things.

Commitment

- is not something we have (like our arm) or something we are (such as male or female);
- is something we *do* or what we *think*;
- is specific thoughts we have about reality and our actions;
- can be changed by changing specific thoughts.

Thoughts about sleep

- can be changed to help us sleep better;
- need to be practiced and used.

The behavior-outcome rules

- are if . . . then . . . statements about our actions and their outcomes;
- influence what we do and how hard we're likely to try to change;
- can be changed if we practice positive ones and look for evidence that they are true.

beliefs about what you think will happen if you do certain things?

2. *Examine what you think about your chances for success.* Some examples of unhelpful behavior–outcome rules are presented on the worksheet entitled "Discovering Your Own Rules". We think it's important to do two things at this point. First, study our examples and the alternatives we provided. See if you can generate some alternatives of your own. Also, try to examine your own thoughts to see what behavior outcome rules you use to guide your own actions.
3. *Once you are familiar with the strategy, begin to change your rules systematically.* Follow the steps in Self-Improvement Task V, use the worksheet provided, and negotiate a self-contract. Once you have

mastered the process, you are ready to begin learning systematic relaxation skills.

Discovering Your Own Rules

Thoughts about Behavior and Sleep:

Thought	*Alternative*
If I wake up in the middle of the night, I'm not going to fall back	If I wake up in the middle of the night, I can fall back to sleep.
If I don't fall to sleep within five minutes, then I'm doomed to lie awake for hours.	If I don't fall asleep within five minutes, then I can lie here and relax and fall asleep very soon.
If I am not in bed by 10:00, then I get revived and I might as well plan on not sleeping for the whole night."	____________________ ____________________ ____________________ ____________________
(Write your own rule here) ____________________ ____________________ ____________________ ____________________	____________________ ____________________ ____________________ ____________________

Thoughts about Your Chances of Success:

If I follow the program, then I probably will not be very successful.	If I follow this program, then my sleep should improve as a result.
If I try to practice new rules, then I am going to get more tense than before.	If I try to practice new rules, then I might start to believe them.
If I keep a daily Sleep Diary, I will not have much time to do anything else.	____________________ ____________________ ____________________
(Write your own rule here) ____________________ ____________________ ____________________ ____________________	____________________ ____________________ ____________________ ____________________

A FINAL WORD

Changing thoughts is not something we commonly think possible, much less attempt to do. But if you can learn how to change your self-talk, your beliefs about reality and your ability to change, you will have gone a long way in learning to improve your sleep. You may also have learned some strategies that can be applied to other parts of your life.

Self-Improvement Task V

Learning New Behavior Outcome Rules

I will help myself improve my sleep by:

1. Identifying one behavior outcome rule about my sleep or about my ability to improve my sleep.
2. Identifying a helpful alternative rule and a self-perception.
3. Practicing my helpful alternative at least two times per day. I will look for and note all evidence that supports the new rule.
4. Completing a self-contract (or use some other method) to help me accomplish these goals.
5. Continuing to keep my daily Sleep Diary and practicing my helpful alternative thoughts. When I have done this for four days, I will move to Chapter 5.

Work Sheet

Behavior Outcome Rules

Self-perception: "I'm the kind of person who . . .

Behavior–outcome rule: "If I . . .
Then . . .

Helpful Alternative

Behavior–outcome rule: "If I . . .
Then . . .

Self-perception: "I'm the kind of person who . . .

I Will Practice this Thought

Evidence

Self-Contract

Goal: Learning New Behavior Outcome Rules

Specific Behavioral Objective

I agree to: ______________________________
(specify behavior)

____

under the following circumstances: ______________________________
(specify where, when,

____

how much, etc.)

____

Environmental Planning

In order to help me do this, I am going to: (1) arrange my physical and social environment by ______________________________

____

and; (2) control by internal environment (thoughts, images) by: ______

____

____

Consequences

Provided by me:
(If contract is kept) ______________________________

(If contract is broken) ______________________________

Provided by others:
(If contract is kept) ______________________________

(If contract is broken ______________________________

- -

______________ Signed ______________________________
(Renewal Date)

Witness ______________________________

Date ______________________________

Part Three

LEARNING TO RELAX

It is 11:10 P.M. Time to go to bed. You switch off the evening news, or perhaps put down what you have been reading or working on, and think about the need for a good night's sleep. "Hmm. I need to sleep well tonight. Tomorrow's meeting is really important, and I need to be up for it. I hope I sleep well tonight. I've got to be on top of the situation tomorrow. I can't afford another night like the last three. I'll just bet I'm not going to sleep."

After going though your "getting ready for bed" routine, you climb into bed still wondering if tonight is going to be good or bad (but probably expecting the worst). "What should I read? I don't want to pick up my novel because I'll get too involved in that. Maybe I can flip through *National Geographic.* No, I'll find that too interesting. I need something boring to put me to sleep. Maybe I'll just read the *TV Guide.* That should do it."

Propping the pillow up behind your back and adjusting your

reading lamp, you start to read an article on the highlights of the new television season and how situation comedies and "give-away" programs are going to be better than ever. The material doesn't excite you greatly, but that's exactly what you want right now. Your mind begins to wander a bit. "This last week has really been something. I have really been under the gun. I sure hope everything turns out okay." Back to new rules for television violence, briefly, and then you notice some tension in your arms and neck.

"It must be catching up with me. I hope I can get some rest this weekend." Even though you feel tired, you notice that you feel a little aroused physically. You feel like you could go out and run around the block a few times. Your body doesn't feel ready, not just yet, to fall asleep. Rolling your head from side to side helps your neck a little bit. You feel some of the muscles crack and a bit of the tension go away, but your wish is that it could become totally limp and relaxed.

Back to the sports events that will be covered next season. Always bigger and better. A good yawn tells you that maybe you can get some sleep, and *TV Guide* isn't really all that stimulating.

The light gets turned off, but back on because you forgot to set your alarm. Better set it for 6:00 so that you have plenty of time to wake up just in case you sleep that long.

"I know I'll be awake before then, but just in case . . ."

The light goes off a second time, you fluff up the pillow a bit, and move into your favorite position.

"The arms are a bit stiff, too, and I still feel like I could work for another hour or so. Maybe I should have finished that correspondence."

Morning comes very early. "I need to relax and get to sleep." Thoughts of the day creep in slowly, and one idea leads to another. "Tomorrow! Need to be prepared for that meeting. Midnight already. Damn! Why can't I stop worrying about it and get some sleep."

Most of us have had experiences similar to this at one time or another, and you may go through it every night. The agony is very real and relief comes only occasionally when you are so exhausted that your body literally collapses. But good sleep need not be reserved for thoses times when total exhaustion takes over. It is possible to learn to do something to reduce your physical and mental tension, and get to sleep more easily and quickly in the process. That's what this section is all about: *learning to relax your mind and your body* so that you can relax at night when you need to sleep *and* during the day so that you can carry on your activities more effectively.

WHY RELAXATION?

Research has revealed two interesting facts about people who have difficulty getting to sleep and staying asleep. First, problem sleepers often have a lot on their minds when they go to bed. It is difficult to fall asleep easily because these thoughts either interfere directly with sleep or are associated with sleeplessness. Second, problem sleepers are often overaroused, physiologically speaking, when they go to bed. In Chapter 2, we spoke briefly about the "process view of sleep," the theory that says that sleep is part of our daily circadian rhythm process. Problem sleepers' circadian rhythms may be desynchronized or simply out of phase with the demands of clock time. Persons with insomnia seem to experience a lot of nervous-system activity as they climb into bed and try to go to sleep. During the day our minds and bodies need to be perked up and working so that we can pursue our daytime activities. But when mental and physical arousal continue into the night, they are likely to interfere with sleep. *Fortunately, we can learn to reduce our mental and physical arousal and tension, and thus learn to get to sleep more easily and to sleep more soundly.*

We present you two techniques to help you relax during the day and at night. These procedures teach you specific ways for lessening physical tension and mental arousal at night. Further, they may help by readjusting your body-rhythm processes. These relaxation procedures do not work automatically; they do not do anything *to you* to help you sleep more easily and better. Rather, they are skills that you yourself can learn and apply with practice. *If you use and apply them, they will help you sleep more normally.**

*You may find, too, that it helps to use other strategies for achieving relaxation. Sexual intercourse is very relaxing for some people, as is reading, a hot shower, or meditation. All these can be used in conjunction with the physical and mental relaxation procedures presented here.

Learning to relax will help you in two ways. First, instead of thinking about the day's events, or whatever you have to do tomorrow or the day after that or even next week, you will learn to concentrate on pleasant internal sensations. Because this requires little thinking on your part, falling asleep is encouraged. Second, relaxation shuts down nervous-system activity because your body and mind can't be active and completely relaxed at the same time. When you relax, sleep will come easily and you will sleep soundly because activity within your body will decrease.

USING THE RELAXATION METHODS

The two procedures we present in Part III are designed to help you relax physically and mentally. The first, called *Progressive Relaxation,* is primarily a physical relaxation procedure, while the second, *Mental Relaxation,* is very useful for relaxing the mind and preventing unwanted and racing thoughts. Bear in mind that both procedures result in physical as well as mental relaxation. You will be finding out which is more helpful or if both are effective for you.

Most people seem to learn to relax best by beginning with Progressive Relaxation. After that is mastered, elements of the mental relaxation techniques can be integrated gradually into your practice until you have learned to relax both mind and body when and where you want to.

Most people seem to learn to relax best by beginning with Progressive Relaxation. After that is mastered, elements of the mental relaxation techniques can be integrated gradually into your practice until you have learned to relax both mind and body when and where you want to.

Before trying to learn the relaxation techniques, read all of Part III and study both procedures carefully. When you feel that you understand them and know the steps involved, begin using them. Some people have found it helpful to record the instructions in a soothing voice on a cassette tape recorder. That way, they don't have to think about the specific steps each time they go through the exercise, but can just lie back and follow the instructions. Also, some very good prerecorded cassette tapes are available commercially and are advertised in *Psychology Today* and other popular psychological magazines.

One final note of caution. *Learning to relax is a skill* and something most of us are not used to using and practicing. Achieving complete results may take time and practice; *don't expect miracles the first time you do the exercises.* Give yourself a chance to try them out; results will come with time. And remember, be patient with yourself. Trying too hard and expecting "quick, 24-hour service" results can make things worse. After all, learning to relax should be a slow, pleasant, and relaxing experience.

5

Learning to Relax Your Body

Progressive (deep muscle) Relaxation was developed in the 1930s at the University of Chicago by Dr. Edmund Jacobson, physiologist and physician. Recently it has become widely used; people are finding it extremely helpful in overcoming a variety of problems: phobias, tension headaches, allergic reactions, and insomnia, to name only a few. Progressive Relaxation works because you cannot be tense and relaxed at the same time. Because the technique can be readily learned, you will be able to use relaxation to get rid of much of the tension you might experience.

The procedure is called *Progressive* Relaxation for two reasons:

1. Each time you use the technique, you notice that you become a little more relaxed than before. The effects

build as you become better at using them. More complete relaxation is achieved in *less* time.

2. In going through the exercises, you will be concentrating on relaxing specific muscle groups one at a time. Your body gradually becomes more and more relaxed as you progress through the muscle groups.

In Progressive Relaxation you will systematically tense and relax the basic muscle groups in your body. You will first focus your attention on a specific muscle group (the arms or the abdomen, for example), tense the muscles tightly, and then release them as much as you can and feel the relaxation that follows. This tension–relaxation cycle achieves two purposes. First, by tensing your muscles and increasing the level of tension *above* your current operating level, you can learn to notice exactly what each muscle feels like when it is tense. It is very helpful in noticing where and how each muscle group feels when you are experiencing tension. Some people are so chronically tense that they have difficulty noticing levels of tension ("Gee, I always seem to feel so tight . . . never really noticed differences . . .").

Second, by first tensing and then relaxing, momentum is built up so that the level of tension drops *below* the point where you started. Each time you tense and relax a muscle, the tension level in your entire body goes lower and lower until you reach the point where little or no tension is present at all. By *focusing your attention* on this process as it takes place, you can eventually reach the point where just thinking and recalling the experiences of release is enough to bring on relaxation. But that comes with relaxing practice! Some persons can "progress" through the exercises rather quickly and use the mental relaxation procedures. Others must take their time and be patient, remembering that trying too hard and rushing it simply makes one more tense.

HOW TO RELAX: SOME INTRODUCTORY INSTRUCTIONS

The next few pages contain some detailed instructions in Progressive Relaxation. We strongly suggest that you study *all* of these directions carefully before trying the procedure on yourself. You might take notes as you go along to make sure you understand the "ins" and "outs" of Progressive Relaxation. Once you feel you have command of these details, then follow the directions for practicing and establishing a schedule for using relaxation.

You will be tensing and then relaxing specific muscles in your body in a certain sequence. This helps you to relax *every* muscle in your body. The tensing and relaxing helps you to relax those muscles perhaps more deeply than they have ever been before.

TAKE YOUR TIME

Plan to take your time. You can't be rushed and expect to achieve full benefit of the exercises. Don't try to squeeze the relaxation practice in between a couple of other pressing appointments. To relax fully, be prepared to spend about 20 to 30 minutes doing the exercises. Set the time aside, be ready to enjoy the feelings that your body will experience, and let your mind and body appreciate the state of relaxation you are bringing about in yourself. After all, you're trying to be good to yourself.

FIND THE RIGHT PLACE

Find a comfortable place and try to make sure that no unwanted distractions are likely to occur. You might tell your secretary not to bother you for the next 20 to 30 minutes. If you are at home, try darkening the room and taking the phone off the hook. When using the exercises at night, be sure that you are prepared to go to sleep immediately afterwards or even during the exercises themselves. At night you can practice while in bed, but we recommend that you not do this during the day. The last thing we want is for you to fall asleep and take a nap during the day. Many people find that a recliner-type chair or the large overstuffed kind with an ottoman facilitates relaxing. Others find it helpful to lie on a carpeted floor or large overstuffed pillows.

TENSING AND RELAXING THE MUSCLES

The tension–relaxation cycles form the heart of Progressive Relaxation. Remember, these tension–relaxation cycles serve two purposes. They teach you to *notice* when you are feeling tension in your various muscles and they teach you to *identify* exactly which muscle groups get most tense in response to stresses in your environment. And the momentum built up from tensing the muscles helps you to achieve more complete relaxation than would be possible if you used only the relaxation part of the cycle by itself.

Tense the muscle *vigorously* so that you really experience what the muscle feels like when it is tense. Be careful not to tense so hard that it hurts you or so that your muscles cramp. You'll have to find that point at which the tension is felt without excessive discomfort or distraction. Tense the muscle quickly, and hold it for 5 to 7 seconds (counting slowly by saying 1,001, 1,002, 1,003, 1,004, 1,005, 1,006, 1,007 to yourself is a good way to judge how long to tense the muscle). As you are tensing, *study* what the tension feels like, *notice* how the muscle feels when tensed, and *experience* discomfort that comes with tension.

When finished tensing, release the tension and relax the muscle *quickly*. Let a wave of relaxation come over the muscle, permit it to become completely limber and relaxed. Allow the muscle to relax quickly so that you can notice the difference between tension and relaxation. Really enjoy the state of relaxation the muscle is experiencing. *Enjoy* and *relish* the state of relaxation for 15 to 20 seconds.

Tense and relax the same muscle group one more time before moving on to the next muscle group. After you have progressed through your entire body, relax for a minute and try to identify where you might still be feeling tension. Go back and tense and relax those muscles where tension is still noticed. Don't expect *complete* relaxation, at first. Be patient with yourself; expect *slow but steady* progress in your ability to relax.

PRACTICING THE TENSION-RELAXATION CYCLES

Before we go further, let's take an example from a couple of the muscle groups to show you what we mean by tensing and relaxing. Practice along so that you get the feel of the cycles.

Let's start with your hand and forearm. (Use your right forearm if you are right handed or your left forearm if you are left handed. If you are ambidextrous, take your pick!) Rest your arm on the chair and make a very tight fist. Notice the tension in your fist, in your knuckles, in your thumb and fingers. Study the tension in the back of your hand and in your wrist. Now notice how the tension is starting to spread up your forearm. Just hold that tension, notice how uncomfortable it is, and realize that the best thing you can do is rid your body of any and all tension.

Now quickly RELAX. Open your fist and let your hand relax completely. Experience the tension flowing out of your hand into the chair and feel the tingly sensation as the muscles release. Take 10 to 20 seconds and just enjoy a warm wave of relaxation come over your hand and forearm.

As a second example, let's try the forehead. Tense your forehead by raising your eyebrows upwards toward the top of your head and wrinkling your brow. Notice the tension first in your forehead—that's often what a tension headache feels like when it first starts coming on. Now notice the uncomfortable tension around your temples and ears and on the top of your head. Hold the muscles tense for 5 to 7 seconds, and then relax quickly. Feel the warm wave of relaxation coming over your forehead. Feel it flow down from the top of your head; let it engulf your forehead and your temples. Relax and enjoy those good feelings of relaxation that follow.

THE MUSCLE GROUPS

We suggest that you first follow the order given for tensing and relaxing the muscle groups. As you become more skilled in relaxing, you may want to follow a different order so that you can develop a relaxation exercise that is completely suited to your needs. That way it will be guaranteed to satisfy you best.

Before practicing the exercises, it's helpful to practice tensing the muscle groups so that you don't have to experiment with that process as you are doing the exercises. *As you read down the list, practice the tension part of the cycle.* Don't begin to do the exercises yet, however. That will come soon after some further instruction. If the methods that we suggest do not seem to be the best way for you to achieve tension in the muscle, experiment a bit (remember, you are a personal scientist) until you find a method that suits you best.

Hands and arms. The first major muscle group that you will be tensing and relaxing are the hands and arms. The tension–relaxation cycles are done separately on four subsets of this muscle group. Begin with the dominant hand and forearm, then tense and relax the dominant biceps, move to the nondominant hand and forearm and finally tense and release the nondominant bicep. These four muscles are worked with separately so that you achieve total relaxation in each muscle.

1. *Dominant hand and forearm*: Make a tight fist to tense the hand and forearm. (This is the group we practiced with in the previous section).
2. *Dominant biceps:* Flex your muscle, bending your arm at the elbow and opening your hand so that it is facing your shoulder. Try to touch your shoulder with your hand while at the same time applying a counter-force to oppose this movement.
3. *Nondominant hand and forearm*: Tense these just like you did the dominant hand and forearm.
4. *Nondominant biceps*: Tense and release these just like you did the dominant biceps.

Notice that each muscle in the group is tensed and relaxed separately and *with care*. It is especially important that you keep all of your other muscles relaxed while tensing and relaxing a specific muscle. (Later on you may combine several groups at one time but for now let's learn how to do it for each one separately.) Focus on one muscle at a time, tense and relax it, and then keep it relaxed while you proceed through the other muscle groups. To do this takes some practice.

Head and face. Three separate muscles are tensed and released in this muscle group: the forehead, the eyes, and the mouth and jaws.*

5. *Forehead*: Tense the forehead just as we practiced previously. Raise your eyebrows up toward the top of your head; feel the tension in your forehead and around your temples and on the top of your head.
6. *Eyes*: Squint your eyes hard and wrinkle up your nose. Notice especially the tension around your eyes, your temples, and your nose. This is often a very tense part of our bodies and one that we neglect frequently when thinking about how tense we are.
7. *Mouth and jaws*: Clench your teeth tightly together and make an exaggerated smile by pushing the corners of your mouth back toward your ears. Notice the tension in your jaw muscles, in your cheeks, and in the front part of your neck. (Don't worry about looking funny—no one is watching).

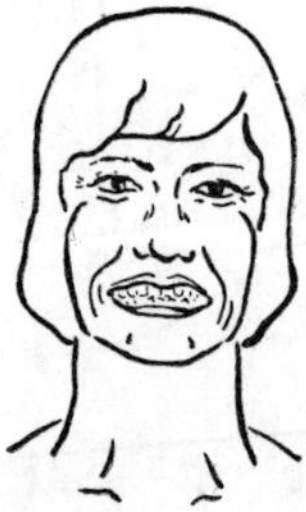

*Incidentally, these relaxation exercises for the head and face are very helpful in reducing tension and migraine headaches, especially in the beginning stages. Some persons also find relaxing the throat, neck, and shoulders helpful in preventing or reducing the pain in headaches.

Throat, neck, and shoulders. Because the neck and shoulders are often extremely tense, we tense and relax them in three ways. Following that, we concentrate on the back.

8. *Neck and throat*: Try to touch your chin to your chest while at the same time applying a counter-pressure to prevent it from touching. The opposing forces will create tension in the back of your neck to such a degree that your neck may actually shake. You will also notice tension in the front part of your neck. (Remember not to overdo it; just enough to really feel the tension.)
9. *Neck and throat*: Use the same counter-pressure technique, only this time try to touch your back with your head and push the opposite way with the opposing muscles. Notice the tension in your throat and in the lower part of your neck.

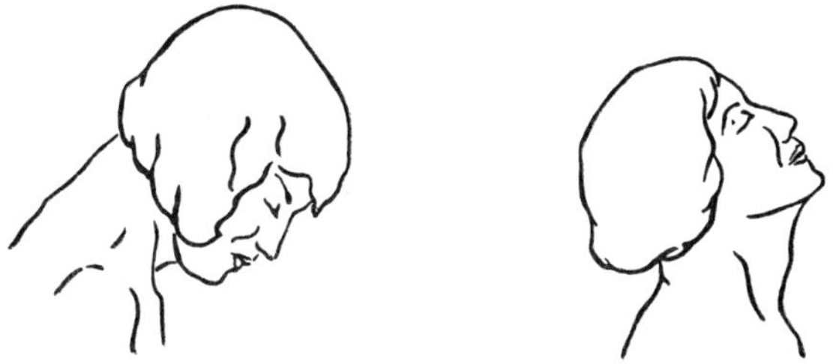

10. *Shoulders and upper back*: Push your shoulder blades back almost as if you were trying to make them touch. Notice the tension across your shoulders and also across your chest.
11. *Shoulders and upper back*: Now repeat the process, only this time push your shoulder blades as far forward as you can. Notice the tension across your back and in the upper part of your shoulders.
12. *Shoulders and upper back*: Shrug your shoulders; try to touch them to your ears. Notice the tension through the upper part of your back and chest.

13. *Chest*: Create tension by taking a deep breath, holding it for several seconds, and then exhaling quickly. Notice the overall level of tension when you hold your breath, and the overall relaxation that occurs as you release the air.
14. *Stomach*: Either pull your stomach in as far as you can, or push it out as far as you can. Again use the five to seven second limit. Tension throughout the abdominal area will result.

The lower body. The buttocks, the thighs, calves, and feet are tensed separately.

15. *Buttocks:* The buttocks are, for many people, a chronically tense part of our bodies. Tense the buttocks by flexing the muscles and pushing down onto whatever surface you are lying or sitting on.
16. *Thighs*: Tense these larger muscles in the upper leg by flexing them vigorously.
17. *Calves*: Be careful as you move into the region of the calves and the feet. These areas can cramp easily, so the first few times you tense and relax these muscles, do so gently and for a few seconds until you find a level that does not cause extreme discomfort or cramping. The calves should be tensed in two ways. First, point your toes down to the ground and notice the tension in the tops of your feet and in your

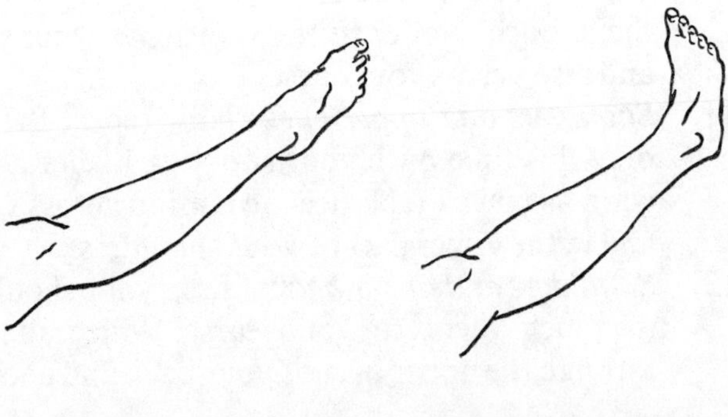

calves. Following that tension–relaxation cycle, point your toes backwards, up toward your head, and notice the tension in the lower calf.

18. *Feet*: Tense your feet in two ways. First turn your feet outward, hold for seven seconds, and then release. Next, turn the feet inward, tense, and release. Notice the tension that results in tensing your feet each way.

WHAT DO YOU SAY TO YOURSELF?

Saying the right things to yourself is a critical and important part of practicing Progressive Relaxation. After all, the objective is to achieve *mental* as well as physical relaxation; you can enhance both by carefully selecting the words you use to talk yourself through the exercises.

Professional psychologists use a very carefully selected set of words and control their voices in some very special ways when teaching people to relax. Try to achieve the same effect when using these procedures to relax yourself.

When tensing a specific muscle, speak very rapidly and in a louder tone (you can either do this mentally or out loud). Your voice should reflect the buildup of tension in the muscles you are working on. The phrases you use can also reflect the tension you are experiencing, such as:

- Feel the tension building up.
- Notice the muscle getting tighter and tighter.
- Study the tension my muscle experiences.
- Really notice what it feels like to be tense.
- Feel the muscles pull and strain . . . hold and experience the tension.

When relaxing, begin to speak slowly and soothingly. Give yourself suggestions of *warmth, relaxation, calm, rest,* and *heaviness* flowing into your muscles. Tell yourself that tension is dissolving and dissipating out of the body. Experience the differences between tension and relaxation.

- Notice and study those good feelings of relaxation that follow.
- Study the differences between tension and relaxation—notice how good it feels to be relaxed.
- Let that warm wave of relaxation come over my entire muscle.
- Notice the tension flowing out of my body.
- Notice the tension collecting and dissipating as I let myself become totally relaxed.
- Completely relaxed, warm and rested.
- More relaxed than ever before, nothing to worry about except allowing myself to relax.
- Just let go . . . relax . . . warmth . . . relaxation.
- Enjoy the calm.
- Rest, relaxation, warmth, heaviness.

LEARNING AND USING RELAXATION

We have provided very careful and thorough instructions in the Progressive Relaxation. We feel it important to cover these details to insure that you achieve the best possible experience and benefit from relaxation. They are good exercises, and will help you *if practiced consistently, and done carefully and conscientiously.*

You are now ready to practice. The checklist on the following pages will help you review the steps. We have also written out a complete set of instructions for you to use the first few times through. Read the instructions carefully. You need not follow them word for word but they will give you an idea of how exercises flow. Some people have found it helpful to record these on cassettes, and then play it back to themselves during their sessions.

After you have the feel of these exercises, try them out a few times. Realize that it will take some practice before you are comfortable with the sequence of the exercises. Then we will talk about setting up a regular schedule for using them.

RELAXING YOUR BODY

Get into your relaxation chair (if you are practicing these exercises during the day) or climb into bed (if you are ready to go to sleep), and take a few minutes to allow yourself to make the transition from your daytime activities to relaxation. Close your eyes and tell yourself that for the next 20 to 30 minutes there is nothing that you need to be concerned about except relaxation. You are going to lie back and let yourself become completely and totally relaxed.

Establish a rhythm in your breathing—begin to take deep, even breaths. Tell yourself how well you are going to feel after spending the next 20 minutes relaxing.

When you are ready, begin the tension-relaxation cycles:

1. Take three deep breaths in order to become completely relaxed. Hold each breath for five to seven seconds to get the full benefit of this exercise. Repeat one more time.
2. Clench your dominant fist. Hold it very tightly and count to 5 very slowly (1,001, 1,002, 1,003, 1,004, 1,005). Now release quickly and let your fingers uncurl. Notice the feelings of relaxation. Now do this again, and really focus in on the tension and then the relaxation you are experiencing in your fist.
3. Flex your dominant bicep. Notice the tension. Relax, tense, and relax again. Notice the warm feelings of relaxation.

4. Clench your nondominant fist. Hold tight. Release. Notice the relaxation. Do this one more time. Let the warm wave of relaxation come over your entire muscle.
5. Flex your nondominant bicep. Notice the tension. Relax and notice the relaxation. Repeat. Notice how your arms are completely relaxed, warm, rested, and calm.
6. Take a couple of deep breaths and notice how calm your arms feel. Enjoy the feelings of relaxing.
7. Tense up the muscles of your forehead by raising your eyebrows as far as you can. Hold it for five seconds and feel the tension building up. Relax quickly and notice how relaxed it feels. Repeat this one more time and let the heavy warm wave of relaxation come down from your hand and begin to cover your face.
8. Close your eyes very tightly. Now release and notice the relaxation. Repeat—just let go—relax, warmth, heaviness.
9. Clench your jaws very tightly and make that exaggerated smile. Release. Notice the feelings of relaxation. Repeat.
10. Take a couple of deep breaths and notice how relaxed the muscles of your arms and head feel. Study and enjoy these good feelings of relaxation.
11. Take a deep breath. Hold it for a few seconds. Now release slowly. Repeat.
12. Now try to touch your chin to your chest, and apply the counter pressure to keep it from touching. Release and notice the difference. Repeat.
13. Try to touch your back with your head but push the opposite way with the opposing muscles. Notice the tension building up. Release quickly and study and enjoy the good feelings of relaxation. Repeat and let your neck become totally relaxed.
14. Push your shoulder blades back and try to make them touch. Notice the tension across your shoulders

and across your chest. Relax, and notice the differences. Repeat.

15. Try to touch your shoulders by pushing them forward—as far forward as you can. Hold, relax, and then repeat. Notice the difference between tension and relaxation.
16. Shrug your shoulders and try to touch them to your ears. Hold, release, and repeat. Notice the feelings of warmth and heaviness in your back, shoulders, and neck.
17. Take a deep, deep breath. Hold it for seven seconds, and exhale quickly. Notice the general feeling of relaxation that results. Do this one more time, and notice how relaxed your whole body is beginning to feel.
18. Tighten up your stomach muscles. Hold them. Now release. Notice the relaxation in your abdomen. Repeat and notice how relaxed your chest and stomach now feel.
19. Tighten up your buttocks. Hold. Release. Notice the relaxation. Repeat.
20. Tense your thighs. Relax quickly and repeat once again
21. Point your toes away from your body. Notice the tension. Now return to a normal position. Repeat and notice the relaxation.
22. Now point your toes toward your head. Notice the tension. Now return to a normal position. Repeat and notice the relaxation.
23. Point your feet outward and notice the tension. Release quickly and repeat.
24. Point your feet inward. Hold. Relax. Notice the relaxation, warmth, and calm in your legs and feet.
25. Just let your body relax for a few minutes. Notice how relaxed, warm, heavy, and calm your whole body feels. Just study and enjoy those good feelings. When you decide that you want to, get up, stretch, and resume your normal activities feeling very refreshed and relaxed.

Progressive Muscle Relaxation

1. Take your time; plan to spend about 20 to 30 minutes relaxing each time you do the exercises.
2. Find a comfortable place to relax. Make sure that no unwanted distractions are likely to occur.
   - When you are practicing during the day, darkening the room may help.
   - When you are practicing at night, be prepared to go to sleep right away.
3. During the tension part of the cycle, tense the muscle vigorously and hold the muscle tense for a slow count of 5 to 7 seconds (1,001, 1,002, 1,003, 1,004, 1,005, 1,006, 1,007). Notice what the tension feels like.
4. During the relaxation part of the cycle, relax the muscle quickly and completely. Let your mind relax and appreciate how relaxed the muscle is feeling.
5. Tense and relax each muscle group twice. After you have completed the entire sequence, go back and tense and relax specific muscles where you still feel tension.
6. Try to keep all other muscles relaxed as you relax specific muscle groups.
7. Follow the order for tensing and relaxing the muscle groups:

   - Dominant hand and forearm
   - Dominant biceps
   - Nondominant hand and forearm
   - Nondominant biceps
   - Forehead
   - Eyes
   - Mouth and jaws
   - Neck and throat (shoulders forward)
   - Neck and throat (shoulders back)
   - Neck and throat (shrug shoulders)
   - Upper back (both ways)
   - Chest
   - Stomach
   - Buttocks
   - Thighs
   - Calves (feet pointed down)
   - Calves (feet pointed up)
   - Feet (pointed out)
   - Feet (pointed in)

8. Don't forget to use your favorite self-suggestions.

If you are using these exercises at bedtime, plan to go to sleep easily and quickly, and sleep soundly through the night.

PRACTICING PROGRESSIVE RELAXATION

Begin now by practicing Progressive Relaxation twice daily. Follow the steps given in Self-Change Task IV.

Plan to practice *twice* daily—once at bedtime and once during the day. Rather than thinking that you will do them

"when I have time," it's probably better to set a specific time for your practice sessions. Build relaxation into your daily routine so it will become a *regular part of your life.*

Self-Improvement Task IV

I will help myself learn to relax physically and mentally by:

1. Practicing Progressive Relaxation *at least* twice daily for a period of two weeks: once during the day and once at bedtime. Each practice session will last from 20 to 30 minutes.
2. Continuing to:
   a. practice my alternative helpful thoughts;
   b. keep my Sleep Diary.
3. Negotiating a self-contract (or my alternative strategy) helping to be systematic and consistent in learning to relax.

When I have completed this assignment, I will begin to learn Mental Relaxation in Chapter 6.

Self-Contract

Goal: Practice Progressive Relaxation

Specific Behavioral Objectives

I agree to: ______________________________
(specify behavior)

____

under the following circumstances: ______________
(specify where, when,

____

how much, etc.)

____

Environmental Planning

In order to help me do this, I am going to: (1) arrange my physical and social environment by ______________________________

____

and; (2) control my internal environment (thoughts, images) by: ______

____

____

Consequences

Provided by me:
(If contract is kept) ______________________________

(If contract is broken) ______________________________

Provided by others:
(If contract is kept) ______________________________

(If contract is broken) ______________________________

- -

______________ Signed ______________
(Renewal Date)

Witness ______________

Date ______________

6

Learning to Relax Your Mind

Our thoughts, images, and other mental activities can often victimize us. Most of us have struggled with unwanted thoughts, sometimes at the most inopportune times. Maybe something at work is extremely pressing, or perhaps a personal problem has been crying for a solution. Thoughts about the situation keep spinning in our mind, almost as if they were being rolled around in a rock polisher or clothes dryer. One idea leads to another, new features of the situation reveal themselves, and soon we find ourselves totally worked up and out of control. We just keep rehashing the problem without really finding a solution. We may find that we are simply unable to concentrate on anything else during the day or have become so aroused that sleep becomes impossible at night.

The strategies presented here may be just for you if this happens frequently or even occasionally. Many people who report sleeping problems also tell two other facts about their thinking, especially at bedtime. First, they say that it doesn't matter if they have a problem or not. If they don't have something important and pressing to think about, something—*almost anything*—will pop up to capture their attention. Often random thoughts will lead them to think thoughts that turn out to be stimulating. And sleep is subverted once again.

Second, many people do not enjoy thinking about personal problems at night. They report a kind of helpless or depressed feeling, only making them feel worse about things going on in their lives. But they don't know how to turn the thoughts off, and then even get more exasperated and frustrated with themselves.

Perhaps you don't mind it when your mental motor runs at full throttle when sleeping might be the preferred activity. Maybe you sometimes resolve a particular problem or discover a new insight or angle. If you find yourself in this situation, then you must make a choice. You can choose to continue your habit of bedtime problem solving or you can choose to learn and use some procedures to help close out these thought processes. *But realize that the choice is yours.* If you are happy with your present mental activity at night, and that's what you really want to do, then your sleep may be somewhat less than adequate. But you have chosen that alternative. Even those who label themselves "night persons" have a choice. They can learn to organize and plan things more on a "day person" routine. Our body rhythms are important in determining our peak activity hours and those times when rest might be what the body says it wants. But these body rhythms can be altered, sometimes easily, to adjust to other demands. After all, many people adjust to travel and vacations and are able to get in new waking–sleeping routines within a matter of days.

CONTROLLING YOUR THOUGHTS

If you decide that you really prefer to sleep rather than think excessively at night, then you can learn some procedures to shut down these thought processes when you want to and choose to put them into practice. You may be thinking, "Well, yes, but sometimes I *do* have things that require some attention and that need to be solved. What then?" All of us find ourselves in this dilemma, but it is important to realize that *bed is not the right place for those activities.* If we want to learn how to sleep more normally, problem solving and other worthwhile mental activities are best done elsewhere and at other times. (In Chapter 9 some ways are suggested to assist you in organizing your day so that you will have time just for thinking as well as methods for learning to think more productively during those moments you set aside for that purpose.)

STEP 1: WHAT DO YOU ENJOY THINKING ABOUT?

When discussing Progressive Relaxation, we made the point that its benefit is based on the notion that it seems impossible to be physically tense and relaxed at the same time. You simply cannot do both simultaneously—at least not very well! Relaxing your mind is based on the same principle. You cannot be thinking relaxed, peaceful, and calming thoughts while your mind is racing wildly up and down the stairways of your life. Learning to control what you think about means identifying what you want to think about, practicing those thoughts, and then using them when you want to relax.

As a first step, generate a list of scenes that are especially pleasant and relaxing for you. (The worksheet can be used for this purpose.) Some people enjoy thinking about previous trips or vacations while others relish thoughts about the beach, forests, flower gardens, or lakes. Perhaps a movie, play, or concert you have attended or even hope to attend is especially calming. Thinking about single images, such as gems or minerals, put one person's mind completely at rest.

When you write these scenes down, include as much detail as possible. One person generated the following relaxing images:

Scene: A walk in the forest

Pleasant details: It is a beautiful, warm, sunny day. A breeze, gently blowing, caresses my face. I find myself in this valley—a beautiful valley. Tall, green grass is blown gently by the wind so that the top of the grass moves gently back and forth. I am walking down a winding trail through the grass, and come across the most beautiful flowers in the world. Brilliant reds, yellows, blues, golds,

oranges. I smell one of the flowers, and the fragrance is sweet but gentle. Pleasing, really pleasing. Walking further, I come across a grove of trees. I hear the birds in the trees, singing and tending their young. The birds themselves are all beautiful colors. Walking on, I wander upon a babbling brook with clear, clean, cold, fresh water. I lie down by the side of the stream, and look up at the blue, clear sky. I experience only peace, calm, enjoyment, and rest.

Scene: On the beach

Pleasant details: It is the perfect day, kind of overcast but warm enough to be comfortable. The beach is completely isolated except for a few children playing off in the distance. I can feel the sea breeze hitting my face; it is refreshing and relaxing. The sun is warm and contrasts with the coolness of the breeze. All problems and concerns seem to melt as I enjoy this beautiful place. Sea gulls fly off in the distance, circling and landing here and there. I can hear the waves crashing into the shore. I think about the tremendous power and beauty. The sun catches the whitecaps as the water turns over. I walk along, peaceful, contented, relaxed, and calmly happy.

Notice in both scenes that all of the senses are included: sight, taste, smell, and touch. Even pleasant sounds are imagined, and self-instructions to feel relaxed, refreshed, and calm are interlaced with fantasies of being in beautiful places.

Your scenes need not be real. You may prefer to use your imagination in the generation of a pure fantasy.

Pleasant Thoughts Worksheet

1. Scene: ______________________

   Pleasant details: ______________________

2. Scene: ______________________

   Pleasant details:

3. Scene: ______________________

   Pleasant details: ______________________

Your scenes need not be real. You may prefer to use your imagination in the generation of a pure fantasy.

Scene: Swimming with a porpoise (the return of Jonathan Livingston?)
Details: I see myself flying with the sea gulls, looking down on the beach below. Maybe for fun, I swoop down and take a closer look at what some people on the beach are eating. Maybe I'll wait for a chance and sneak off with some of their food. Ah, the perfect opportunity to grab those potato chips. Swoop, and off I go with a mouthful of food. Flying over the water, I notice a cluster of fishing boats and some porpoises playfully swimming around them. What fun! Swooping down to the water, I become a porpoise, swimming around the boats, bobbing up and down. Moving swiftly through the water, I notice some tasty morsels of food. Not bad, this porpoise food. I decide to try my hand at some of those tricks porpoises are known for. Swimming rapidly, I jump and swoop over the bow of the boat. Feel the exhilaration as I emerge from the water and sail over the boat. See the people amazed at my agility and grace.

Writing down your scenes is more than busy work. It's very important that you prepare in advance exactly what you will think about so that you can do it easily and without effort when you want to relax your mind during the day and at night so you'll fall asleep more easily.

USING YOUR SCENES TO RELAX

When you have developed a list of three or four scenes, proceed to use them to achieve mental relaxation. The following exercises combine some imagery to assist you in calming your mind with your own pleasant scenes to enhance your relaxation.

Be patient with yourself as you begin to learn mental relaxation. Complete concentration, even with pleasant images, requires practice. Don't get upset if unwanted thoughts intrude. That happens even to the most practiced masters of yoga and meditation who are trained in this type of mental relaxation. Just recognize that this can happen and treat these thoughts calmly. Tell yourself that the thoughts will soon pass if you don't pay attention to them and return to your pleasant image. Don't fight them, just let them pass. This is where the patience comes in. If you get upset about all these thoughts racing by, then you give them attention and that simply encourages them.

Some people have found it helpful to imagine a burning candle from time to time. The flame is upright when thoughts are on target. If unwanted thoughts do pop into your mind, imagine that they are a gentle breeze blowing the flame and making it flicker slightly. But breezes always flow by, and take with them your unwanted thoughts. The flame returns to its upright and still position, and brings your mind back to its pleasant relaxing images.

Please read the instructions all the way through at least *two* or *three* times. Commit them to memory or record them on tape if you prefer. Find a quiet place to practice, and be sure that you won't be disturbed or distracted by the telephone or anything else. You may wish to take the telephone receiver off the hook while you practice. After all, you are busy learning something important.

TOTAL MENTAL RELAXATION

First, get very comfortable. Lie down, if you can, and loosen restrictive clothing such as tight-fitting shirts or blouses. Loosen your belt and take off your shoes if that makes you feel more comfortable.

Close your eyes and take a couple of deep breaths. Hold, and then exhale slowly. Tell yourself that you are going to experience complete deep relaxation.

In order to prepare your body and mind for rest, tense and quickly release *all of the muscle groups in your body at the same time.* Notice that warm wave of relaxation beginning to engulf your entire body. Repeat the tension-relaxation cycle and study and enjoy these good feelings of relaxation, heaviness, and warmth that follow.

Focus your mind on a single image (a white spot, a single color, or a simple object). If you have trouble making a mental picture, try focusing on the word "calm" or "let go," saying it to yourself in a slow and steady way. As you focus your mind on that image or the calming words, concentrate on relaxing your various muscle groups in turn. Start with your arms. Notice how heavy and relaxed they are starting to get. If necessary, you might want to actually tense (for about five seconds) and then relax them. That may help you achieve greater relaxation. Then move to your head and face. Feel the energy coming down from the top of your head being released and dispelled. Feel the beginning surge of that warm wave of relaxation coming over your forehead, your eyes, and your mouth. Slowly, gently, feel the heaviness, the warmth. Your neck and shoulders are often very tense. Just let them go. Focus your attention on the back of your neck, down across your shoulders. Let them relax. Feel that wave of relaxation beginning to spread down your entire body. Enjoy this growing feeling of pleasant relaxation. Let the midbody become relaxed—the stomach, the back, and the buttocks. Finally, relax your legs and feet. Just let them go limp and enjoy the relaxed, heavy feeling of your body.

Next, imagine an escalator. You are standing at the top and the escalator is moving down. As you go down the escalator, count from one to ten. As you say each number, take a deep breath and let it out slowly. Say to yourself, with each number, that you are getting "more calm," "more relaxed," and "more peaceful." The quiet, pleasant tranquility is beautiful and encompassing.

Imagine your first scene. Notice the details and enjoy the relaxation you are now experiencing. When you are ready, move on to the second and third scenes. Experience the scenes with *all* of your senses. If distracting thoughts come into your mind, remember the candle. It's okay. They'll pass. Let the thoughts go. Just return to your peaceful, relaxing scenes.

When you are ready, count down from five to one. As you count down, begin moving various parts of your body. Stand up slowly, stretch, and tell yourself that you will feel more relaxed and calm for the rest of the day. If you are doing this before sleeping, continue to imagine your scenes, and tell yourself that you will soon be asleep and that you will sleep peacefully and beautifully all through the night.

USING RELAXATION

We cannot repeat too often that learning to relax, like any skill, *takes time, patience, and practice.* But always remember that learning to relax is a physical and mental skill that you can learn to use with tremendous benefit to you, *both* during the day as you go about your activities, as well as at night as you are trying to sleep. Sleeping well depends on living well. Tense and hectic days make for turbulent and troubled nights.

The need to build relaxation experiences into your daily routine is crucial. Being more relaxed must become a more normal routine part of your life, much like eating an unhurried good dinner or brushing and flossing your teeth.

It's important to realize that relaxation is not something to be done only on weekends or a personal luxury confined to those occasions when you have extra time. Almost everyone is busy—too busy—and most of us take on more than can be easily accomplished in the day and night we are allotted by the earth's revolutions. (We still haven't learned how to live on 24 hours a day!) Most of us enjoy being stimulated and undertaking challenging activities. Unfortunately, we often fail to take the time to pursue those activities that have no immediate utility—the practical "payoff" is not obvious—or those which are not required of us. Learning to relax is admittedly more difficult and time consuming than popping a pill to calm down during the day or to sleep at night. (Our modern culture has taught us a bad lesson: "Better living through chemical solutions." Most of us have learned it too well and yearn for some instant curative: "Gee, Doc, can't you give me something to take . . .?") Our approach may be more demanding at first, but once you get into the routines we are teaching in this book, it will certainly seem easy and natural. We believe these techniques are certainly more helpful and more healthy than simply taking pills. *If you arrange your schedule so that you practice relaxation consistently and systematically, you can control yourself and not have to use pills and suffer the problems that go along with using chemicals.*

PRACTICING THE PROCEDURES

We recommend that you begin with Progressive Relaxation and practice it consistently for at least two weeks. Once you have mastered it and can go through the cycles easily, then you begin to use mental relaxation. You might begin by using mental relaxation at the end of the Progressive Relaxation. *Do this gradually,* and as you proceed, you can begin to shorten the length of time in the tension-relaxation cycles and spend more time relaxing your mind. Remember, it is you who must tailor and cut out a pattern from what we've offered that best suits you.

Plan to practice relaxing *at least two times every day.* One natural time, of course, is as you are retiring and preparing to go to sleep. As you get into bed, make sure that all routine matters (e.g., doors locked and the cat out) are taken care of. Turn off your light. If you have a spouse, say goodnight in a relaxed fashion. Begin relaxing with the real expectation—that sleep is just a short time away.

It is equally important to relax at least once during the day. Sleep is part of a total daily cycle of sleep–wakefulness and one phase of a daily rhythm we all experience. When you think about it, it is very unrealistic to expect to be tense all day and then to relax immediately at bedtime when trying to sleep. By relaxing during the day, by slowing the pace and reducing at least some of the tension, we can slow down the tension buildup at night.

Some people have experienced and noticed some sensations that may require some explanation while practicing and using relaxation. At least they will be less mystifying if you are prepared for them.

You may lose track of time, especially as you begin to experience deeper states of mental and physical relaxation. Just try to let yourself relax and enjoy the total calm experienced by your body and mind. If you are afraid of going too long, you might set a clock with an unalarming alarm or arrange to have someone remind you when a certain amount of time has elapsed. That way you won't have to keep thinking about the time as you are trying to relax.

Some people have also reported tingling or spinning sensations, also signs of relaxation. Just let your body go with the feelings and enjoy them. You might even incorporate those sensations into your fantasies.

Sneezes, itches, and similar annoyances need not be distracting. Just deal with them calmly and continue relaxing.

MAKE A SELF-CONTRACT

A self-contract is provided at the end of the chapter. You may wish to use one to help you get into the regular habit of practicing your relaxation. Many people find that making promises very specific and tangible really helps them put their best of intentions into practice. But if you strongly object to putting your promises down in black and white, that's okay. Be sure that your reluctance to use a written contract is not a "reasonable excuse" to avoid doing something. A self-contract is just one way of holding ourselves a bit more accountable. For most of us, every bit helps.

Fill it out, complete with reminders and rewards, to help you use relaxation consistently and systematically. We have found that it can be a good idea to involve someone else in your contract as well.

Don't forget to continue self-monitoring. That way, you can follow the progress you make as you learn and practice relaxation. Keep up your efforts to use your new adaptive thoughts about sleep in conjunction with relaxation. The combination of the two should be most helpful.

When you feel that you have mastered the relaxation procedures, continue with the next chapter. Until then, we hope that you enjoy learning this new, helpful, and healthy skill.

Self-Change Task V

I will help myself learn to sleep well by:

1. Practicing mental relaxation at least twice a day at the end of my Progressive Relaxation exercises. I will do this for two weeks.
2 Continuing to practice alternative helpful thoughts.
3. Continuing to keep my Sleep Diary.
4. Negotiating a self-contract, involving at least one other person, if possible (or some alternative strategy), to help me be sysematic and consistent.

When I have completed this assignment, I will be ready to move to the next section.

Self-Contract

Goal: Learn Mental Relaxation

Specific Behavioral Objectives

I agree to: ______________________________
(specify behavior)

____

under the following circumstances: ______________________________
(specify where, when,

____
how much, etc.)

____

Environmental Planning

In order to help me do this, I am going to: (1) arrange my physical and social environment by ______________________________

____

and; (2) control my internal environment (thoughts, images) by: ______

____

____

Consequences

Provided by me:
(If contract is kept) ______________________________

(If contract is broken) ______________________________

Provided by others:
(If contract is kept) ______________________________

(If contract is broken ______________________________

- -

______________________ Signed ______________________
(Renewal Date)

Witness ______________________

Date ______________________

Part Four

SKILLS FOR SPECIAL PROBLEMS

Progressive and Mental Relaxation form the heart of what you will be doing to help you obtain more restful sleep at night. Their impact can be tremendous; their effects on your life can be pervasive. In addition to helping you sleep better, they can make your daytime activities more pleasant and productive. It may seem paradoxical, but slowing down and becoming more relaxed about everything will help you accomplish *more*, especially in terms of improving the quality of your life.

In this part of the book we present three more strategies to help you improve your sleep. These procedures build on the basic relaxation skills you are mastering and are designed to help you overcome specific sleep problems you may experience.

A TIME TO CHANGE

We have arrived at an important transition point. Everyone with a sleep problem needs to learn and master the skills presented so far: systematic self-observation, changing thoughts, and physical and mental relaxation. From here on, you can be selective in choosing and using those skills that apply to the specific sleep problems you experience. Here's where the personal scientist notion becomes especially important. It's up to you to decide what you need to learn, and to try things out systematically to see if they do you any good.

In Part Four we start you on the road to analyzing and adapting procedures to your sleep difficulties.

Cognitive Focusing (Chapter 7) helps you to return to sleep when you wake up during the night. Many persons experience this kind of disrupted sleep, and cognitive focusing skills can help by teaching you to return to sleep without difficulty.

Environmental Control (Chapter 8) teaches you methods for looking at your physical and social surroundings to see what changes might be made to improve your sleep. We are often not aware of the contribution that a changed environment can make to improved sleep.

Problem Solving (Chapter 9) is the mark of a real personal scientist. It's impossible to write chapters for every contributing factor that you might experience (we'd end up with a 20-volume encyclopedia). But you can learn to analyze your remaining sleep difficulties and devise and try out methods that seem suited to problems you identify.

We recommend that you *read all of Part Four through at least once.* When you understand the steps involved in each technique, *then go back* and start to learn and use the procedures one by one. Feel free to vary the order in which you learn so that your own needs and interests are met. But be sure to *give yourself enough time and practice* to master each one. Only by using the procedures on a day-to-day basis can you experience fully the benefits they can provide.

7

Cognitive Focusing: Relaxing in the Middle of the Night

LYNDA. *Lynda went to bed as usual around 11:00 p.m., skipping the late night news wrap-up and feeling ready for a good night's sleep. It had been a busy day in the classroom, and tomorrow's field trip to the tide pools to study starfish, sea urchins, and other similar creatures promised excitement.*

"Should be exhausting. Gina will be sure to fall into the water, and Bob will no doubt be regaling me and everyone else with little known facts about marine biology. I hope the day's fairly enjoyable. At least it provides a break in the routine."

Progressive and mental relaxation brought calmness quickly: ". . . tense and release, and feel the warmth come over my body . . . focus on the pleasant, beautiful valley . . ." and sleep soon followed. Restful oblivion.

Lynda found herself awake some time later. "I wonder what time it is? 2:30 a.m. Damn! I don't have to get up until 6:00. I probably won't get back to sleep. I don't want to lie awake for a couple of hours." She found herself even more awake and aroused by her anger and apprehension.

"Maybe a glass of milk will help." The house was slightly chilly, causing her to wake up some more. The milk tasted good. As she was leaving the kitchen her eye caught some unpaid bills on the counter causing her to wonder how she would pay all of them and go on vacation, too. (A few spoonfuls of chocolate chip ice cream also hit the spot.)

Lynda was now really awake. "The only thing to do is to go back to bed where it's warm and cozy." She could at least try to get to sleep once again.

"I need to get back to sleep. Maybe I'll just lie still, breathe regularly, and stay calm. I hope it works, because I need to be rested for tomorrow!"

"No chance. 3:00 a.m. I need to get to sleep." One thought led to another, and soon Lynda's mind wandered back to the bills.

"Let's see. If I pay $10.00 to Standard Oil, I can save $20.00 to pay the rest of that charge account off." Money problems solved, Lynda returned to her teaching. "Raymond is still quite a problem . . ." and so on until 4:00 when Lynda fell asleep out of sheer exhaustion. Needless to say, getting up at 6:00 was its own trial. Lynda kept thinking how much more enjoyable the day at the beach could have been with some more sleep.

WHAT'S HAPPENING?

Does this sound familiar? This kind of disturbed sleep bothers most people. It's not uncommon to awaken once or twice during the night. But this can become a problem *if* it takes you a long time to get back to sleep, *if* you cannot fall asleep again at all, or *if* you are bothered by many awakenings. Remember that these awakenings by themselves are not important. It's only as they make you feel fatigued and tired the next day that you need to be concerned about them.

Let's take a close look at Lynda's situation. Notice that when she woke up, she was instantly worried about falling back to sleep. These thoughts woke her up completely. The walk to the refrigerator and her nighttime munching aroused her even more. Her worries and concerns had run rampant by the time she returned to bed. Only sheer exhaustion put her back to sleep.

WHAT'S THE ALTERNATIVE?

Getting back to sleep in the middle of the night requires that you learn to relax your mind so that thoughts of any kind have less of a chance to get started in the first place.

The principle is clear. It is necessary to do something *positive* so that troublesome thoughts don't get out of control and arouse you so that sleep becomes totally impossible. You can teach yourself to relax when you awaken in the middle of the night and focus your mind on pleasant and calming thoughts. It is possible to learn how to get back to sleep quickly and easily. Some people relax using Progressive and Mental Relaxation Exercises to get back to sleep. You may want to use these as a first step. But many persons don't feel physically tense, and don't notice excessive mental activity. We developed a shorter method for use during the middle of the night. Its strength comes from its giving you something calming to do *immediately* as you awaken. If your mind can focus on positive and peaceful thoughts, you won't awaken more, and you can return to sleep with a minimum of difficulty. Let's review the steps involved, and then discuss how you might put them into practice.

THE STEPS IN COGNITIVE FOCUSING

Use these steps when you *first* notice that you are awake. First, tell yourself something calming and reassuring:

> It's the middle of the night, but I'll soon be back to sleep and resting peacefully.
>
> I see that it is 2:00 a.m., but there's no need to worry.
>
> Sleep will come soon if I just allow myself to relax.
>
> Just stay calm and relaxed, and sleep will come quickly.

These, of course, are only a few of the possibilities. See if you can generate a list of your own relaxing self-statements.

Next, take two deep breaths and concentrate on relaxing your body. Imagine that all of the tension is draining out of your body as you breathe in and out. Focus momentarily on the various muscle groups (head, arms, torso, and legs) to make sure that your entire body is becoming relaxed completely. If you notice tension in any of these muscles, you might want to tense and relax them to achieve total physical relaxation.

Third, take five deep breaths. As you take each breath, you will count to yourself (not aloud) beginning with "one" and moving up to "five". As you recite each number, tell yourself: "As I count, I'm getting more and more calm and relaxed, peaceful and serene."

> "1: Feeling rested and relaxed." Deep breath.
>
> "2: Getting more relaxed. Arms and legs heavy and warm." Deep breath.

"3: Not a worry in the world." Breathe.

"4: Feeling sleepy. I should be back to sleep soon." Breathe deeply.

"5: Feeling totally relaxed and wonderful." Breathe.

Continue breathing deeply. Focus upon a pleasant and relaxing image. Let your mind be totally captivated and engulfed by the image. Some persons prefer single simple images like gems or minerals. Others enjoy conjuring up thoughts about pleasant nature scenes or social interactions. Design your personal images according to your own preferences.

If extraneous thoughts come into your mind, don't be alarmed by them. Remember that candle flame. The unwanted thought blows the flame slightly. But your thought, like the wind, goes away. As the candle flame returns upright, your thoughts become focused, pleasant, relaxing, and calming.

The Steps in Cognitive Focusing

1. When you first notice that you are awake, tell yourself something calming and reassuring.
2. Take two deep breaths, and relax your body.
3. Take five deep breaths. Count from one to five and tell yourself that you are getting more relaxed with each breath you take.
4. Focus your thoughts on a pleasant and peaceful image. If you like, use the candle flame image to rid your mind of unwanted thoughts.

LEARNING TO RELAX IN THE MIDDLE OF THE NIGHT

Begin by practicing cognitive focusing at the end of your regular relaxation exercises. Do this for at least a period of four or five days until you are able to relax when you use them.

When you finish your regular relaxation exercise, imagine you are in bed and that it is the middle of the night. Picture yourself waking up; immediately use cognitive focusing to relax and fall back to sleep. Once you feel that you have mastered cognitive focusing, try using it at night when you awaken.

Beware that cognitive focusing is not an easy skill to master. Three things could happen:

1. You may not experience immediate and dramatic results. Be prepared to be patient with yourself; give yourself time to master the technique. Don't give up if you don't experience immediate success the first night or so.
2. Sometimes cognitive focusing may work and sometimes it may not.

Therefore, we are warning you not to be frustrated or discouraged if you're not completely successful the first time

Self-Improvement Task VI

Learning Cognitive Focusing

I will begin to help myself learn to fall back to sleep at night by:

1. Practicing Cognitive Focusing during the day at the end of my Progressive and Mental Relaxation Exercises. I will do this for at least four or five days.
2. Trying it out at night when I awaken once I have practiced Cognitive Focusing and notice that I can relax using it.
3. I will continue to:
   - practice Progressive and Mental Relaxation during the day and when going to bed;
   - practice alternative helpful thoughts;
   - keep my Sleep Diaries; and
   - congratulate myself.
4. I will negotiate a self-contract (or use some alternative strategy) to help me be systematic and consistent in learning Cognitive Focusing.
5. Once I have learned Cognitive Focusing, I will move to Chapter 8.

you use Cognitive Focusing or if it occasionally fails to give you the desired result. There's a third possibility, too: Cognitive Focusing may not work at all for you. In such cases, be prepared to work further to solve your problem. The rest of this book is designed to help you do just that. In Chapter 8 we tell you how to design an optimal sleep environment, and in Chapter 9 we give you a systematic way for analyzing your sleep problems and finding methods for solving them.

A FINAL NOTE

Nighttime awakenings are often associated with high levels of daytime tension and/or a depressed mood. Part V contains three chapters to help you reduce stress and tension and improve your mood. You might consider studying and using those chapters carefully if you feel bothered by either of those problems. They may offer the key that unlocks your sleep difficulty.

Self-Contract

Goal: Learning Cognitive Focusing

Specific Behavioral Objectives

I agree to: ______________________________
(specify behavior)

____

under the following circumstances: ______________________________
(specify where, when,

____

how much, etc.)

____

____

Environmental Planning

In order to help me do this, I am going to: (1) arrange my physical and social environment by: ______________________________

____

and; (2) control my internal environment (thoughts, images) by: ______

____

Consequences

Provided by me:
(If contract is kept) ______________________________

(If contract is broken) ______________________________

Provided by others:
(If contract is kept) ______________________________

(If contract is broken) ______________________________

- -

______________ Signed ______________________________
(Renewal Date)

Witness ______________________________

Date ______________________________

8

A Time and a Place for Every Purpose

WHAT'S RIGHT AND WHAT'S WRONG?

Eating cotton candy may be okay (to some people at least) in the middle of the afternoon at the circus. If friends told you that they had cotton candy for breakfast, you might wonder about their health and worry about how they are feeling. Screaming at the top of your lungs and jumping up and down vigorously is a fairly normal activity in the last ten seconds of a championship football game when the score is tied and your team is in field goal position. Raucous laughter is expected when you watch your favorite comedian, play, or movie. But screaming vigorously or laughing heartily when viewing a Greek tragedy or when confronted with depressing news might cause others to wonder about your sanity—or, at the very least, about your manners.

The point is clear. Few things we do are right or wrong in and of themselves. Judgements about our actions can usually be made only in relation to *when* and *where* those actions take place.

TIMES AND PLACES AND WHAT WE DO

Places and times can also influence what we do. Just noticing that it is noon may cause you to think about food to such a degree that hunger pangs even start. Many smokers report that they smoke more in some situations than in others: with a cup of coffee, watching television or reading, driving a car, or sitting in a favorite chair and relaxing. Specific thoughts also tend to occur more frequently in some circumstances or certain times of day. Standing under the shower in the morning might be your cue to begin planning and organizing your day. Hearing the clock chime 3:00 p.m. may remind you that it is time for the cup of coffee that you *always* need to carry you through the rest of the afternoon.

TIMES AND PLACES AND SLEEP

Your sleep problems might also be related to times and places in which they occur. Many people find that they overeat only at certain times (in the evening watching television) or in certain locations (in the family room). Controlling overeating may require that they eat only at certain times and places and that they avoid eating in "high risk" places like standing in the kitchen by the refrigerator.

People with sleeping problems often recognize that they have a lot on their mind and that they often feel physically tense when they go to bed. These thoughts interfere directly with sleep, and intense mental activity can also lead to physical arousal. Excessive thinking and physical arousal are similar to anything else we do: *They tend to occur more in certain situations and at certain times.*

Thinking and physical activity are okay and are really enjoyable. It's where and when they occur that cause problems. Unfortunately, problem sleepers engage in these activities at the wrong times and in the wrong places. Persons with insomnia often find that their sleeping environment—the bed, bedroom, and bedtime—can become a signal for these arousing activities. And, as you well know, it's quite difficult to think and be alert physically and asleep at the same time.

TIIE SLEEP RHYTHM

Time has a very special relationship to sleep because our bodily functions ebb and flow on a daily cycle. Waking, non-REM, and REM sleep, three different *states* of being and experience, occur as part of this rhythmic process. Many physiological processes follow the same pattern.

Problems in our daily body rhythms can occur in one of two ways. Some of the physical processes can get out of phase with the others. Some scientists have suggested that narcolepsy (sudden irresistible sleep attacks) represents the onset of REM sleep at the wrong time. Insomnia for some persons might be caused by similar out-of-phase processes.

A person's different body rhythms may all be fluctuating in harmony, but the person's entire circadian rhythm may be out of phase with the environment around him. This is the common jet lag problem. Flying east from San Francisco to Yugoslavia will transport you from a place where your body time was in harmony with clock time to a place where you are out of phase with the environment. Your peaks in San Francisco coincided with those times of the day when you expected to be most alert, and you reached your low point when you and most people expected sleep to occur easily. Your world in

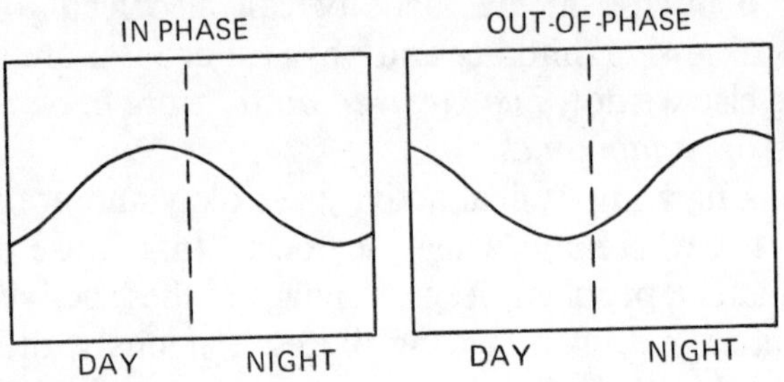

The common "jet lag" experience. The in-phase person's circadian rhythm peaks during the day and declines at night; he feels alert during the day is ready to sleep at night. The out-of-phase person (or one who has traveled recently) finds himself declining during the day (feeling fatigued) and peaking at night (experiencing insomnia). It is possible to get back in phase by establishing a regular sleep schedule.

Yugoslavia has turned you upside down. Until your body has a chance to adapt, you'll be trying to carry on daytime activities when your body cries "Sleep!" Your attempts to obtain slumber will be countered by body signals that say "I'm ready to go!" Traveling from the West to the East Coast produces the same experience, although less dramatically. The first few days are disturbed because your body's rhythm is suddenly expected to change. It will adapt gradually if you are patient and maintain a fairly standard routine in the new environment.

Being out of phase with the outside environment may not be intolerable if you can design life to meet your optimal sleep and alert times. People commonly describe themselves as "night people" or "morning people," and manage to arrange their lives so that they sleep when most ready and are pursuing important activities when their body functions are peaking.

Problems can arise, however, if you seldom permit your body to adjust to a consistent schedule, if you prevent your body rhythms from settling into harmony with clock time.

DWIGHT. *Dwight was a normal, relatively well-adjusted junior, doing all right in high school and progressing well socially. He had managed to get his driver's* *license and had obtained a part-time job frying hamburgers and french fries at the local fast-foods restaurant across from the high school. He was in good physical health, with one major exception. He found himself having more and more trouble in getting adequate sleep since he began high school two years ago. His sleep patterns were getting more and more variable and erratic. He maintained a reasonably stable routine during the week. He went to bed around midnight, fell asleep about 1:00 or 1:30, and got up for school at 7:15. School work, athletic events, extracurricular activities, and the part-time job kept him quite busy during the day.*

Weekends were always greeted enthusiastically because they meant extra sleep and a chance to catch up on rest. On Friday evening, Dwight usually worked until midnight, hung around work for a half-hour talking to some of his buddies, came home, and relaxed for awhile. He finally went to bed around 2:00 or 2:30, after checking out the late movie. The best part came on Saturday morning

when he could sleep in as long as he wanted, usually until 10:30 or 11:00. Saturday was low key. He worked in the afternoon and evening, and then stayed up even later. Sunday meant sleeping in until around noon, maybe 1 p.m., along with some recreation or chores.

School returned predictably on Monday, and Dwight, wanting to feel rested and prepared for the day, would attempt to go to bed and to sleep at his regular time around midnight. Only now, instead of taking only an hour to fall asleep, Dwight regularly lay awake until 2:00 or 2:30, tossing and turning and wondering why sleep was such a chore. On Monday morning 7:15 came awfully early; he always felt washed out. On Monday night he was able to get to sleep somewhat more quickly. Finally, by Tuesday, he had settled back into his weekday "routine."

Dwight was not giving his body's rhythms a chance to adjust to any regular routine or establish a stable harmony with clock time. Just as he might begin to slip into a pattern on Wednesday or Thursday, the weekend would arrive and his patterns would be thrown into disarray once again.

LEARNING NEW PATTERNS

Times, places, and your sleep are related in three ways:

1. Places and times can influence what we do and think. This means that your bed and bedroom and the time you customarily go to bed may be signals for you to think and plan and worry.
2. Judgements that we and others make about our actions are often done so in relation to when and where they occur. *Thinking and planning are not, in*

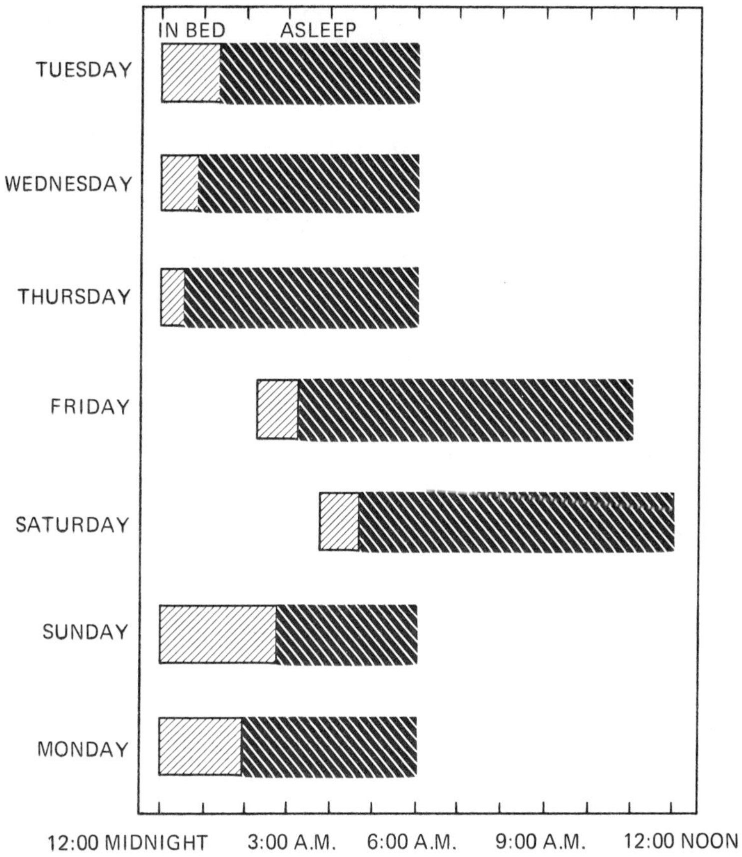

Dwight's sleep patterns through the week. The shaded portion represents the time he is in bed but not asleep, and the dark portion represents the time he is actually sleeping. Notice how the weekend sleep patterns tend to disrupt constantly his circadian rhythm cycles.

and of themselves, inappropriate and improper. It's only when we engage in those activities when we want to sleep that trouble results. (The choice, of course, is yours. You may prefer to lie awake and think in bed. That's okay, if that's what you really want to do.)

3. Our bodies may need a more consistent schedule to establish a regular rhythmic pattern in harmony with the clock schedule we must keep.

In the rest of this chapter we offer you some procedures that make use of what we know about the relationships among times, places, body rhythms, and your actions and thoughts. We first present some general strategies useful for anyone with a sleep problem. Once you have mastered those, we introduce you to some procedures for analyzing your own sleep-related activities. This information is then used to help you make changes in habits that may be preventing satisfactory sleep.

BREAKING OLD HABITS AND BUILDING NEW ONES

Associations between places, times, and activities are learned, having been built up by repeated practice. Fortunately, we can adapt to new situations—it's one of the strongest survival mechanisms we as humans possess. We can adjust to a variety of conditions and situations because we can learn quickly. We are fortunate in being able to break old habits and learn new ones.

Replacing one habit with another involves following six simple rules. These rules should help you accomplish two objectives. First, they will help you to establish new, more helpful habits and eliminate actions that prevent good sleep. Practice and more practice is all that is required. But you must be willing to work to rehearse and use good sleep habits in the bed and bedroom, and engage in other actions at other times and in other places. Second, they will help your body establish a normal and regular body rhythm. Your sleep–wake cycle can then function so that you sleep at night and are alert during the day. Let's review the rules and then talk about how you might put them into practice.

ESTABLISHING GOOD SLEEP HABITS

1. Lie down intending to go to sleep only when you are sleepy. Let your body tell you when it's tired. Don't go to bed because "It's 10:00 and I always go to bed at 10:00." If you go to bed when you are sleepy, you are more likely to fall asleep right away, reinforcing the association between bed and sleep. If you are not sleepy, you might possibly toss and turn for awhile, begin to think, and get mentally and physically aroused. That would only reinforce the old-habit patterns we are trying to eliminate.

Some people might worry that they won't get enough sleep doing this because the time they have to get up cannot change. But that's exactly the point. By establishing a fixed time for getting up and allowing your bedtime to vary, your body can determine just how much sleep you do need in order to function well. Remember, not everyone needs eight hours of sleep.

2. Don't use your bed for anything except sleep. Bed and bedroom are for sleeping. Anything else done there will only reinforce the notion that a variety of actions are appropriate in that setting. If you usually watch TV in bed, climbing into bed may be enough to signal you to begin thinking thinking about things related to what you've seen on TV. But if bed is reserved for sleep (and, of course, sexual activity), then climbing into bed will be a strong cue for you to fall asleep.

3. Get up and go into another room if you are unable to fall asleep. The objective is for you to associate bed and bedroom with sleeping. Don't allow yourself to engage in other activities because if you do, your new habits will not have a chance to become a natural part of your routine.

4. Repeat these steps as often as necessary. The new habits will come only with repeated and consistent practice.

5. Get up at the same time every morning. This is especially important. It's important to permit your body to establish a regular body rhythm pattern. As tempting as it might be, don't get up later on weekends; this is when most persons disrupt their body rhythms. Take heart for this rule need not be followed forever. Once you have established a fairly consistent rhythm, it will be possible to vary the time you get up within certain careful limits. But we think it to your advantage to establish consistent rhythms before you permit yourself to deviate from the routine.

6. Do not nap. By now, the reason is obvious. Napping can throw your body rhythm off schedule, and make it more difficult for you to sleep at night. By taking daytime naps you will not give yourself the opportunity to establish a harmonious sleep–wakefulness rhythm and strengthen positive associations between your sleep environment and what you want to do there—sleep.

GETTING STARTED AND KEEPING AT IT

Follow the directions in Self-Improvement Task IX, and negotiate a self-contract with your helper to help you follow whatever procedures you have devised to help you remain consistent and systematic.

Being systematic and persistent is especially important as you work to learn these new and more helpful actions. Habits, especially well-established ones, are very hard to break and can be unusually resistant to change. Replacing them with more helpful ways of behaving and thinking may not come easily. As you begin to apply the six rules for "Establishing Good Sleep

Habits," be patient with yourself and with the procedures. We've reminded you to be patient with yourself several times now. It's advice we all seem to need often.

Don't expect to change over night; it will probably take awhile before your new habits will become second nature, a comfortable "automatic" part of you. But most important, don't allow yourself to slip back into your old ways through carelessness, neglect, or discouragement. Practicing these patterns will not be easy at first. It's never easy, and always takes a while to adjust to new routines. But we think that the effort and readjustment will be worthwhile, and that your work will pay off.

Remember, too, that you've gotten this far and you can be justifiably proud of your progress. Give yourself some strokes along the way, too.

WHAT NEXT?

Once you have implemented the six basic rules and feel confident that your old habits are beginning to fade and your new habits are becoming part of who you are, then you're ready for the next set of exercises, presented in Chapter 9. These help you discover other factors in your environment and other actions you do that may be associated with unsatisfactory sleep. Most important, you can learn some methods for changing them.

Times, Places, and Sleep

1. Places and times can have a strong influence on what we do, and can signal certain actions and thoughts.
2. Actions and thoughts are often judged to be inappropriate or appropriate according to when and where they occur.
3. Our bodies need a fairly regular sleeping-waking schedule so that it can establish a consistent daily rhythm.

Establishing Good Sleep Habits

1. Lie down intending to go to sleep *only* when you are sleepy.
2. Don't use your bed for anything except sleep.

   (Sexual activity is the only exception to this rule—unless it leaves you agitated and awake rather than pleasantly contented and tired.)
3. If you find yourself unable to fall asleep, get up and go into another room.

   Stay up as long as you wish and then return to the bedroom to sleep. Although we do not want you to watch the clock, we do want you to get out of bed if you do not fall asleep immediately.

   Remember, the goal is to associate your bed with falling asleep quickly! If you are in bed more than about ten minutes without falling asleep and have not gotten up, you are not following this instruction.
4. If you still cannot fall asleep, repeat Step 3.
5. Get up at the same time every morning.
6. Do not nap.

Self-Improvement Task IX

Establishing Good Sleep Habits

I will help myself learn good sleep habits by:

1. Deciding which of the six basic rules for establishing good sleep habits I want to follow. I will also plan a specific time to put them into practice.
2. Negotiating a self-contract

   or

   Planning to use another strategy to help me be consistent and systematic.
3. Continuing to:

   a. Keep my Daily Sleep Diaries;
   b. Practice alternative helpful thoughts;
   c. Practice Physical and Mental Relaxation; and
   d. Practice Cognitive Focusing so that I can reduce the amount of time I am awake in the middle of the night.

When you have practiced these new habits for at least 7 days, move to Chapter 9 to:

- learn how to analyze your sleep environment and other actions possibly associated with poor sleep; and
- learn how to use this information to learn to sleep better.

Self-Contract

Goal: Establishing Good Sleep Habits

Specific Behavioral Objectives

I agree to: ____
(specify behavior)

____

under the following circumstances: ____________________
(specify where, when,

____
how much, etc.)

____

Environmental Planning

In order to help me do this, I am going to: (1) arrange my physical and social environment by: ____________________

____

and; (2) control my internal environment (thoughts, images) by: ______

____

____

Consequences

Provided by me:
(If contract is kept) ____________________

(If contract is broken) ____________________

Provided by others:
(If contract is kept) ____________________

(If contract is broken) ____________________

- -

____________________ Signed ____________________
(Renewal Date)

Witness ____________________

Date ____________________

9

Looking Closely and Planning Wisely

In our clinical experience, the combinations of procedures we have presented so far have helped many persons struggling with occasional and frequent insomnia improve their sleep.* Changing beliefs about sleep, learning to relax mind and body at bedtime, focusing thoughts when waking up in the middle of the night, and establishing good sleep habits have helped many persons learn to sleep better.

But there are exceptions, and the next four chapters will help you analyze the reasons for these exceptions and do something about them.

*Note that we are not saying that everyone's sleep should be improved by these procedures. Don't think that something necessarily is wrong with you if you have not experienced improved sleep (assuming that you have practiced the strategies as recommended). We do urge you to read on and continue trying the techniques out. Again, be patient.

At this point in the program, you might be experiencing one or a combination of two possible sleep patterns:

- Your sleep may have improved *most of the time.* But there are some nights when your sleep is still disturbed—despite the fact that you use everything you know.
- Your sleep has not improved despite the fact that you have really given these strategies an honest and wholehearted effort and have attempted to use the procedures consistently and systematically.

If either of these descriptions apply to you, then it will be worth your while to learn the skills presented in this and the remaining chapters. These lessons are devoted to looking closely at possible causes of your sleep problems and devising solutions to meet your needs. Even if you feel that your sleep problem has been solved, become familiar with these strategies before proceeding to Chapter 13. *Maintaining your progress will require that you are able to solve difficulties and setbacks quickly and efficiently when they arise.*

SELF-ANALYSIS: WHAT'S IT ALL ABOUT?

The daily Sleep Diary has two important purposes: It gives you *immediate feedback on your efforts and serves as a yardstick to measure your progress.* The data you have collected gives you a day-by-day record of your progress, your ups and downs, and where to improve.

We invited you to adopt a scientific perspective to improve your sleep. That meant looking, gathering data, developing hunches, experimenting, and gathering more data as a way of successfully solving your problems. We asked you to be prepared to *abandon your favorite assumptions in an effort to find effective solutions to your problems.*

Now you can use your personal-scientist skills to the fullest. *Your continued improvement depends on your ability to devise creative solutions to your problems, and move on courageously to new ones if the old methods don't work.*

WHAT'S GOING ON?

Two sources will be used to complete the first step of your assessment and planning procedure: the daily Sleep Diary and the Self-Assessment Chart.

The daily Sleep Diary contains a comprehensive record of your sleep since you started the program and gives us an invaluable account of events, environments, and situations that may be associated with better sleep and with less than good sleep.

First, let's take a good close look at sleep by graphing some selected factors such as how long it normally takes you to fall asleep, how many times you wake up at night, and how many hours you sleep each night. Once you have it graphed (take a look at Jim Stone's data for an example), pick some nights (five to ten) when you slept especially well and an equal number of nights in which you slept poorly. If you have no or few poor sleep nights, don't worry. You must really be on the right track and that's great!

> ***JIM STONE.*** *Jim Stone graphed his data (Fig. 9-1). Note that he originally experienced problems both in getting to sleep initially and in waking up and staying awake for several hours in the middle of the night. The two relaxation strategies helped him reduce the amount of time needed to get to sleep initially. Note also he started to go to sleep much more quickly during the night when he*

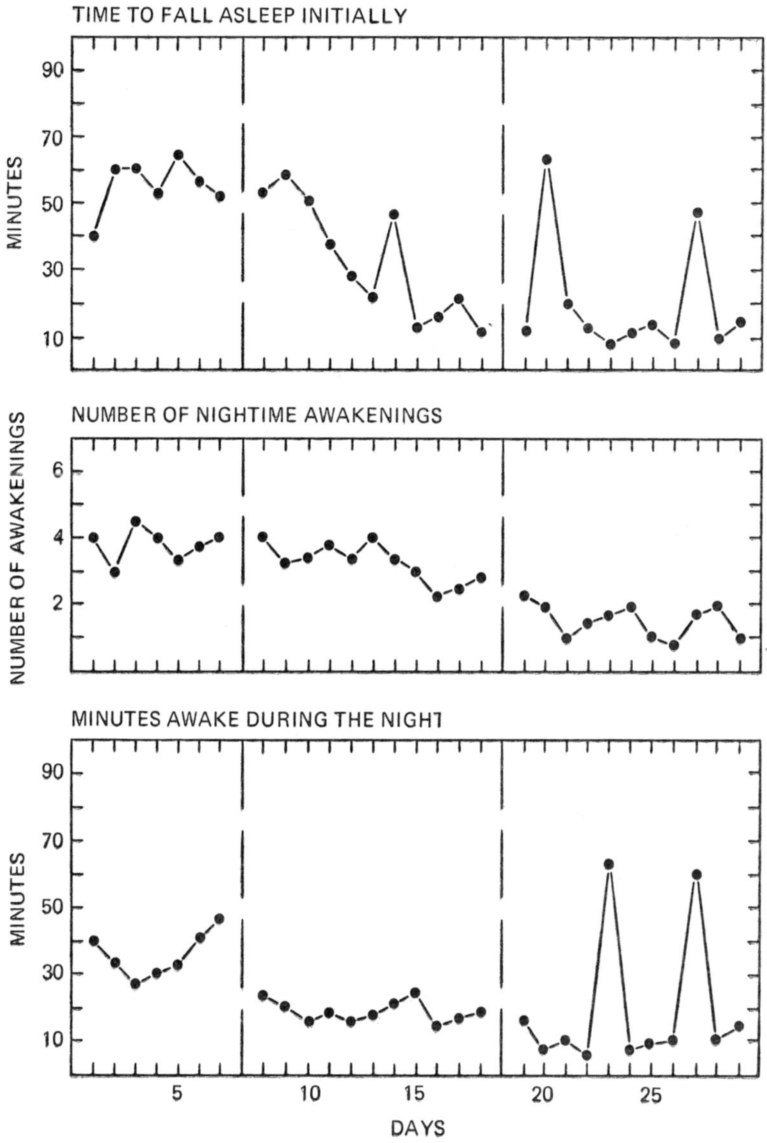

Jim Stone's sleep patterns as he progressed through the steps in How to Sleep Better. This formed the basis for his self-analysis and problem solving.

started practicing physical and mental relaxation. Difficulties in nighttime awakenings were reduced further when Jim learned cognitive focusing and when he began following the "Rules for Establishing Good Sleeping Habits." However, notice his occasional lapses. To begin his self-analysis, Jim chose nights 14, 20, 23, and 27 as "poor sleep nights", and nights 15, 16, 17, 18, 19, 21, 22, and 24 as "good sleep nights".

The next step involves digging out your daily Sleep Diaries to make use of the wealth of information recorded there. Find the diaries for the nights you have selected, and sort them into two piles, "good" and "bad" nights. Next, take a close look at what you wrote down, focusing on four specific categories:

1. Physical arousal when going to bed.
2. Thoughts when going to bed.
3. Activities between dinner and bedtime.
4. Bedtime activities.

As a first step, leaf through the two piles to see if anything stands out to distinguish good and poor sleep nights.

JIM STONE (Continued). *Jim used the Self-Analysis Worksheet to discover any differences between the two kinds of sleep nights. Note two features of his self-analysis. First, level of physical arousal when going to bed and activities from dinner to bedtime seem to be the same on good and poor sleep nights. But some interesting differences emerge when looking at "Thoughts when Retiring" and "Bedtime Activities." Before he wrote information down in the Self-Analysis Worksheet, Jim had no awareness that specific differences in his actions might end in better or worse sleep.*

This exercise comprises the first step in self-analysis. Before going any further, take some time—as much time as you need—to analyze your own Sleep Diaries. Write your responses on the Self-Analysis Worksheet and then you'll be ready to start the second step in self-analysis: brainstorming.

Self-Analysis Worksheet

Name Jim Stone

Dates: From March 29 to May 17

	Good Nights	Bad Nights
Daily Sleep Diary Number of nights	8	4
Physical arousal	4.5	5.0
Thoughts upon retiring	Daytime accom-plishments Vacation plans	Tomorrow's schedule Problem situation
Activities from dinner to bedtime	Television Novel reading Playing with children	Television Playing with children Read novel
Bedtime activities	Talk to spouse about pleasant events Stay in bed once there	Talk to spouse about finances, kid's problems Get up several times to do things I forgot to do
Brainstorm		
Other factors		

BRAINSTORMING

Now that the analytic part of self-analysis is behind us, we can treat ourselves to the luxury of being playful, adventurous, and creative. (All are excellent and necessary qualities of a good scientist, and especially of a good personal scientist.) Brainstorming begins with the unlikely question:

> If I wanted to make my sleep really bad, what could I do? How would I set up conditions to make sure that I would experience fitful, disturbed, and terrible sleep?

This exercise shouldn't be hard; after all, you have had a lot of practice in sleeping poorly.

Here are some items that one group generated:

- have the phone ring every half hour
- think about problems
- plan tomorrow's schedule
- reflect upon your negative personality characteristics
- drink at least three cups of coffee after 8:00 p.m.
- make several phone calls just before going to bed
- have an argument with your spouse
- think about something you're afraid of
- take a long afternoon or early evening nap

How many can you add to the list? Unleash your creative juices—write down *anything* and *everything* that comes to mind.

JIM STONE (Continued). Jim brainstormed with his wife, and together they came up with six items that led to poor sleep, which he listed on his Self-Analysis Work-

sheet. Note that Jim found some of the things associated with poor sleep not thought of previously, including thoughts ("beat" myself mentally), actions (take a long nap), and physical features of his surroundings (warm bedroom).

List as many items as you can. It might be helpful to ask someone who really knows your sleep habits to join you. Once you have generated a list of possible items, go through and pick out those items that really do lead to less than satisfactory sleep for you and list them on your Self-Analysis Worksheet.

MORE OBSERVATION

There may be other factors, occurring during the day, or those that don't seem especially related to sleep, that could make a difference in how you sleep. Our task right now is not to evaluate the reasonableness of what we write down. Rather, like the scientist, we are "sleuthing," following every hunch to make sure that every clue gets careful consideration.

As a final step in self-analysis, we suggest that you take a few more days to observe and note any other daytime and nighttime activities possibly related to good and poor sleep. *Be especially careful to note daytime activities;* they may be more important than is apparent.

Record anything that you do during the day or at night that seems related to your sleep.

JIM STONE (Continued). *Jim was able to identify four additional factors. Good sleep nights were marked by a transition between evening activities (especially intense reading) and going to bed, and physical exercise during the day. Poor sleep nights seemed to be associated with outside noises and busy days.*

IT'S UP TO YOU

You now have the basic information you need to complete your self-analysis. Use the worksheet provided, and complete the information requested by:

- Examining your daily Sleep Diaries
- Brainstorming
- Observation

Take your time and complete the Self-Analysis Worksheet with care. What you discover will aid you invaluably in solving

Self-Analysis Worksheet

Name: Jim Stone

Dates: From March 29 to May 17

	Good Nights	Bad Nights
Daily Sleep Diary Number of nights	8	4
Physical arousal	4.5	5.0
Thoughts upon retiring	Daytime accomplishments Vacation plans	Tomorrow's schedule Problem situation
Activities from dinner to bedtime	Television Novel reading Playing with children	Television Playing with children Read novel
Bedtime activities	Talk to spouse about pleasant events Stay in bed once there	Talk to spouse about finances, kid's problems Get up several times to do things I forgot to do
Brainstorm		"Beat myself mentally Take long naps Really warm bedroom Make a phone call Think about unfriendly exchange with co-worker
Other factors	Transition between work and bed Physical exercise during day	Noises outside Tense, uptight day

your remaining sleep problems and any you might experience in the future. Once a careful assessment has been completed, the rest of the process is straightforward—identifying the problem is three-quarters of the battle. Once you have done that, the solution usually will be obvious.

Self-Improvement Task X

Self-Analysis

I will help myself overcome my remaining sleep problems by:

1. Assessing differences in my daytime and nighttime actions, thoughts, and physical surroundings on good and poor sleep nights by:
   a. examining my daily Sleep Diaries from good and poor sleep nights;
   b. brainstorming; and
   c. observing
2. Summarizing these differences on my Self-Analysis Worksheet
3. Negotiating a self-contract or
   Using another strategy to help me be consistent and systematic
4. Continuing to:
   a. Keep my daily Sleep Diaries;
   b. Practice alternative helpful thoughts;
   c. Practice and use physical and mental relaxation;
   d. Practice cognitive focusing to reduce the amount of time I am awake in the middle of the night; and
   e. Following the rules for Establishing Good Sleep Habits

When I have completed my self-analysis, I will move to the second half of this chapter to learn how to use this information to devise solutions to the problems I have identified.

Self-Analysis Worksheet

Name ______________________________

Dates: From ______________ to ______________

	Good Nights	*Bad Nights*
Daily Sleep Diary Number of nights	________	________
Physical arousal	________	________
Thoughts upon retiring	________	________
	________	________
	________	________
Activities from dinner to bedtime	________	________
	________	________
	________	________
Bedtime activities	________	________
	________	________
	________	________
Brainstorm	________	________
	________	________
	________	________
	________	________
	________	________
Other factors	________	________
	________	________
	________	________

Self-Analysis Worksheet

Name ____

Dates: From ____________________ to ____________________

	Good Nights	*Bad Nights*
Daily Sleep Diary Number of nights	________	________
Physical arousal	________	________
Thoughts upon retiring	________	________
	________	________
	________	________
Activities from dinner to bedtime	________	________
	________	________
	________	________
Bedtime activities	________	________
	________	________
	________	________
Brainstorm	________	________
	________	________
	________	________
	________	________
	________	________
Other factors	________	________
	________	________
	________	________

Self-Contract

Goal: Completing a Self-Analysis

Specific Behavioral Objectives

I agree to: ______________________________
(specify behavior)

____

under the following circumstances: ______________________________
(specify where, when,

____

how much, etc.)

____

Environmental Planning

In order to help me do this, I am going to: (1) arrange my physical and social environment by: ______________________________

____

and; (2) control my internal environment (thoughts, images) by: ______

____

____

Consequences

Provided by me:
(If contract is kept) ______________________________

(If contract is broken) ______________________________

Provided by others:
(If contract is kept) ______________________________

(If contract is broken) ______________________________

- -

______________ Signed ______________________________
(Renewal Date)

Witness ______________________________

Date ______________________________

USING THE DATA TO GUIDE YOUR ACTIONS

Your personal change program will be marked by two strategies: *doing more of those actions that lead to good sleep and less of those actions that lead to less satisfactory sleep.*

> ***JIM STONE (Continued).*** *Jim's self-analysis led to the discovery of several important clues relating to his activities, thoughts, surroundings, and sleep. Let's see if we can summarize them briefly.*
>
> *From the daily Sleep Diary, Jim learned that thinking about business, hashing over problems, discussing heated issues with his wife, and popping in and out of bed several times to complete unfinished business led to poor sleep. Through brainstorming, he realized that thinking unpleasant thoughts about himself or his day's activities, taking a long nap, reading something stimulating, or trying to sleep in a warm bedroom usually led to the same result. Finally, especially tense days and outside noises seemed related to poor sleep.*
>
> *Conversely, pleasant thoughts, "mellow" conversation with his wife, daytime physical exercise, and transition time between work and bed seemed related to better sleep.*

SUMMARIZE AND RANK ORDER

Jim's next step involved lumping these observations into some major categories. He chose a three-way classification system.

	Poor Sleep	*Good Sleep*
Thoughts:	Negative thoughts about myself; Negative thoughts about my work; Negative thoughts about my co-workers; Thinking about problem situations	Positive thoughts about myself; Positive thoughts about future
Activities:	Phone calls late in evening; Long nap; Up and down before settling down; Tense during day; Negative conversation with wife	Physical exercise; Talk about pleasant events with wife; Transition time
Physical surroundings:	Warm bedroom; Outside noises	

Based on what he knew about himself and some hunches he had about his own reactions, Jim next attempted to rank his observations in order of importance. He asked himself the question: *Which of these really requires some immediate actions, and which ones can wait?*

Jim decided that the big difference between good and poor sleep nights for him involved two key factors.

- His thoughts when going to bed played a big role. If he retired with negative thoughts, poor sleep would surely result. If, instead, he was able to have pleasant thoughts, he usually slept well.
- Almost as important were his conversations with his wife. If they were able to talk about pleasant events and topics, his mind was put at ease. But if their conversation revolved around difficulties or problem situations of any kind, disturbed sleep was almost certain to result.

FINDING SOLUTIONS

Jim's next step involved solving the problems. The solution usually becomes relatively straightforward once the problem has become identified precisely and correctly.

Your solutions can come from two sources. We have included three chapters in Part V to teach you how to manage and solve problems commonly experienced by persons with insomnia. One or several of the skills presented here may be just what's needed to take you the rest of the way in solving your sleep difficulty:

- **Chapter 10** will teach you how to relax during the day at those times when tension rises and gets out of hand. Learning to keep from getting too excited and overwrought during the day will help you sleep at night because your body and mind will be more ready to relax.
- **Chapter 11** will teach you ways to think differently about yourself. Negative self-thoughts, especially at the wrong times, can really work to prevent good sleep. Learning to look at yourself differently should take you a long way to improved sleep.
- **Chapter 12** will assist by teaching you that your world can be viewed from a variety of perspectives. A negative, down-in-the-dumps point of view often is associated with poor sleep, while a more optimistic outlook can lead to improved sleep. Learning to view your world more positively may be just what you need. (There is more to it than just telling you to think positive!)

JIM'S SOLUTIONS

Jim found that his thoughts upon retiring were his central problem. At a first step, he decided that Chapters 11 and 12 were just what he needed. By learning new ways of thinking about himself and the world about him, Jim reasoned that he might be able to retire with positive thoughts all of the time.

He decided to tackle his second problem at the same time. He and his wife made a contract. *They both agreed to talk only about pleasant events at bedtime.* If either brought up a negative topic, a signal was used (the index finger across the lips) and the conversation was stopped immediately and the topic changed. It took a little time for them to get used to this unusual routine, but once started it kept going under its own momentum. Both Jim and his wife found going to bed much more pleasant than ever before!

NOW IT'S YOUR TURN

You now have the basic skills and background for finding solutions to those things that might still be related to poor sleep. The process requires only that you be *creative* in analyzing your problems and *courageous* in proposing and trying solutions.

Don't be intimidated by the detailed analysis that Jim completed; his was quite involved. Some simpler examples are presented in the table on page 174. We felt it important to present a comprehensive example of how the process works so you could get a really clear idea of how to proceed. It basically consists of four major steps:

1. *Self-analysis:* Examine your daily Sleep Diary, brainstorm, and observe to see what you can find out about things that are different on good and poor sleep nights.
2. *Summarize and rank order:* Classify your observations into some major categories and rank them in order of importance.

	Factors Influencing Sleep	*Solution*
Patricia Landry	Trying to sleep in room that is too warm leads to poor sleep	Be sure that heat is turned down at night; buy electric blanket with dual controls
	Physical exercise during day improves sleep	Start a regular program of physical exercise (jogging, brisk walking, and using stairs instead of elevator
	Talk with husband about finances	Discuss only pleasant events with husband during late evening
Spencer Graham	Finishing work and trying to go to sleep right away	Learn to manage time better so that a transition time between work and bed can be scheduled
	Afternoon nap leads to poor sleep	Find active thing to do between 4:00 and 5:00 when fatigue is most likely
	Going to bed when not sleepy	Go to bed only when sleepy; try out different times
Tammy Williston	Neighbor's porch light sometimes shines in my eyes	Move bed and fix curtains
	Think about my failure to accomplish everything well	Study Chapter 11 to learn to think differently about myself
	Phone calls late at night	Take phone off hook at night; ask people not to call after 10 p.m.
Joe Guzicki	Experience excessive tension throughout the day	Study and practice cue-controlled relaxation in Chapter 10
	Exciting and stimulating reading from 10:00 to 11:00	Read less exciting material or watch television during the hour prior to bedtime

Self-Improvement Task XI

Finding Solutions and Trying Them Out

I will help myself learn to sleep better by:

1. Devising and implementing solutions to the problems I have identified by:
   a. Summarizing observations from the Self-Analysis Worksheet into some major categories and ranking them in order of importance;
   b. Determining if the skills taught in Chapters 10, 11, and 12, apply to the problems I identify;
   c. Devising my own solution if necessary; and
   d. Trying my solutions out and seeing if they work
2. Negotiating a self-contract, or
   Planning to use another strategy to help me be consistent and systematic.
3. Continuing to:
   a. Keep my daily Sleep Diaries;
   b. Practice alternative helpful thoughts;
   c. Practice and use physical and mental relaxation;
   d. Practice cognitive focusing to reduce the amount of time I am awake in the middle of the night; and
   e. Follow the rules for Establishing Good Sleep Habits

When I have satisfactorily solved the problems I have identified, I may want to:

- Peruse the material presented in Section V to see if any of these skills might be helpful, or
- Study Chapter 13 to find ways to maintain my progress.

3. *Find solutions:* Use the skills presented in Chapter 10, 11, and 12 (if these apply to the problems you have identified) or plan to do *more* of those things that promote good sleep and *less* of those things that lead to poor sleep.
4. *Experiment:* Put your solutions into practice and see what happens. If you improve, continue using your strategy. If no change results, try your hand at further self-analysis or devise new solutions.

WHAT IF I'M OKAY?

If you have no problems that require immediate solution, than we suggest two steps. Leaf through Part V to see if there are any techniques there that may be beneficially used by you at this time. It's not necessary that they be learned only in response to specific problems you experience. Actually mastering some of the skills might be beneficial simply in terms of enhancing your life and helping you feel better.

Second, everyone should study Chapter 13, since we stress the importance of maintaining your progress. *It is important that your gains be consolidated so that your current sleep problems remain solved and so that you can deal with new ones if they come up.*

Self-Contract

Goal: Completing a Self-Analysis

Specific Behavioral Objectives

I agree to: ______________________________
(specify behavior)

____

under the following circumstances: ______________________________
(specify where, when,

____
how much, etc.)

____

Environmental Planning

In order to help me do this, I am going to: (1) arrange my physical and social environment by: ______________________________

____

and; (2) control my internal environment (thoughts, images) by: ______

____

____

Consequences

Provided by me:
(If contract is kept) ______________________________

(If contract is broken) ______________________________

Provided by others:
(If contract is kept) ______________________________

(If contract is broken) ______________________________

- -

______________ Signed ______________________
(Renewal Date)
Witness ______________________
Date ______________________

Part Five

DAYTIME BEHAVIOR AND NIGHTTIME SLEEP

Demands may seem constant and the pressure to perform well is always present in our busy lives. Some alcoholic refreshment and a big evening meal may soothe our frayed nerves at the end of a busy day and help us gather strength to face tomorrow. Yet these "tranquilizers" may not always work, and we may sometimes find ourselves spending most of the evening, even into the early morning, trying to wind down from the day.

Insomnia is not a problem isolated only to the times that we attempt to sleep. Sleep and wakefulness make up an intimate and daily cycle. Anyone who has experienced poor night's sleep knows well the toll it takes the next day. We feel tired and may have difficulty concentrating on tasks that need to be accomplished. If poor sleep persists for a few days, we may find ourselves viewing problems as momentous and insurmountable. Irritability and depression may find their way into our behavior.

The reverse is also true. *What we do during the day has an enor-*

mous impact on how we sleep at night. It's unrealistic to expect to be "under the gun" all day long and then to come home, relax instantly, and fall asleep blissfully. It's unreasonable to be tense all day long and expect to fall asleep at night as if we didn't have a care or concern in the world. *Learning to act more relaxed and positive during the day will take us a long way in improving our nighttime sleep.*

Part V is designed to help you start looking at your daytime behavior to see how it might be contributing to your poor sleep. Besides looking at what you're doing during the day we suggest three basic techniques for improving the quality of your daytime actions so that improved sleep will result.

Instant Relaxation (Chapter 10) helps you identify those times and places that you experience daytime tension and learn to relax quickly when you find yourself in stressful situations.

Thinking Positively About Yourself (Chapter 11) can be important in helping you improve your mood and reduce tension. Many of our anxieties result from the ways in which we evaluate our actions in various situations. Looking at ourselves differently can help improve sleep by improving mood and reducing tension.

Thinking Positively About Your World (Chapter 12) can also help improve mood and reduce tension by giving us a different view of our world and the various activities that make up our day.

Again, these techniques assume that you have mastered Progressive and Mental Relaxation and can use them easily and to your advantage. (If you haven't yet mastered them we strongly recommend that you try to do so before going any further.)

We present only three possibilities for changing daytime activities to improve nighttime sleep. Other strategies, revealed by your self-analysis exercises in the last chapter, may be more important for you. Some people have turned to time management, while others have realized that some form of physical exercise is most helpful. We have listed several good resources for solving other daytime problems in the Suggested Readings section. If you have identified a particular daytime activity that either interferes with or promotes improved sleep, we suggest that you use these resources to design your own continued sleep improvement program.

10

Relax! Don't Get Uptight

HOW CAN I STAY RELAXED?

"Relaxing is well and good, but who could afford to relax with all my responsibilities? I can't relax! I *need* to be geared up so that I can finish everything I have to do."

This is one of those "half truths" that gives us so much trouble. Some tension is needed, but too much is as bad (often worse) than not enough. Stress can be beneficial up to a certain point and even improve our performance in certain situations. But often it feeds upon itself, gets out of control, and interferes with our performance. Too much tension causes us to engage in endless and unproductive worrying. Excessive stress and tension can take its toll on our physical well being too, leading to problems such as high blood pressure, tight muscles, migraine headaches, and insomnia (as you well know).

Remaining *calm* and *relaxed* can enhance performance in many situations. Even a mild amount of stress can block certain thinking processes, leading us to behave less effectively than when we are more relaxed. Can you remember trying (when feeling stressed) to add long columns of numbers in only a few minutes? Mistakes come very easy.

Being "geared up" sometimes carries with it the belief that we must be working very hard because we feel like we are expending so much energy. But expending a lot of energy and working productively don't always go together. *Managing stress and reducing tension during the day may take us a long way toward being more creative and more efficient in our work.* That may seem untrue, but it fits the experience of many people. "Trying harder" and doing more are not always better for us or for others.

Many of us find ourselves in surroundings that trigger stress regularly. Deadlines, the pressure to perform well, our own high standards, and the demands of running a home may appear to be constant and unrelenting. Recall that in Chapter 3 we talked at length about *selective perception.* The way that we respond to something is often a function of how we view it. We may be choosing to react with tension to situations that may not require it. Have you ever had the experience of being engaged in an important and busy activity for an extended length of time? The pressure on college students at the end-of-semester examinations is a good example, as are preparing for vacation, remodeling a house, or meeting a deadline. The next few days can be difficult to handle after the task is finished. Even though demands have diminished, you may feel that you should be busier than you are, doing something rather than pursuing your activities more leisurely. It often takes time to realize that it is no longer necessary to rush about frantically; you can calm down and "take your time" to relax and enjoy yourself.

But it's not necessary to respond with stress even when we are under pressure. It is possible to learn to remain relaxed and still get important tasks accomplished. It is possible to feel better about what you are doing, meet your responsibilities creatively and efficiently, and sleep well at night. You can learn how to respond to pressure without getting excessively aroused and tense.

That's what Instant Relaxation is all about—learning to relax throughout the day despite what is going on around us. Progressive and Mental Relaxation are very effective in inducing deep physical and mental relaxation, but it may not be practical to use these every time you feel tense. But once a person has mastered relaxation skills, it is possible to get some of the same feelings of relaxation simply by using a cue or self-instruction.

In this chapter, you learn how to experience relaxation in those important situations in which you need it the most. You'll learn to notice when you *first* begin to experience stress and tension, and then to use these initial signs to signal you to use Instant Relaxation. You will also learn to identify tension-arousing situations and alter some of these problem situations so that your tension may not have a chance to get started in the first place.

Learning to do this will involve three steps:

1. We will lead you through some exercises to help you identify exactly *how* you experience anxiety.
2. We will help you notice the conditions in which stress is typically felt.
3. We will demonstrate some procedures for either relaxing in the situation or changing it altogether.

IDENTIFYING EXPERIENCES OF ANXIETY

Anxiety is a common term we use to describe our states of heightened tension. Sometimes we may be tense because of specific circumstances, but at other times we may not really know the reason for our anxiety. (Such anxiety is sometimes called "free floating" because the experience of feeling aroused is not directly tied to particular situations.) It's important to note that anxiety is not something we "are" or "have." Rather, *anxiety refers to a group of specific reactions we experience in certain situations.*

Most of us notice anxiety in one or a combination of three ways. We experience anxiety *physiologically* (a racing heart felt in our chest, rapid breathing, or sweating palms). Anxiety is often felt *physically* (hands shaking, stuttering, or twitching). Anxiety might also affect our *thought patterns* (thinking "I'm really getting uptight," or "Boy, am I blowing this one," or worse yet, "Wow. This will be a total disaster"). These thoughts interfere with the kind of clear thinking that would allow us to cope with whatever situations in which we find ourselves.

There are various methods you can use to find out how you respond when you're anxious. First, think back to the most recent time when you were really anxious. Try to imagine the scene as vividly as possible. Who was there? What did things look like? What was being said? Next, imagine that you are back in that situation now; try to include as many details as possible. Use all of your senses: sight, smell, hearing, touch, and taste. What were you experiencing? Go over the details of the situation as they unfolded. As you *relive* the scene, observe your reactions. As you re-experience the stress and tension associated with that situation, identify your reactions. The checklist we provide may help you to notice your stress and tension actions.

If someone else (a spouse, friend, or possibly the person working with you on your self-contracts) can help, a second very useful exercise can be used. Prepare a list of topics (for example, "What is Anxiety," "Friendship," "The Value of Work," "Courage," or "Confidence") on 3 × 5 index cards. Note that each of these topics is something most of us know about; but they are rather general and thus require some thought. Put these cards into an envelope. Taking turns, each

Stress and Tension Responses

Physiological

1. Increased heart rate ________
2. Increased breathing rate ________
3. Perspiration ________
4. Queasy stomach ________
5. ________________ (other) ________
6. ________________ (other) ________

Physical

1. Shaking ________
2. Stuttering ________
3. Muscle twitch ________
4. Increased muscle tension ________
5. ________________ (other) ________
6. ________________ (other) ________

Patterns of Thought

1. "I'm really getting uptight" ________
2. "I'd better get out of here" ________
3. "I'm really making a mess of this." ________
4. ________________ (other) ________
5. ________________ (other) ________

person reaches into the envelope, pulls out a card, and is allowed 30 seconds to prepare a 2-minute speech on the topic listed on the card. The objective is to give the speech and at the same time identify some of the feelings of stress and tension you experience. After each person has had the opportunity to speak, let everyone check on his reactions and talk further to compare and contrast personal experiences of anxiety. Those playing the game with you can also give you feedback on what they noticed about your actions as you were speaking.

These two exercises (and any others you can dream up) will give you the opportunity to observe your stress and tension in two different situations. This is very important information, as you will be using this knowledge to know when to relax. You should now be prepared to observe your reactions in everyday life situations.

TAKING A LOOK AT YOUR ENVIRONMENT

The next task involves watching yourself as you go through the day to identify two things: (1) your stress and tension reactions; and (2) those events or situations that may "cause" you to experience anxiety. Keep a three by five index card handy to serve as a convenient recording device and also as a cue for your self-observation. Whenever you experience stress and tension, indicate four items on the card:

1. The time of day;
2. The event that caused your anxiety;
3. Your particular experience of anxiety; and
4. What happened as a result

In completing his own self-assessment, Jerry was quite surprised to discover that he experienced anxiety more than he ever realized, and that some things that he had been tolerating for years were real problems.

Notice several things about Jerry's self-assessment card for Monday, July 14. First, he filled in all of the categories. If the notes are left general, it is not possible to know *exactly* without specific information what happened each time you feel anx-

Jerry's Self-Assessment Card

Time	*Event*	*Experience*	*Result*
7:30 a.m.	Car swerved in front of me on freeway.	Tension in neck. Angry thoughts ("You stupid ass!").	Started worrying about accidents and insurance. Upset that I got so angry.
8:00 a.m.	Thought about tasks for day.	Thoughts about ability and the time to get job done. ("Ummmm, can I do it? Well. . .")	Spend one-half hour feeling overwhelmed. Starting to get angry about demands.
12:00 p.m.	Meeting client for lunch.	Sweaty palms. Pain in neck and shoulder blades.	Did not enjoy lunch. Hard time really listening to client.
5:30 p.m.	Wife tells me about her lousy day.	Tightness in lower neck and shoulders. Irritating thoughts: "Why can't she just once say something good. Always bitching. . ."	Felt fatigued and depressed. Drank three dry martinis. Starting to worry about completing reports. Where's the time to do it.

ious. Second, thoughts can also cue stress and tension (as when Jerry got to his desk and saw all of the work piled up for the day). Third, Jerry noted that he experienced anxiety both physiologically and mentally and that the effects were usually undersirable. This was quite a revelation to him, as he had previously considered anxiety as a good stimulus for action.

TIME TO OBSERVE

Use the next four days to note your own stress-producing events and the particular anxiety reactions you have in each situation. *Do this carefully and consistently.* The more details the better. Like a scientist trying to figure out the "facts" involved in a problem, you are on the lookout for a lot of detailed information. Don't worry about flooding yourself with information at this point. You may want to complete a self-contract to make sure you'll get the task done. After several days of observation, you should not only have a clearer picture

of the way you experience anxiety, but you should also have some "hunches" about what causes it and what results in your feeling tense. Using this information, stress and tension can be changed in one or a combination of two ways. You can change the environment, and/or learn to use Instant Relaxation.

LEARNING TO MANAGE STRESS

CHANGING THE ENVIRONMENT

Your self-observation should have revealed those events that typically produce stress in you. Some of these might be changed so that stress and tension can be prevented from occurring. Jerry might go to work a bit earlier or somewhat later to avoid the heavy rush hour traffic. He could also make an agreement with his wife that she tell him only pleasant events when he first arrives home in the evening. The worksheet entitled "Changing the Environment" provides some examples which one client found feasible and practical. Use the worksheet to plan changes in your environment.

Another way that the environment can be changed is by communicating your feelings of stress and tension. This helps in two ways. First, instead of brooding and ruminating about your current unpleasant experience, the straightforward expression of your feelings can alter the actions of others and breaks the cycle of unproductive thinking.* Second, expressing an honest feeling can change our environment. Telling your wife when she confronts you at the front door with a stream of complaints that "Fran, I always feel more anxious and angry when you greet me like that," can be a first step in helping her to act more positively when you first arrive home. If one of your

*Bertrand Russell, the great philosopher, once observed, "Worry is like a rocking horse. It keeps you going but gets you nowhere."

teenage children were to say "Gee, Mom, I always feel uptight when you speak to me like that," it might be helpful to change your behavior for your child's benefit.

Changing the Environment

Situation	*Possible Changes*
Commuting to work in rush hour traffic.	Leaving home and work at a different time to minimize traffic difficulties.
Rushing from appointment to appointment.	Schedule appointment with brief breaks (e.g., 10 minutes) in between for relaxation.
Arriving at work feeling overwhelmed about tasks to be done.	Clear desk before leaving work on previous night; make list of tasks to be accomplished with time allotted to each.
Children's excitement when you arrive home in the evening.	Arrange for a 15-minute rest and relaxation period when you first arrive home.
Supervisor (boss) asks you (as he often does) to get out a report 10 minutes before it's time to leave.	Set up appointment with your supervisor. Express how your tension interferes with being efficient and suggest an earlier time for routine requests. (Emergencies are a different matter.)

Notice that the above expression contains two features. It begins with the acknowledgement "I." Telling someone "You make me uptight," would only put them on the defensive. Rather, you are saying, "This is my reaction to the situation." It also contains the expression of a genuine feeling. The worksheet entitled "Expressing Feelings of Tension" provides some further examples of ways to express your feelings honestly and yet appropriately in tension-arousing situations.

Expressing Feelings of Stress and Tension

Situation	*Possible Expression*
Spouse tells you about children's bad behavior.	"I really get upset when you talk to me about the children when I first get home. I realize you're upset. Can we set aside some time later tonight to discuss what we might do?"
Boss calls you in to examine your progress in recently assigned project.	"I have great difficulty responding to your request on such short notice and doing what I feel is a first-rate job. In the future, would it be possible for you to give me some advance warning?"
______________________	______________________
______________________	______________________

Use the worksheet to plan some statements you might use. It's often helpful to rehearse these scenes in your imagination or to practice them with someone else to make sure that you can use them with ease. Please note that we are not naive about the often overrated power of expressing one's feelings. "Telling it like it is" can sometimes make matters even worse, especially if you "unload" ten years of bottled anger in ten minutes. Rather, we believe that a careful, specific, and personally tailored approach to expressing yourself can work wonders. *It make a huge difference in just how you express yourself to another person.* Your boss, for example, may seldom express genuine feelings and may consider such behavior as "hogwash . . . a bunch of psychiatric nonsense." However, your wife or husband, your mother or father, or your roommate may be much more approachable.

It's not always possible to change the social or the physical environment to remove its stress-producing elements. In situations that cause stress but cannot be dealt with in these two ways, it is possible to induce feelings of relaxation instantly, and thus keep stress effectively under control.*

LEARNING INSTANT RELAXATION

Learning to relax in tense situations requires practice. After identifying exactly how you experience stress and tension in your everyday life and noticing those situations in which you are most likely to feel anxiety, you are now ready to learn how to relax. We recommend that you proceed carefully through the following steps to learn this skill.

It is important to first master the Progressive and Mental Relaxation procedures. Plan to practice them at least twice a day for a period of two weeks until you reach the point where you can achieve total and complete physical and mental relaxation by going through the exercises. It may take some of you longer than two weeks to accomplish this objective but that's

*We recognize that sometimes it is crucial, in the long run, to make some major decisions about one's career, one's marriage, one's basic life style. Others may not cooperate with you and may even create more pressure. Clearly, the complex process of clarifying one's values and identifying short- and long-term goals for one's life is important, but is beyond what we can discuss here.

okay. *The important thing is to be able to relax totally when using the strategies.*

When you have reached that point, you can begin to practice Instant Relaxation, a quickie method of using relaxation when you begin to feel tense.

STEP ONE: PRACTICE

First, tense all of your muscles in your body at the *same time.* Study the tension all over your body and notice what it feels like. After all of the muscles are tense, take a deep breath and hold it for five seconds. Let all of the air out and relax your muscles by giving yourself the command, "Relax, let go." Try this a few times to see what it feels like. Practice this for a few days until you can achieve fairly complete relaxation simply by tensing your muscles, holding your breath, and then releasing with the self-instruction, "Relax."

STEP TWO: PUTTING IT INTO PRACTICE

The next step involves going through this same procedure when you notice feelings of stress and tension. These feelings can be used to discriminate when you are getting tense and can cue your use of Instant Relaxation. Begin by imagining a stress-inducing scene, perhaps one that you noted when you were observing when and where you tended to become anxious. Imagine that scene vividly, and try to re-experience the feelings of tension. Now tense, hold your breath, and release using your self-instruction, "Relax." Practice this procedure several times daily until you notice that your tension goes away with Instant Relaxation.

As you become more skilled in using Instant Relaxation, use it in real-life situations when you begin to feel tense. Start by using it when your tension is relatively low and you will feel comfortable in trying it. Begin using it in more difficult situations even as you master the procedure. Often it is helpful to use a cue (for example, looking at a favorite bracelet, ring, wristwatch, or some other object) to remember to use Instant Relaxation.

The objective is to use Instant Relaxation when you first notice the tension arising in your body. This will help prevent your stress from getting out of control. You might also plan to use it in those situations in which you have commonly experienced stress in the past. That way anxiety won't have a chance to get started, much less run rampant.

SOME FURTHER REMARKS

Use the Checklist to monitor your progress as you begin to learn to use Instant Relaxation. Relaxation is a helpful skill; its use is not widespread and it may seem rather different from the kinds of things you do in your daily life. But its helpful possibilities remain endless, and only depend on you to use them to the fullest.

As you begin to use Instant Relaxation, a note of caution is in order. Instant Relaxation is effective when you first feel the tension coming on. If you wait until you are overwhelmed with anxiety, you may find that it is ineffective and this may cause you even greater anxiety. Relaxation takes practice. Use it first in fairly safe situations and move on to progressively more difficult situations only after you have mastered the easier ones.

Checklist for Learning Instant Relaxation

1. Identify how you experience stress and tension.

   Have you:

   a. imagined previous stress-arousing situations to identify your stress and tension reactions? ________
   b. tried the spontaneous-speech game to identify stress and tension reactions as you were engaged in an activity? ________
   c. used other exercises that you dreamed up to identify stress and tension reactions? ________

2. Take a look at your environment.

   Have you:

   a. self-observed for at least four days to assess when, and under what condition you typically experience stress? ________
   b. further identified how you experience stress and tension in your daily life? ________

3. Changing the environment

   Have you:

   a. identified those situations that might be modified to reduce your stress and tension? ________
   b. identified how you might modify those situations? ________
   c. identified those situations in which it would be appropriate to express your feelings of stress and tension? ________
   d. practiced expressing your feelings in your imagination and/or rehearsed them with someone else? ________

4. Learning Instant Relaxation.

   Have you:

   a. practiced Progressive and/or Mental Relaxation for at least two weeks? ________
   b. practiced tensing all of the muscles in your body, holding your breath, and then releasing all at once with the self-instruction, "Relax?" ________
   c. practiced inducing Instant Relaxation while imagining a stress-inducing scene? ________
   d. practiced using Instant Relaxation in real-life situations? ________

Self-Improvement Task VII

Learning Instant Relaxation

I will help myself learn to sleep better by:

Following the checklist for learning Instant Relaxation in:

1. Identifying experiences of stress and tension
2. Assessing my environment
3. Changing my environment
4. Practicing Instant Relaxation

Continuing to:

1. Practice and use Cognitive Focusing
2. Practice and use Progressive and Mental Relaxation
3. Practice and use alternative helpful thoughts
4. Keep my Sleep Diary

Negotiating a Self-Contract or
Using some other procedure to help me be systematic and consistent.

Self-Contract

Goal: Learning Instant Relaxation

Specific Behavioral Objectives

I agree to: ______________________________
(specify behavior)

____

under the following circumstances: ______________________________
(specify where, when,

____
how much, etc.)

____

Environmental Planning

In order to help me do this, I am going to: (1) arrange my physical and social environment by: ______________________________

____

and; (2) control my internal environment (thoughts, images) by: ______

____

____

Consequences

Provided by me:
(If contract is kept) ______________________________

(If contract is broken) ______________________________

Provided by others:
(If contract is kept) ______________________________

(If contract is broken) ______________________________

- -

______________ Signed ______________________________
(Renewal Date)

Witness ______________________________

Date ______________________________

11

Thinking About Yourself

"WHAT A PIECE OF WORK IS MAN . . .

Long ago we discovered how to record our thoughts so that they would last a few years. Since that time we have not stopped marveling at our capacities and potential. Our ability to think and reflect on what we perceive sets us apart from our animal ancestors. Renè Descartes, the famous seventeenth century French philosopher, used thought to establish his existence. *"Dubio, ergo sum,*—I doubt, therefore I am" told him that he existed because he could doubt. You may not find it necessary to go to such lengths to prove to yourself that you exist (Descartes was trying to find an indisputable foundation upon which to build a philosophy), but his point is compelling.

We can think, and that gives us a remarkable ability to fashion our world to meet our needs, wants, and even our dreams.

But the ability to think is a double-edged sword. It helps us strive and achieve, but it carries with it problems and difficulties. Not all of our collective musings and mutterings have been worthwile or even beneficial. On a more personal level, our thoughts and reflections can be good or they can be harmful. E. B. de Vito captures the spirit quite succinctly in his poem "Words." The words we use and the thoughts we have can make us afraid, soothe our nerves, cause us to be tense, fascinate us by their brilliance, or bring us happiness and peace.

WORDS*

There are words that make us
Shudder, wince:
Wormwood, persimmon,
Alum, quince.

There are words that soothe
And tranquilize:
Slumbering, rainbows,
Butterflies.

There are words that tighten,
Words that roil:
Tension, turmoil,
Chaos, spoil.

There are words that shimmer,
That beguile:
Stars, ships, peacocks,
Firelight, smile.

And always, words
That make life full:
Love, laughter, home,
Peace, beautiful.

E.B. de Vito

***The Christian Science Monitor*, September 9, 1975. Reprinted by permission.

FLEXIBILITY IS THE WAY

The ways we perceive and think about ourselves and our world are no *more* than *our* perceptions and thoughts. We have *chosen* (and there are some definite choices involved) to look upon reality in a specific way, *but this doesn't mean that reality is really the way we see it.* Our way of viewing ourselves and the world is valid, but it represents one limited point of view. It's always important to realize that there may be other ways to view and think about something.

"Is the image below two faces or a vase?" is a meaningless question. It can be neither and both at the same time, *depending upon how you choose to view it.* Most things in life can be viewed from a variety of perspectives, all of which capture part of the truth but none of which is complete by itself. A sunset provides a good example. The nature enthusiast may revel in the brilliance of the colors, the roses, scarlets, deep blues and purples, and the

Two faces or a vase?

gold and yellow hues. The physicist may be more interested in measuring the wave lengths and refraction patterns, while the psychologist may be fascinated by how different individuals perceive these colors. The ecologist might show alarm: a brilliant sunset can mean a fouled atmosphere!

Which is correct? They're all correct! All of these individuals have a unique perspective. Most important, they could all be the views of one individual wearing different "thinking caps" at different times. The point is clear: *the way we perceive and think about reality is not carved into stone.* Our thoughts and perceptions can be changed. In fact, learning to perceive yourself and your world in different ways may help you improve your sleep and also change other aspects of your life as well.

DAYTIME THOUGHTS AND NIGHTTIME SLEEP

A CASE IN POINT

JACK. *Jack was a hard-working middle-level executive in a large electronics firm. He, like all of us, battled the "middle-age midbody bulge," but found that two or three vigorous games of handball each week kept his weight (and his girth) within reasonable limits. Being a family man, he derived a great deal of pleasure from his wife and five children, although he did worry occasionally about his capabilities of being a good husband and his ability to rear his children to be independent, hard working, and creative.*

Jack's sleep difficulties, beginning about one year ago, included problems in falling asleep initially and subsequently waking up too early in the morning.

Sometimes he thought he lay awake for as long as two hours before falling asleep and could take from one to two hours to fall back to sleep once awakened. Sometimes he would lie awake until it was time to get up for work.

A combined and personalized version of Progressive and Mental Relaxation provided considerable relief in solving Jack's problems in falling asleep initially. Once he mastered these procedures, sleep came easily and quickly most nights.

Nighttime awakenings, however, remained a problem. Usually waking up around 3:00 a.m., Jack reported both physical tension (sweating and a racing heart) and almost immediate and intense mental activity. His thoughts were usually free floating, and might revolve around work and his ability to perform there, difficulties any members of his family might be experiencing, feeling disgruntled at the performance of his colleagues and decisions of his supervisors, or what was needed to improve his handball game. Cognitive focusing brought some help

*in reducing the severity of these nighttime awakenings. On three nights out of seven during a recent week, use of the technique immediately upon awakening allowed him to return to sleep quickly. But on the other four nights, Jack reported that his level of physical and mental tension upon awakening was too intense for cognitive focusing to work.**

Following the personal assessment procedures in Chapter 9, Jack realized that his typical modes of thinking about himself, his work, and his family might be interfering with his ability to sleep well. Jack knew that he was a perfectionist and that he measured his performances against very high standards. He often found himself downcast during the day, and his thoughts at night had a depressed and almost helpless quality. Jack was well aware that he was skilled at seeking out and dwelling upon the negative. His thoughts spontaneously and instantaneously gravitated in this direction when he was awakened at night.

It was then that he realized that learning to think differently about himself and his world might be beneficial. His previous impression was that such changes might be feasible only with at least two or three years of psychotherapy. The systematic self-administered procedures presented here made him stop and consider that important changes might be made on his own. With that optimism, he decided to venture forth.

THE WORLD VIEW

Jack's thoughts about himself, his work, and his family emphasized his failings, dissatisfactions, and general discontent. These in turn led to more frequent, intense, and

*Remember, we indicated at the end of Chapter 7 that other procedures are often needed to overcome the nighttime arousal problem.

pessimistic thoughts and feelings. The negative thoughts appeared immediately in his mind when he awakened at night. Because they were so arousing, he was alert instantly and thinking intensely. A vicious cycle was then established.

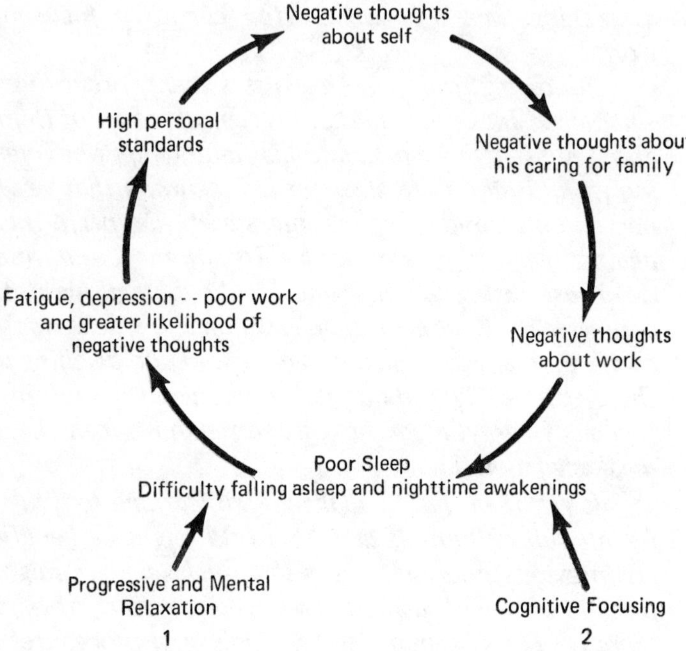

Jack's negative thinking cycle.

Negative thoughts lead to more negative thoughts to poor sleep to fatigue and feelings of inability to cope to further negative feelings. But it is possible to interrupt his cycle to bring about change. In Jack's case, cognitive focusing brought some relief but was clearly not enough. Because something more was needed, Jack decided to attempt to change his thoughts about himself and his world. Although he could have started anywhere, he chose to begin with his thoughts about himself and his personal evaluations of his actions.

CHANGING YOUR THOUGHTS ABOUT YOURSELF

Learning to evaluate your own actions differently may require changes in two areas: (1) in the standards you use to judge yourself and your performance in specific situations; and (2) in noticing your positive as well as your not-so-positive performances during the day. Rather than making global judgments about global activities ("I feel lousy about what I failed to get done today") it may be more helpful to begin making separate judgments about the specific activities in which you participated.

STEP 1 WHAT DID YOU DO TODAY?

The first step in changing your thoughts about yourself involves taking time at the end of the day to list some of your activities. Let's first talk about what we mean by an activity. "I went camping this weekend" is a description that is very general, while "I got home, changed my clothes, hung up my suit, and fixed a martini" is extremely specific. Try to find some middle ground when you write down your actions: don't be too general, but don't be extremely specific either. Getting home might be summarized as "I arrived home and changed my clothes." The camping weekend, on the other hand, might be split up into several separate activities: "I drove to the mountains, hiked back five miles, and then pitched the tent".

Two other points about activities are important. An activity is something you *do* (including thinking and daydreaming), but it should not include things you don't do. "Thinking about the dinner party on Saturday" (something you did) is an activity, while "failing to return Mr. McKee's phone call" (something you did not do) is not.

Before you list your own activities, take a look at three Jack came up with. Notice that he listed three very different kinds of activities: one relating to his work, and a second having to do with interactions with his children. His third activity was a daydream about some specific ways to improve his handball game.

Now's your chance to begin. Turn to the blank worksheet on page 214 and note three activities you did today. Remember, not too specific or too general, and make sure that all of the activities are something you did rather than did not do.

STEP 2: YOUR FIRST REACTION

The second step requires you to record your reactions to your actions. *What do you think about the way your performed? How do you judge the way you spent your time? Did you do well or did you perform poorly?*

The next three columns on the worksheet will help you identify your reactions and your reasons for reacting that way. Three pieces of information are requested: an initial reaction, rating that reaction as positive or negative, and the standards or criteria you used in reaching that decision about your actions.

Writing these things down is especially important. It's possible to feel vaguely uneasy about a day or something we have done without really taking the time to discover the source of our discomfort. Writing this information down helps us be reflective and specific.

> ***JACK (Continued)*** *Let's take a look at Jack's worksheet to see how he judged his own actions. The three actions listed for Tuesday, April 12, received three different kinds of reactions. Jack rated his performance at the research meeting very negatively, berating himself for not speaking more than he did. His standard stipulates that he*

Thinking about Myself

Date April 12 Day Tuesday

Actions	Initial Reactions			A New Look	
	One First Thought	*Rating*	*Standards*	*Positive Accomplishment*	*Trial Standard*
1. Attended research meeting					
2. Played with children					
3. Thought about handball					

should speak up more often. He was a bit more tolerant with himself about the time he spent playing with his children. He believes that his children should have his full attention when he is with them, and because he found himself somewhat preoccupied, he was slightly dissatisfied with himself. He did manage to rate his handball fantasies positively, although he admitted privately that he felt guilty about the time he spent thinking about a trivial activity. After all, he could have devoted his mental energies to problems at work!

Now it's your turn; register your areactions on your worksheet. Be honest and be specific. Take your time. Examining your standards is an important step in beginning the change process. Just try to list them without trying to evaluate them. Change comes next.

STEP 3: THERE'S A POSITIVE SIDE, TOO

Step 3 brings the challenge. *Learning to think differently about your own actions means taking deliberate steps to change your usual ways of judging yourself and your actions. Remember, thoughts are relative and changeable. Like other things we do, they are habits that can be changed only by practice.*

Learning to look at yourself differently involves two steps. First, we ask you to note something positive you did in those situations in which you viewed yourself negatively. We don't want you to become a "Pollyana," seeing everything through rose-colored glasses. Our purpose is to help you realize that, even though improvement is possible (and there's always room for improvement), there was something laudable that you did. *Breaking a cycle of negative self-thought means giving the praiseworthy equal billing with the blameworthy.*

In addition to noting something positive about what you did, we also ask you to try using different standards in evaluating your performance. The criteria you are using cur-

Thinking about Myself

Date: April 12 Day: Tuesday

Initial Reactions (One First Thought, Rating, Standards) — A New Look (Positive Accomplishment, Trial Standard)

	Actions	*One First Thought*	*Rating*	*Standards*	*Positive Accomplishment*	*Trial Standard*
1.	Attended research meeting	Poor performance Failed to speak enough	–	Should speak up in meetings more often	I made one point that no one else thought of and which influenced the outcome	Perhaps the quality rather than the quantity of my remarks is important
2.	Played with children	OK—was a bit preoccupied	So-so	Children should have my full attention	children enjoyed themselves	my preoccupation is expected sometimes; if it does not show, perhaps I should not worry about it.
3.	Thought about handball	Good—solved a problem about my return	+	Fun to think productively while driving home	OK	OK.

rently may never permit any self-strokes.

An exaggeration? Maybe slightly but certainly not that far from the ways that many of us treat ourselves. Why be your worst enemy when it is possible to be more of a friend, to show yourself to a little bit of kindness?

JACK (Continued) *Let's see how Jack handled this one. He decided that his thoughts about his handball game were probably acceptable. The drive was long and he was tired; thoughts about work would not have been productive anyway. Regarding playing with his children, Jack realized that his children enjoyed themselves during the 20 minutes he devoted to them, despite his preoccupation. Sharon and Terry, his younger children, didn't notice anyway. When it was time for dinner, they even remarked on how much fun the game had been. Jack realized that his preoccupation, if minimal, might be all right. After all, many fathers spend no time at all with their children.*

Jack finally came to the really difficult item. He wracked his brain trying to come up with something positive about his performance at the research meeting. Even though he didn't quite believe it, he decided to write it down anyway. He had made one point during the discussion that everyone else there had overlooked completely. The point was central to the problem they were trying to solve and his contribution changed the thrust of the discussion dramatically. "Maybe quality is more important than quantity. After all, Leonard speaks a lot and many times he just fills the air with words. People really don't listen very closely to what he has to say." Jack decided to try a new standard: quality as more important than quantity.

It's your turn again. Try your hand at generating some positive reactions to the actions you've listed. Some of your initial reactions, like Jack's, may already be positive. Others may be neutral or negative and may require balancing with the positive. One final point. *You may not believe what you have written down, and it's possible that you are not ready to subscribe to your new standard. That's okay. For now, the important thing is merely to generate the positive thought.*

STEP 4: TIME TO PRACTICE

Learning to look at the positive, to be willing to view your actions from a variety of perspectives, requires practice. Doing anything differently means working at it until it becomes second nature and part of who we are. It's not enough to list the positive. Think about it a bit and then move onto your next activity without giving it further thought (that's why just telling people to "relax" or "think positive" seldom works). It's important that you begin to *contemplate the positive* until that way of thinking becomes part of who you are. Positive thinking takes regular ongoing practice just as a good tennis serve does.

We can recommend some useful strategies; you may want to devise your own after looking these over and trying them out.

- Set aside specific times to mentally review your actions and your positive reactions. Try it while traveling to and from work, when performing routine chores (housework or yardwork), when engaged in personal hygiene tasks (brushing your teeth, going to the bathroom or taking a shower), or when placed on "hold" on the phone. Make sure that you choose a time or situation that is happening each day, and preferably several times each day. It's important that you practice regularly and frequently.

- Choose an activity that you do rather frequently. Some

frequent activities are drinking a cup of coffee, having a cigarette (if you smoke), talking on the phone, looking at the clock, eating, and walking. Make a deal with yourself: *before* you engage in that activity, *you must think about one of actions and your positive reaction to it.*

- Each day after you have listed your actions and your positive reactions, write them on a three by five card. Put the list where you will see it frequently: in your pocket or purse, attached to your pack of cigarettes, or next to the phone. Each time you look at the list, think about what you have written down.

These represent only three possibilities. But note what they have in common. They each associate practicing your new thoughts with frequent activities, making it difficult for you not to practice and rehearse the new way of thinking.

STEP 5: GIVE IT A TRY

Follow the steps in Self-Improvement Task XI. Try the techniques out and see for yourself if any positive changes result. Learning to think differently may seem strange or impossible, but if habitual negative personal reactions do seem to fit, what have you got to lose? Nothing really! And, what's more important, you may find yourself feeling better about who you are and what you can do. You might even sleep better in the process!

Self-Improvement Task XI

Changing Your Thoughts about Yourself
I will help myself learn to sleep better by: 1. Learning to think about myself differently by: a. Listing at least three important activities every day; b. Writing down my personal reactions and the standards I used to judge my activities; c. Indicating a *positive* side to any negative reactions I've had; and d. Setting time aside to *practice* my positive reactions. 2. Negotiating a self-contract (or some other procedure) to help me be systematic and consistent. 3. Continuing to: a. Practice alternative helpful thoughts; b. Chart my progress in my Sleep Diary; and c. Practice Progressive and Mental Relaxation. 4. Maintaining my progress by practicing problem-solving and using other personalized change strategies I have developed for myself.

Thinking about Myself

Date__________ Day__________

	Actions	Initial Reactions		Standards	A New Look	
		One First Thought	*Rating*	*Standards*	*Positive Accomplishment*	*Trial Standard*
1.						
2.						
3.						

Self-Contract

Goal: Changing Thoughts about Myself

Specific Behavioral Objectives

I agree to: ______________________________
(specify behavior)

____

under the following circumstances: ______________________________
(specify where, when,

____
how much, etc.)

____

Environmental Planning

In order to help me do this, I am going to: (1) arrange my physical and social environment by: ______________________________

____

and; (2) control my internal environment (thoughts, images) by: ______

____

____

Consequences

Provided by me:
(If contract is kept) ______________________________

(If contract is broken) ______________________________

Provided by others:
(If contract is kept) ______________________________

(If contract is broken) ______________________________

- -

______________ (Renewal Date)

Signed ______________________________

Witness ______________________________

Date ______________________________

12

Exploring Your Thoughts About Life and Your World

You can also *expand* the ways you think about your world using methods just like the ones you've just learned. We're not saying that you should become a starry-eyed, "pie-in-the-sky" person, unable to see through anything but rose-colored glasses. But we are recommending balance. Nothing is *totally* bad, yet we can too easily get used to seeing only the negative. *Being realistic demands that we see both the positive and the negative. Our personal well-being may demand that we emphasize the positive over the negative.*

You may have heard about the "self-fulfilling prophecy." If we believe that someone is basically unfriendly, that person might sense our attitude and be unfriendly toward us. Our chances of enjoying ourselves at a party may be increased if we anticipate having a good time there. Fear of getting nervous and uptight at a job interview may cause us to be nervous and uptight.

The same holds true for our view of our world. If we view things negatively, they may be more likely to turn out that way for us. If, on the contrary, we can begin to see the positive sides of things, these more positive benefits may begin to come our way. At the very least, we will have learned to balance our view and see things from a variety of perspectives.*

> ***SALLY.*** *Sally was an 18-year-old junior-college freshman who had suffered from insomnia for last two years. Falling asleep at night had bothered her most of the time, but recently she found herself waking regularly around 1:30 in the morning and lying awake for at least an hour before being able to fall back to sleep. Knowing about the harmful side effects of sleeping pills (her grandmother had been hooked on them), Sally decided to take some positive action to overcome her sleep difficulties. She knew that if she let it go any further, she would be more and more tempted to start taking pills, a one-way downhill street she wanted to avoid traveling at any cost.*
>
> *Progressive and Mental Relaxation helped considerably, reducing her time to get to sleep from 1 to 2 hours nightly to 15 to 30 minutes on most nights. This range was acceptable to Sally; she enjoyed reviewing her day for awhile before falling to sleep anyway. But she realized that her sleep difficulty centered on the thoughts she would have during the day and when she awoke at night. She noticed that she sought out and emphasized the negative. One example revolved around a get-together with her very closest friends from high school. Although Sally still regarded herself as close to these friends, and*

*This question of how we view ourselves and the world around us—our beliefs—is a fundamental one in religion, philosophy, and science. It is also important for you to consider in trying to solve problems as a "personal scientist."

had even encouraged Marie to make the arrangements to "get the old crowd together for a night out," Sally found herself having more and more negative thoughts about it as the day approached for the gathering. "I'd probably be bored by all of them, and they're not going to be too interested in me anyway. We'll probably talk about the same old things and go to the same old places. I'm not really sure that I want to go. I'm not sure it's going to be all that fun, anyway. Maybe I'll make an excuse and just stay home."

As it turned out, Sally went to the get-together, but had a terrible time. Everyone else seemed to enjoy themselves but Sally was downcast, quiet, and removed. Everyone commented on her distance, but not to her, of course. Sally's friends figured that she was in "one of her moods," and left her alone for the evening.

Sally's mother asked her about the evening and got a glum report. "It was all right. People really seemed distant though. They just avoided me more and more as the evening went on! It was really kind of a bummer!"

In thinking back on the evening, and telling more people about it, Sally could only dwell on what a "downer" the whole evening had been. Worse yet, she realized that she made her own bad time, leading her to berate herself for being so ". . . stupid and moody."

It's obvious that Sally created her own "bummer." Her negative anticipations led her to be reclusive. Naturally everyone avoided her because they were all set to have a good

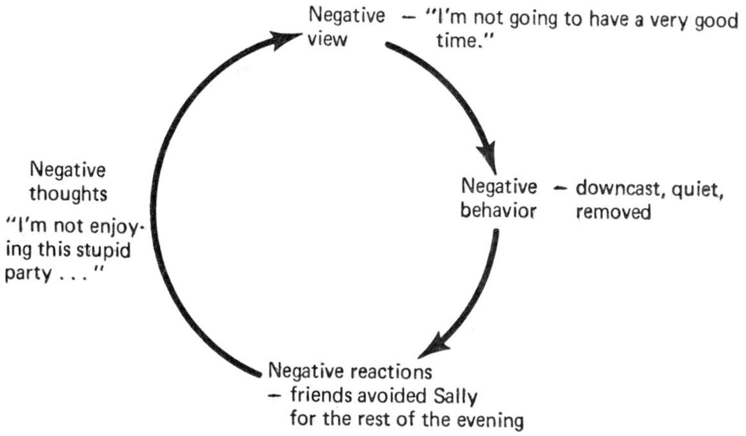

How might a different view have made Sally's evening different?

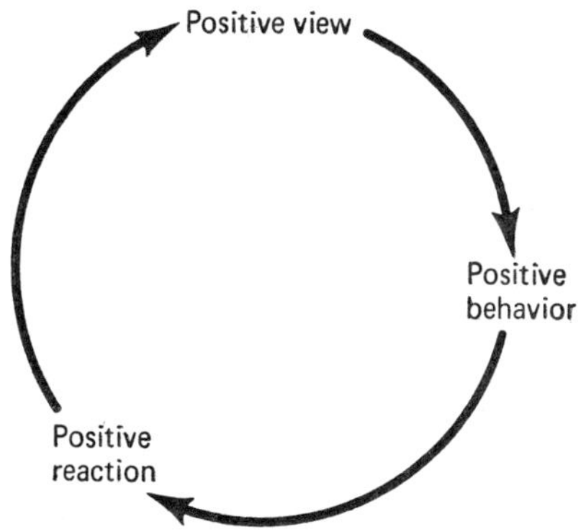

The self-fulfilling prophecy.

time. Think of how different her evening might have been had Sally been able to approach the evening differently. A neutral attitude might have permitted her the option of enjoying her friends. Her negative anticipations removed completely any possibility of having a good time. If you often find yourself in a similar position, then the strategies for change presented here may be just for you.

THE PAST AND THE FUTURE

It's helpful to learn to *balance* our evaluations of both the past and the future. In looking at the past, the key is learning to dwell on the positive as well as the negative. In anticipating the future, everything hinges on finding ways to increase enjoyment in your life. This may involve learning to pick out and contemplate the positive and pleasant sides of upcoming events, planning personal activities arranged purely for your own enjoyment, and learning to look forward to them.

LOOKING BACK MAKES NOW MORE PLEASANT

Negative thinking drains our energies into unproductive channels. Mulling over the "downers" of the past can prove especially depressing because nothing can be done to change it. At the very least, it's probably better to forget the past rather than grind on its unpleasantness. More helpful is the ability to recall the positive sides of what has happened, or at least to view it with some balance.

Learning to view the past in an expanded way can be accomplished using methods very similar to the ones we tried in Chapter 11. Following the steps involved, we want to:

1. List three recent past activities,
2. Write down your initial reaction to those activities,
3. Rate your reaction as positive, neutral, or negative,
4. Make explicit the standard or criterion you used.

Steps 1 through 4 tells us where we stand now. For those actions rated negative or neutral, we will take one additional step in balancing our view with the positive side as well. This may not be easy, but no one ever promised that changing long-standing habits was simple for anyone. This "balancing act" proceeds in three steps:

1. List one positive aspect of the activity,
2. Try a new standard (and write it down) so that you can have a positive reaction in addition to the one you've already listed,
   and
3. Practice your new reaction by:
   a. setting aside *specific times* to review mentally your positive reactions;
   b. planning to *rehearse* your positive reaction prior to some activity you do rather frequently;
   c. writing your positive reactions on a three-by-five index card and *place* the card in some conspicuous place; and
   d. Thinking about what you have written down each time you look at the list.

Sally tried this strategy in reflecting back on the reunion. She chould have chosen to continue to view the evening totally negatively.* She could have proceeded that way, but what good would it have done? Why not remember the *positive*?

*It's important to realize that we are not doomed to view things in any specific way. Whether we realize it or not, we make choices about how we look at our world.

WHAT ABOUT THE FUTURE?

Notice that the way she anticipated the evening with her friends was a major ingredient in Sally's "bad time menu." As the evening approached, Sally kept thinking more and more about how she might be bored by her old friends, about how the group would talk about "the same old things and the same old places." There's little chance that Sally could have had a good time after approaching the evening in that frame of mind. How different the evening might have been with a positive (or at least neutral) outlook.

Again, we want to emphasize that we are not starry-eyed and naive. People certainly do things that turn out to be less than positive. Not everything we do turns out the way we want, and it's silly to believe that we can breeze through life above the clouds.

But we do have two biases:

Why turn something potentially positive into something negative by anticipating the negative (and perhaps making it come true)?

Why focus on the negative once something is over and done with?

Instead, why not approach the future with at least a neutral attitude? If possible, a positive attitude may enhance whatever enjoyment might be possible. In thinking about the past, acknowledge the negative, resolve to behave differently in the future, but spend your mind's time on the positive. Life is too short (and sleep too precious) to spend your time doing anything else.

The rest of this chapter is devoted to teaching you two strategies for learning how to think differently about the future. One emphasizes identifying and contemplating the positive sides of things we do frequently; the second involves planning activities that we will enjoy and learning to think about them in positive ways.

WHY DREAD THOSE THINGS WE HAVE TO DO ANYWAY?

Our lives are filled with the routine and the predictable. Getting up in the morning, preparing for the day, traveling to work (if we work outside of the home), engaging in our jobs, eating lunch, working in the afternoon, returning home, eating dinner, and working and relaxing in the evening comprise a typical schedule for most of us.

We can view our days with dread (and, if we do, they *will* probably be dreadful) or we can learn to tune in on the positive to build some balance into our view of things.

BUT MY WORLD IS DREADFUL

Your world may be dreadful, but a variety of reasons might be responsible. Reducing them to their simplest form, two things might be involved: (1) your environment may be presenting major irritants, constantly causing dissatisfaction; and (2) your view of your world may emphasize the negative. Thus we're not trying to lay the blame entirely on you if you find yourself constantly downcast and brooding. Your environment, especially people around you, can be involved.

If your world has some minor irritations, then perhaps it might be worthwhile to divert some energy to identify precisely what those are and doing something about them:

> Perhaps there are some tasks you have to do all of the time that you really don't enjoy. Can someone else do them?

Perhaps your spouse or close associate has been doing some minor but irritating things lately. Can they change if asked in the right way?

Perhaps there are some features of your daily routine you loathe. Can they be changed or made more enjoyable?

Perhaps you are associating continually with people who grate on your nerves. Can you manage to be around them less frequently?

Don't be afraid to experiment; try doing something about those small irritants. You have only your irritation to lose. But if there are some major irritations, and these are continual and complex, then some form of professional assistance might be beneficial. Major financial difficulties, marriage problems, troubles with your children, job dissatisfaction—none are trivial and unimportant. People sometimes live with them long beyond the point that they should. At the very least, exploring the possibility of changes with a skilled professional can't hurt; it may lead you to some positive changes.

NO MATTER WHAT, YOUR THOUGHTS ARE IMPORTANT

Even if you have some minor irritants (and who doesn't?), or some major difficulties, *how you think about what you do is still important.* Contemplating only the negative can only lead to depressed feelings and inaction. Balancing a negative view with the positive may help by allowing you to evaluate your situation from all sides—at least more than one side—and forestall glum and downcast feelings. Being on top of things mentally may be necessary before you can take action. And, if your world isn't all that bad or if it's not possible to make some minor changes, why continue to dwell on the negative? Why not choose to let the positive come through as well?

STARTING WITH THE EVERYDAY

One useful approach to thinking differently about things involves permitting ourselves to think differently about those everyday mundane things we do.

It's first important to become practiced at looking at the specifics, at seeing things in their related parts rather than globally. In most things we do, there are some elements that are more inherently enjoyable than others. Lumping everything together under some vague heading may make it impossible to separate those good pieces from the less enjoyable.

> *GINA.* *Gina listed four activities she performed with great regularity. She began with these activities because she realized that she had mixed feelings about each of them, but was never sure why. However, her negative feelings usually won out. This not only increased her general stress and tension, but could also tip the scales between a predominantly positive or fairly negative day.*
>
> *As a first step, she tried to write down some pieces of each of these activities that she considered important. She tried to be specific without going into all of the minute details.*
>
> *As a second step, she assigned a rating to each component part: "+" meant mostly positive, while "–" was mostly negative. "so-so" meant mostly a neutral reaction. The exercise was revealing. No wonder her reactions to performing these tasks fluctuated wildly! Never before did Gina realize that she had different reactions to the different things she did everyday. When she did start to dread doing some of them—and this happened often during those wee morning hours lying awake in bed—it was always the negative that was emphasized.*
>
> *Gina realized, of course, that the negative components were just as essential as the positive and were really unavoidable. But she was aware of the fact that she did*

have control over those parts of upcoming events that she chose to mull over in her mind.

The next step required practice in thinking about the positive rather than the negative. Gina decided that the easiest place to begin would be in anticipating the drive to work. Rather than dreading the short drive on the freeway and the hunt for a parking place, why not focus on the enjoyment usually derived from her new FM stereo car radio and the drive down pleasant Miller Lane on her way to the freeway?

How would she remember to do this? Negative anticipations about driving to work usually occurred in the middle of breadfast, and while she was on her way to work. She decided to use two strategies.

First, before drinking the first (and most enjoyable) cup of coffee, she would rehearse mentally the positive feelings she expected to have from the radio and Miller Lane. And second, while driving, she would focus on the pleasant reactions to both component parts.

GIVE IT A TRY

1. List some major global activities which are part of your daily routine.
2. Write down the component parts; be specific.
3. Rate each of these component parts; think for a while about what you may have learned from this exercise.
4. Begin with one of the activities, one in which you have both positive and negative reactions to the component parts.
5. Develop a strategy for rehearsing the positive components.

Again, you have nothing to lose and everything to gain. Your outlook on your day cannot help but improve, and you may find yourself sleeping better as well.

Looking at Things Closely

Global Activity	*Component Parts*	*Rating*
Eating breakfast	Drinking morning coffee	So-so
	Reading entertainment page and reviews	+
	Eating eggs	So-so
	Putting dishes in dishwasher	–
Driving to work	Listening to FM stereo	+
	Driving down Miller Lane (country road)	+
	Driving on freeway	–
	Finding a parking space	–
Preparing for sales meeting	Arranging statistics	–
	Brainstorming sales strategy with Peter	+
	Discussing audiovisual presentation	So-so
Returning phone calls	Beginning to return calls	–
	Crossing completed calls off list	+

PUTTING THE POSITIVE IN YOUR LIFE

Thinking about the future—and enjoying it—need not be limited to our routine activities. *Indeed, many of us may fail to treat ourselves to pleasant and pleasurable activities very often, events and outings we plan solely for our own personal relaxation and enjoyment.* Planning positive activities for ourselves and then thinking about them before they happen can take us a long way in improving our outlook on the world and in reducing our tension level. This general positive change in our thought, feelings, and tension can help to contribute to improved sleep.

1. Plan one or two positive activities to be completed sometime within the next week.

2. Write down why you think these activities will be positive. Specify those aspects of the activity you expect to be enjoyable.
3. Set aside two times per day to think about your upcoming positive activity. Try to experience the good feelings you expect from the activity.

PLANNING POSITIVE ACTIVITIES

Your first reaction might be to say: "That's just fine. But my schedule is already full and there's absolutely no room to add anything else to my already overcrowded day."

But that's precisely the problem! Your day may be full, but crowded with "must dos" rather than "want to dos." Our response is to start small. The activity planned need not be extravagant, time-consuming, and disruptive. It's probably better to begin with something that can be accomplished rather easily.

We have listed some activities selected by people like yourself. In addition to the fact that all of them are simple and easy to perform, notice some other important features. First, the people selecting them chose these activities because they were reasonably certain to enjoy them. They had done them before and knew they had a fairly good chance to relish these activities once again. Second, enjoying these activities did not

Activity Planning

A walk in the park at lunchtime
Breakfast with Mimi
Handball after work
Practicing guitar
Movies on Friday night
Walking on the beach
Sunday brunch at The Gazebo
Watching sunset on Saturday
Shopping on Tuesday evening
Reading *The Adams Family*

depend on anyone else enjoying them. They might be shared with someone else, but that someone else would not have to influence the personal satisfaction and pleasure involved. The breakfast with Mimi would be enjoyed by itself, and would not depend on Mimi's reactions. Making your enjoyment of an activity dependent upon someone else's pleasure may set you up for disappointment.

Take a few minutes now and decide on one or two activities you might enjoy doing in the next week or so. Remember, choose activities that:

- can be put into your present schedule;
- you are reasonably certain to enjoy; and
- do not depend on someone else's enjoyment.

WHAT ARE YOU GOING TO ENJOY?

The next step is most critical because it involves determining specifically those aspects of the activity that will be enjoyed. Often we can enjoy an activity but never really take the time to find out why. To really get pleasure from planning and thinking about future activities, as well as doing them, it helps to know where the pleasure comes from, to discriminate those parts of the activity that are especially enjoyable. This means listing all of the component parts of the action and deciding which of the parts brings you the most pleasure.

We have listed three parts of each activity that people choosing them expected to enjoy. Notice that there's nothing spectacular or extraordinary about the items listed. They are all quite ordinary. But (and this is really important) *they do represent tuning in and paying attention to those elements we can expect to enjoy.* Too often, they are simply forgotten or neglected, or relegated to second place behind the negative side of things.

Now it's your turn. Take the activities you've listed and indicate two or three pieces of the activity that you expect to enjoy and relish. Remember, be specific and list those things that you are reasonably sure to enjoy.

Pleasant Activities

Activity	*I Plan to Enjoy*
A walk in the park at lunchtime	Looking at flowers Noticing birds Quiet reflection
Breakfast with Mimi	Eating omelette Talking to Mimi about book I'm reading Relaxing in the morning
Handball after work	Exercising vigorously Competing with Dave Shower afterwards
Practicing guitar	Being by myself Listening to guitar Mastering chord
Movies on Friday night	Eating popcorn Seeing Jack Nicholson act Eating dinner out
Walking on beach	Listening to ocean Watching birds Collecting seashells
Sunday brunch at Gazebo	The Ramos Fizz Reading the entertainment section of the Sunday paper Eating Eggs Benedict
Watching sunset on Saturday	Being alone Noticing the colors against the clouds Studying the sounds
Shopping on Tuesday evening	Looking at new blouses Dinner out Buying new shoes

Pleasant Activity Worksheet

I have planned, as a pleasant activity, to: ______________________

____

____

on: ____
(specific day and time)

I will enjoy:

1. ____
2. ____
3. ____

I will practice thinking about these pleasant activities:

1. ____

____

2. ____

____

PRACTICING AND DOING

The final step involves two parts. We not only want you to do the activity at the time you said you would, and to enjoy it as much as you can, but also to practice thinking about the activity and to experience *now* the pleasure you will feel in the future.

In thinking about and anticipating the activity, it's important that you use all of the imagining skills we have presented in this book. *Set time aside, be sure that no distractions are likely to interfere, and let your mind create a vivid picture of the activity you have planned. Let yourself really experience and enjoy the pleasure you will find in doing the activity.*

Be sure to set aside specific times to practice and anticipate. Once you program this part of the exercise into your daily routine, it, like so many other things, will go by the boards and get lost in the press of events.

Above all, remain flexible. If things don't turn out as planned, don't give up. There may be other parts of the activity that can be enjoyed as well. Or it may be necessary to plan again. Go easy on yourself. You are learning something new, but it is worthwile to take your time and enjoy the process of change.

A FINAL NOTE

These exercises may seem far afield from nighttime sleep. But in many ways they may be getting to the heart of your sleep problem. We started out with the notion that sleep is not divorced from the rest of our life but intimately associated with everything we do. Sleep seems to be related to our daytime mood and tension level. Improving mood and reducing daytime tension may take you a long way to better sleep. Better sleep, in turn, will lead to improved mood and reduced tension. It's a way of starting a positive kind of "vicious" cycle.

Self-Improvement Task XII

I will help myself learn to sleep better by:

1. Planning a program for changing my thoughts about past events, everyday routine actions, or for planning future enjoyable activities.
2. Using the self-contract (or some other procedure) to help me be systematic and consistent.
3. Continuing to:
   a. Practice alternative helpful thoughts;
   b. Chart my progress on my Sleep Diaries; and
   c. Practice Progressive and Memtal Relaxation
4. Maintain progress by practicing problem-solving and other personalized-change strategies I have developed for myself.

Part Six

MAINTAINING YOUR PROGRESS

13

Maintaining Your Progress

Writing a book to help persons overcome a problem leaves us feeling pleased, but also slightly uncomfortable. It is heartening to realize that we may have presented you with some alternatives to your sleeping problem, solutions that you wouldn't have considered seriously if you hadn't read our book. This is especially satisfying to us if the only remedy you knew about before was drugs. We get a great deal of pleasure in knowing that you have read our book, applied some of the principles and procedures, and experienced improved sleep as a result.

PILLS AND PRESCRIPTIONS DON'T FIT

Many kinds of problems, especially medical ones, are easily treated once they are correctly diagnosed. In many cases, the treatment is so obvious and well accepted that physicians can be accused of malpractice if they fail to follow a standard procedure. Pneumonia, for example, is caused by a specific bacterial agent that can be eliminated by penicillin. Once pneumonia is identified, treatment with some type of penicillin becomes almost mandatory (unless, of course, the person is allergic to it). An appendicitis attack is another example. If the physician realizes that the patient is afflicted with an infected appendix, removing it surgically is not questioned. The person can refuse the operation, but the doctor's responsibility has been fulfilled: correctly identifying a physical problem and prescribing a standard remedy to restore health.

Insomnia, as you know by now, is not one of these kinds of maladies. Disturbed and restless sleep is not a single and unitary "disease" cureable with the prescriptions of a tried and true remedy. *Treating insomnia with drugs usually causes more problems than it solves.*

Knowing this is both bad and good for you. On the one hand, you lose the security of a pat and precise solution to your sleep problem. You lose the ease of a prescription and the lack of effort required of you in a simple remedy such as a sleeping pill.

But you also gain. Many people bothered by disturbed sleep report that they feel *victimized* by their problem. Poor sleep just "happens" to them and they feel unable to do anything about it. *We have attempted to teach you some ways to take charge of this problem, to exert personal control where you formerly felt powerless.* In becoming a personal scientist—examining, looking, generating hunches, trying out solutions—you have learned to solve your own problems. You have elevated yourself from a victimized state to one in which you clearly can command your actions and what happens to you.

PUTTING YOURSELF IN THE DRIVER'S SEAT

Our uneasy feeling stems from the distinct possibility that you may have improved only partially. Worse yet, your sleep might not have improved at all, despite your consistent and systematic use of the strategies presented.

We sleep about one-third of our lives and probably spend more time sleeping than in any other single activity. It becomes extremely difficult to pin down everything that influences the quality of our sleep. This is especially true from our vantage point. In writing a book to meet the needs of a variety of people with a variety of sleep problems, we realized that it was possible to write chapters forever to cover the multitude of conditions that might relate to different people's problems. But we limited ourselves to presenting basic skills that we have found necessary for everyone to use. These include the techniques presented in Part II (self-observation and cognitive ecology) and Part III (Physical and Mental Relaxation).

Beyond that, *our goal had been to provide you with methods for analyzing your own sleep problems and the conditions associated with them, and procedures for developing your own solutions based on what you find out about yourself and your actions.* Parts IV and V are written to include those solutions commonly needed and requested by many people.*

But your sleep may be disturbed for other reasons, and improvement may require solutions other than those presented here. Perhaps intolerable work conditions or the strains of an emotionally demanding relationship are taking their toll. Maybe you need to manage your time more efficiently or program some physical exercise into your day.

Only you know what's needed for you! This is the heart of our message. If you have learned anything from this book, we sincerely hope that it has provided a helpful way of viewing and solving your sleep problems. Consistent with our personal-science philosophy, *we cannot solve your problem for you.* Even those clients with whom we work directly receive the same

*In addition to the sections on cognitive focusing (Chapter 7), situational control (Chapter 8), stress management (Chapter 10), and mood management (Chapters 11 and 12), we also considered sections on time management, physical exercise, nutrition and diet, other relaxation procedures, and assertive training. Obviously, we had to stop somewhere!

message: *Only you can solve your sleep problem.* If you have acquired some tools to accomplish that objective, then we can feel satisfied that we met one of our major goals.

WHAT NEXT?

You may have experienced one of three results:

- Your sleep may not have improved at all, despite your conscientious and systematic use of the strategies presented.
- You may have experienced some improvement, but may feel that your sleep could get better still.
- You may feel satisfied with the progress you've made and want to make sure that your very real gains are maintained.

NO IMPROVEMENT AT ALL

If you were systematic and conscientious in your attempts to use the strategies presented, and experienced no improvement as a result, be especially cautious and careful.* Don't blame or beat yourself for failure. *Don't feel that your case is hopeless, or that you are mentally imbalanced, or that your only recourse is drugs.*

You may need more assistance than can be provided in a book. You may need the services of someone who can brainstorm, problem-solve, and help you be consistent and systematic. Having a problem and seeking professional

*Be honest with yourself! We advised, in Chapter 1, that careful attention and consistent effort were required. It is unrealistic to expect improvement if you gave the procedures only a halfhearted or occasional try.

assistance does not imply that you are "crazy" or abnormal. To the contrary, it shows good sense to seek the services of someone with whom you can work to solve your problem. At least it doesn't hurt to try, and using a professional is far better than returning to drugs or despairing of a solution altogether.

Four resources might be used to identify someone who could be of assistance. First, of course, you can consult your family physician, who may be able to refer you to someone specializing in the nondrug treatment of sleep disorders. Second, you can look in the yellow pages of your telephone directory under "Psychologists." Usually there is some indication of their specialty or theoretical orientation, but you can always phone and talk with people to see if they might be interested and capable of helping you. Your local county mental health association or the department of psychology at a nearby college or university might also suggest useful alternatives. If all else fails, you might contact the sleep clinics and laboratories listed in the Resource Materials or drop us a letter. We would be glad to help in any way we can.

SOME IMPROVEMENT

It's also possible that you experienced some improvement in your sleep, but feel that more gains could and should be made before your sleep is really sound and restful.

At the very least, it's important that you maintain the progress you have made and not let yourself slip back into your former unhelpful sleeping practices. Be sure to proceed with the next section (Working to Maintain Your Progress) so that the changes you have been able to realize can become part of who you are.

Further improvement may require other steps as well. If you have found some relief and improvement, chances are that you are on the right track and that you have a good beginning command of the techniques and procedures. You may simply need to practice them more before further gains can be realized.

The problem-solving exercises in Chapter 9 may also help you further identify other solutions. If you feel it necessary, it may be useful to seek outside professional assistance.

Most important, *realize that you have made a significant beginning.* You have come part of the way, and that part may have involved the most difficult steps. Further improvement may require only minor refinements to achieve more satisfactory results.

WORKING TO MAINTAIN YOUR PROGRESS

If you have experienced partial or even extremely satisfactory improvement in your sleep, it's an important task at this point to make sure that your gains are maintained. It's easy to slip into a medical frame of reference and think of yourself as "cured" in a traditional sense of the term. Getting rid of a cold, for example, usually means following some simple recommendations (take aspirin, drink a lot of liquids, and get plenty of rest). Once cured, it's no longer necessary to follow that advice. In fact, people might wonder about you if you did.

Sleep difficulties are different. They are not "diseases" but *life-style problems requiring you to learn new ways of thinking and acting.* We have carefully avoided the "pill-and-prescription-zap-you're-cured" approach because we believe that it is wrong. Overcoming insomnia means:

- identifying new ways of thinking and acting;
- learning and practicing them; and
- using them so that they become habits—part of who you are.

You are never "cured" of your disturbed sleep. *Rather, you can sleep better as long as you continue to practice new and helpful actions.* Our goal now is to help you find ways to do this.

YOU ARE NEVER FINISHED

Sorry, but that's the reality of chronic sleep problems. *It's a good idea to plan to practice your sleep strategies until they become second nature.* They should become part of your daily and nightly routine, so much so that they are done without special effort, concentration, or planning. It's easy to become lax with ourselves and to begin slipping when activities are not a real part of our daily routine. But how often do you forget to brush your teeth in the morning? Some people who get hooked on physical exercise report that they feel an uncomfortable gap in their day when they fail to exercise. When you don't follow through on your helpful sleep routines, you should feel that something important has been omitted from your day.

KEEP A MAINTENANCE CHECKLIST

You have probably found that two or three of the strategies we presented really work for you, while the others may or may not provide any help. The strategies that really do the job for you are the ones you need to continue using on a daily basis.

To help you continue practicing your helpful sleep habits, we suggest that you keep a "Maintenance Checklist," a simplified version of the daily Sleep Diary that allows you to:

1. Select two or three strategies that hold the key to your success;
2. Keep track of your consistency in practicing them; and
3. Chart your sleep to make sure your gains are maintained.

Ray's Maintenance Checklist is presented here. Notice first that he identified four strategies he felt he needed to continue practicing. Three of them, Behavior-Outcome Rules, Progressive Relaxation, and Cognitive Focusing, were presented in the text. The fourth, a noontime swim, was selected because Ray found that swimming was relaxing and restful. It really did seem to positively influence his sleep.

Keeping the checklist was crucial to Ray's maintenance. Not only did it allow him to monitor his practice carefully, but it also gave him an overview of the relationship between his habits and his sleep. Notice, for example, that his sleep Tuesday was poorer than on the other days. Notice also that he failed to practice Progressive Relaxation at bedtime and that he did not swim at noon. By contrast, sleep on Wednesday and Thursday were much improved and Ray was much more conscientious in practicing the procedures

A blank checklist has also been provided at the end of the chapter for your use. Continue to use it as long as is necessary. *Remember, helpful sleeping habits and better sleep need to become part of who you are.*

CONTRACTS AND SOCIAL SUPPORT

Admonitions and even the best of intentions aren't always enough for some of us to continue practicing even those habits that we know are good for us. Sometimes we need outside assistance, and even find that the ongoing collaboration of someone genuinely interested in us can make the difference between success and failure.

You know yourself better than anyone. Maybe you realize that sticking to your program and practicing good sleep habits really won't be a problem because good sleep is such a blessing.

On the other hand, your past track record may tell you that it is possible to slip into old pattrns very easily. Take steps right now to keep you moving in a positive direction. Developing

Ray's Maintenance Checklist

Week 5/16 to 5/23

Helpful Sleeping Habits	*M*	*Tu*	*W*	*Th*	*Fr*	*Sa*	*Su*
1. Practice Behavior Outcome Rules	✓	✓	✓	✓	✓		
2. Practice Progressive Relaxation	✓		✓	✓			
3. Practice Cognitive Focusing	✓	✓		✓	✓		
4. Swim at noon	✓		✓	✓	✓		
5.							
6.							
Sleep latency	15	10	10	15	20		
Minutes awake after sleep onset	15	20	15	10	15		
Total sleep time	7	6½	7	7	6½		
Sleep rating (0 = poor, 3 = great)	2	1½	2½	2	2		

supports for yourself doesn't mean that you are weak or that you lack willpower. To the contrary, *prudent planning means that you know yourself well and can take steps to set things up so that you will be able to do what you want to do when you want to do it* (and that's willpower in action).

We have suggested two methods in this book to help you be consistent and systematic: self-contracts and social support. If you have found either or both of these helpful, we suggest that you continue to use them now as you move to maintain your progress. You may have identified other strategies especially helpful to you. Continue to use whatever procedures are useful so that you can maintain the progress you've made.

WHAT IF I START TO SLIP?

A second strategy may also be required. You may, at times, find yourself faced with especially trying circumstances (pressure at work or at home, family crises, etc.) that influence your sleep. Or you may discover that your sleep is slipping back gradually to its former undesirable patterns. If either begin to happen, you shouldn't be surprised. It is not necessary to panic. Just realize that these things can happen to anyone who has ever had a sleep problem. What is required is that you take steps to do something about it.

You may need to:

1. Plan ahead for circumstances that may disrupt your sleep (vacations, trips, or pressure at work or at home) so that they don't catch you by surprise and so that you have a plan ready to put into action should problems occur.
2. Begin using more of the techniques to prevent complete relapse.
3. Keep daily Sleep Diaries once again to chart your sleep carefully and to identify circumstances currently associated with good and poor sleep.

4. Using problem-solving (Chapter 9) to devise other strategies you may need to use to manage current problems.

Points 1 and 2 recognize the fact that previously you were able to identify and use various techniques to improve your sleep considerably. Planning ahead for special circumstances and beginning to use more strategies merely requires that you be prepared to reinstitute, for a short period of time, those routines that you know are helpful.

Points 3 and 4 take into account the fact that new problems and circumstances can arise and interfere with your sleep. There's no cause for alarm or panic. It's only necessary that you begin keeping Sleep Diaries and engage in further problem solving. If necessary, you can doff your "personal scientist" cap and begin experimenting with new and needed solutions.

YOU KNOW YOU CAN DO IT

If you have experienced any improvement in your sleep as a result of trying some of these principles and techniques, one important realization may hold the key to your continued success. Whereas poor sleep seemed inevitable and mysterious before, you now realize that *you can take active steps to learn to sleep better.* Even if problems do occur or minor relapses do happen, you know that the problems can be overcome and that the relapses need only be temporary. *You know that you have the resources and the skills to improve your sleep.*

This is the basis of our approach to helping persons improve their sleep without using drugs. If you have learned nothing else from us, we hope that you have taken this message to heart and that you really believe it. And we sincerely hope that you continue to believe it as you continue to improve your

sleep. If your sleep has improved even a small amount, we will have considered our efforts totally worthwhile. If you have learned that it is possible to take command where you were formerly powerless, then you have taken major strides. Keep up the good work!

Maintenance Checklist

Week ________ to ________

Helpful Sleeping Habits	*M*	*Tu*	*W*	*Th*	*Fr*	*Sa*	*Su*
1.							
2.							
3.							
4.							
5.							
6.							
Sleep latency							
Minutes awake after sleep onset							
Total sleep time							
Sleep rating (0 = poor, 3 = great)							

Part Seven

RESOURCE MATERIALS

Appendix A

Behavioral Self-Management in the Treatment of Insomnia: Clinical and Research Issues

Applying psychological procedures to treating problems that are traditionally considered medical presents a formidable challenge to the health care professions. Current medical practices were designed primarily to treat infectious disorders, but are often inept in dealing with today's major health problems: degenerative diseases resulting from maladaptive behavior patterns (cf. Glazier, 1973). Preventing and curing coronary heart disease, tension and migraine headaches, depression, and essential hypertension may require that persons learn to live differently, rather than merely ingest chemical agents three times daily.

Insomnia has been conceptualized traditionally as a nonspecific medical problem related to chronic anxiety and depression or transient life stresses. It has been typically treated by pharmacological means, prescription or otherwise. In concert with the recent interest in treating insomnia psychologically, research evaluating behavioral procedures has proliferated within the past few years (cf. Knapp, Downs, and Alperson, 1976; Montgomery, Perkins, and Wise, 1975). This appendix is designed to acquaint the professional reader and interested lay person with this growing research literature. We have attempted to provide theoretical and empirical justification for the conceptualization of insomnia we have adopted and for the treatment strategies suggested. We have also highlighted major methodological issues that need to be addressed in future clinical research in this area; and discuss selected considerations important in the clinical treatment of insomnia.

We first present a rationale for nondrug approaches to the treatment of insomnia, followed by a general overview and review of behavioral strategies evaluated to date. We then discuss two research issues ignored to date in this research: the kinds of data used to verify the efficacy of treatment and the preponderance of analogue studies. The final section is devoted to three clinical and research issues: the importance of careful individual assessment and differential diagnosis; the need for broadly based multicomponent treatment strategies; and the potential benefit in using a variety of research approaches.

THE NEED FOR NON-PHARMACOLOGICAL TREATMENTS

The development of nonpharmacological procedures for treating insomnia is both relevant and timely. Large scale random surveys both in England (McGhie and Russell, 1962) and in the United States (Karacan, Williams, Salis, and Hursch, 1971; Kales, Bixler, Leo, Healy, and Slye, 1974) have estimated that at least 15 per cent of the population suffers from insomnia. In a prospective study of the risk factors in coronary heart disease, stroke, and cancer, Hammond (1974) surveyed 1,064,004 people and found the 13 per cent of the men and 26.4 per cent of the women complained of insomnia. Because of its prevalence now and in the past, recommendations for its treatment abound and typically include procedures for controlling both cognitive and physical arousal. Binns (1842) refers to a story told by Rabelais concerning: . . . some monks, who oppressed with wakefulness, resolutely addressed themselves to prayer, and before they had concluded a dozen aves, or pater nosters, we forget which, they fell asleep." Evans (1935) also suggested prayer because of its spiritual and soothing qualities. From a different theoretical perspective, Farrow (1925) recommended that one paint large imaginary threes (because of its unconscious phallic significance) extremely slowly on a large mental blackboard by means of an imaginary brush and tin of white paint. Jacobson (1938) proposed that progressive muscle relaxation be used.

But sleep medications (called hypnotic drugs) have received the lion's share of the research-and-development dollar and remain the most common treatment for insomnia. An estimated $170,000,000 was spent on prescriptions for hypnotic drugs in 1970 (Balter and Levine, 1971). Most drugs currently available are, at best, inappropriate for the treatment of insomnia and, at worst, dangerous. Both inter- and intra-subject data indicate that the majority of hypnotic drugs lead rapidly to *tolerance* and *dependence*. Sleep usually improves initially when a person begins taking sleep medications. With chronic use, however, tolerance develops and sleep returns quickly to baseline or may become even *more* disturbed than before drugs were started. Increased dosage may improve sleep temporarily, but again tolerance develops and dependence also results simultaneously. Abrupt termination of hypnotics may lead to a total inability to sleep for several days. These negative consequences generally cause a return to hypnotics. If dosage has been especially heavy, abrupt termination may lead to convulsions (cf. Dement, 1972b; Dement and Guilleminault, 1973; Kales and Kales, 1974).

Hypnotic drugs also produce alterations in sleep structure, suppressing rapid-eye-movement (REM) and delta (Stages 3 and 4) sleep below levels observed before beginning the use of the drug. If termination of hypnotics is attempted, the person typically experiences severe withdrawal reactions in the form of REM rebound (increases in vividness of REM mentation progressing to nightmares). A vicious cycle is thus established: poor sleep leads to the use of hypnotics, but worsened sleep is not attributed to drug use and the person increases their use. The insomniac continues to use the drug, not because it treats the problem, but because termination results in highly aversive consequences.

Alcohol and other drugs are also used frequently to obtain relief.

A recent telephone survey of adult insomniacs in the San Francisco Bay Area (cf. Spiegel, 1973) revealed that 40 per cent of the sample used hypnotics frequently, and 26 per cent used them occasionally. A full 33 per cent used alcohol to eliminate sleep disturbance, while 14.3 per cent frequently used the potentially lethal combination of hypnotics and alcohol together. The complaint of insomnia may also be implicated in the development of alcoholism (Bayh, 1972).

An effective nondrug treatment for insomnia is needed: (1) so that persons can learn to sleep well without using hypnotics; and (2) so that persons who have used hypnotic drugs can learn to terminate usage and find an effective nondrug means for insuring adequate sleep.

BEHAVIORAL TREATMENTS: AN OVERVIEW

Research involving behavioral strategies for treating insomnia is summarized in Table A-1. Treatments have ranged from autohypnosis, EMG and EEG biofeedback training, autogenic training, systematic desensitization, progressive muscle relaxation, to situational ("stimulus") control procedures. A common hypothesis forms the basis of these diverse techniques: insomnia results from hyperarousal. It is postulated that wakefulness, even in experimentally sleep-deprived subjects, is maintained by interoceptive and exteroceptive stimulation. In spontaneously occurring insomnia, these stimulations play on the central nervous system to maintain the waking state, often in spite of the person's attempts to fall asleep (Kleitman, 1963; Monroe, 1968). Various modes of relaxation training are designed to assist the person in decreasing both cognitive and physical arousal at bedtime. Situational-control procedures are designed to separate cues for sleep from stimuli evoking cognitive and physical arousal.

Increasingly sophisticated methodological controls are also evident in this research. Nicassio and Bootzin (1974), for example, used both placebo and wait-control groups in addition to two active treatment groups. The use of a placebo group provided an important control, as subjects in this group showed some improvement, but treat-

TABLE A-1

Behavioral Treatments for Insomnia

Study	*Subjects and Severity Level*	*Treatments*	*Design*	*Dependent variables*	*Results*
Classical conditioning					
Poser et al. (1965)	1 adult male, severe	Classical conditioning (140 trials)	Case study	Sleep EEG	No evidence of conditioned sleep
Evans & bond (1965)	1 adult male severe	Systematic desensitization, classical conditioning	Case study	Sleep diary	SD = no improvement CC = improvement
Stimulus control					
Bootzin (1972)	Adult, female, severe	Stimulus control	Case study	Sleep diary	Latency reduced to 10 min; sleep time increased by 2 to 4 hrs;
Bootzin (1973)	78 adults, severe	Stimulus control; Progressive Relaxation; Placebo; Wait-control (sessions variable)	Group factorial	Sleep diary	SC > PR > placebo= and wait-control;

TABLE A-1—Continued

Behavioral Treatments for Insomnia

Study	*Subjects*	*Treatments*	*Design*	*Dependent variables*	*Results*
Tokarz & Lawrence (1974)	50 students, moderate	Stimulus control; temporal control; stimulus and temporal control; placebo; wait-control (4 sessions)	Group factorial	Sleep diary Roommate observation	Treated groups improved; Control groups showed no improvement.
Haynes et al. (1974)	4 adults, severe	Stimulus control (Reverse Design)	Single-subject experiment	Sleep Diary	All subjects showed improvement; 2 of 4 subjects showed no reversal-effect.

TABLE A-1—Continued

Behavioral Treatments for Insomnia

Study	*Subjects*	*Treatments*	*Design*	*Dependent variables*	*Results*
Progressive relaxation					
Geer & Katkin (1966)	29-year-old female, severe	Single-item desensitization (14 sessions)	Case study	Retrospective self-report	Occasional insomnia (once every 1–2 weeks)
Hinkle & Luther (1972)	7 adults, severe	Relaxation + imaginal rehearsal (4 sessions)	Single group	Sleep diary	4 subjects extremely improved; 3 subjects moderately improved
Weil & Goldfried (1973)	11-year-old female	*In vivo* and taped relaxation	Case study	Retrospective self-report	Tapes discontinued after 6 weeks; 3- and 6- month follow-up confirmed maintenance
Haynes et al. (1974)	14 students, moderate	Relaxation; Placebo (6 sessions)	Group factorial	Sleep diary	Both groups improved significantly, but PR superior to placebo.
Borkovec & Werts (1976)	36 students, moderate	Progressive Relaxation; Placebo; Wait-Control; (4 sessions)	Group factorial	Sleep EEG; Sleep diary	All groups reduced latency to Stage 1 from baseline to week 3; improvements shown by Progressive Relaxation group to week 4 superior to other groups; no differences among groups in self-reported improvement.

TABLE A-1—Continued

Behavioral Treatments for Insomnia

Study	*Subjects*	*Treatments*	*Design*	*Dependent variables*	*Results*
Autogenic Training/Self-Hypnosis					
Kahn et al. (1968)	16 students moderate	Autogenic training (4 sessions)	Single group	Retrospective self report	3 subjects dropped; 11 of 13 subjects reported improvement.
Fry (1963)	28 adults, severe	Self-hypnosis	Single group	Retrospective self report	26 subjects improved and stopped using medications.
Traub, et al. (1973)	7 adults, severe	Autogenic training (reverse design)	Single-subject experiment	Sleep EEG; sleep-diary	All subjects reported improvement; EEG: 3 subjects improved on latency; 2 subjects increased delta sleep

TABLE A-1—Continued

Behavioral Treatments for Insomnia

Study	*Subjects*	*Treatments*	*Design*	*Dependent variables*	*Results*
<u>*Comparative Relaxation Strategies*</u>					
Borkovec & Fowles (1973)	37 female college students, moderate	Progressive relaxation; Hypnosis; Placebo; Wait-control (3 sessions)	Group factorial	Sleep diary	3 treatment groups improved significantly
Borkovec et al. (1973)	24 female adults, moderate	Progresive relaxation; Desensitization + Progressive Relaxation; Desensitization alone (3 sessions)	Group factorial	Sleep diary	No differences among groups
Steinmark & Borkovec (1974)	48 college students moderate	Progressive Relaxation; Desensitization; Placebo; Wait-control (4 sessions)	Group factorial, (counter-demand instruction for first 3 sessions)	Sleep diary	During negative demand: Progressive Relaxation and Desensitization groups improved; During positive demand: Placebo groups improved.

TABLE A-1—Continued

Behavioral Treatments for Insomnia

Study	*Subjects*	*Treatments*	*Design*	*Dependent variables*	*Results*
Comparative Relaxation Strategies (Contd)					
Nicassio & Bootzin (1974)	30 adults, severe	Progressive relaxation; autogenic Training; Placebo; Wait-control (4 sessions)	Group Factorial	Sleep Diary Spouse questionnaire; Pupil constriction	Progressive Relaxation and Autogenic Training groups showed significant improvements in sleep.
Gershman & Clouser (1974)	20 students, moderate	Relaxation; Desensitization; Wait-control (8 sessions)	Group factorial	Pre–post estimates of sleep behavior	Relaxation and desensitization improved in latency to sleep onset.
Borkovec et al. (1975)	56 students, moderate	Progressive relaxation; Relaxation with tension-release cycles omitted; Placebo; Wait-control (4 sessions)	Group factorial; counter demand instructions for first 3 sessions	Sleep diary	Negative demand: Progressive Relaxation significantly greater improvement than other groups; Positive Demand: Progressive Relaxation only group significantly different from no-treatment group.

TABLE A-1—Continued

Behavioral Treatments for Insomnia

Study	*Subjects*	*Treatments*	*Design*	*Dependent variables*	*Results*
Pendleton & Tasto (1976)	29 adults, moderate	Progressive relaxation; Metronome-conditioned relaxation; Metronome-induced relaxation; Wait-list control	Group factorial	Sleep diary	Treated groups same at posttreatment; all different from controls.
Freedman (1976)	18 adults, severe	EMG Biofeedback; Progressive relaxation; Placebo	group factorial	Sleep EEG; Sleep Diary	Biofeedback and Progressive Relaxation reduced latency to sleep onset.
Ribordy (1976)	adults, moderate	Progressive relaxation; Systematic desensitization; Cognitive distraction; Wait-control	group factorial	Sleep diary	All treatment groups reduced latency to sleep onset; controls showed no change.

TABLE A-1—Continued

Behavioral Treatments for Insomnia

Study	*Subjects*	*Treatments*	*Design*	*Dependent variables*	*Results*
Comparative Relaxation Strategies (Continued)					
Mitchell & White (in press)	13 adults,	Incremental (Progressive Relaxation, Mental Relaxation, Cognitive Control taught in 2-week periods, each followed by 3-week practice); Accelerated (no practice session); Delayed (learned cognitive control only).	group factorial	Sleep Diary	All groups reduced latency significantly; Incremental and Accelerated superior to Delayed.
Woolfolk et al. (1976)	24 adults, moderate	Progressive relaxation; Meditation; Wait-list control	Group factorial	Sleep diary	Both treatment groups improved significantly in latency, controls did not change.
Biofeedback					
Raskin, et al. (1973)	6 adults, severe	EMG training + home relaxation practice (40 sessions)	Case studies	Sleep diary	5 subjects improved ability to fall asleep

TABLE A-1—Continued
Behavioral Treatments for Insomnia

Study	*Subjects*	*Treatments*	*Design*	*Dependent variables*	*Results*
Feinstein et al. (1974)	12 chronic severe	SMR central (13 Hz) feedback; Alpha (occipital 10 Hz) feedback; Central (10 Hz) feedback; Central (15 Hz) feedback (25 (25 sessions)	Group factorial	Sleep EEG Sleep diary	4 subjects receiving SMR (13 Hz) training showed decrease in latency, movements during sleep; increase in percentage of REM and cyclicity of sleep stages.
Hauri & Good (1974)	10 chronic severe	EMG training (13–16 sessions)	Case studies	Sleep EEG; Sleep diary	Some nonsignificant improvements noted in sleep latency, minutes awake after sleep onset, and total sleep time.
Montgomery et al. (1975)	7 chronic severe	EMG training (18 sessions)	single group	Sleep rating	Reduced muscle tension; reduced perceived difficulty in falling to sleep and increased perceived restfulness of sleep.
Haynes, et al (in press)	24 chronic severe	EMG training, Relaxation Instructions; Control.	Group factorial	Sleep diary	Treatment groups different from control group on slege latency.

TABLE A-1—Continued

Behavioral Treatments for Insomnia

Study	*Subjects*	*Treatments*	*Design*	*Dependent variables*	*Results*
Attribution					
Storms & Nisbett (1970)	42 college students, moderate	Placebo +: Instructions to expect arousal; Instructions not to expect arousal	Group factorial	Daily sleep diary	Arousal subjects reduced sleep latency; nonarousal subjects stayed same.
Davison et al. (1973)	15 college students, moderate	Relaxation + 1,000 mg chloral hydrate +: "Optimal dosage" instructions; "Weak dosage" instructions.	Group factorial	Sleep diary	Greater maintenance of change by "weak dosage" subjects.
Kellogg & Baron (1975)	42 college students, moderate	Pill (administered vs. withheld) Reason for participation (high vs. no)	2 × 2 Anova	Sleep diary	Subjects given pill but not given reason showed placebo reaction; other subjects showed no reaction.

ment strategies produced effects beyond those accounted for by placebo factors. Steinmark and Borkovec (1974) further controlled expectancy and demand effects in analogue research using counter-demand instructions. Previous research using college students with moderate insomnia (e.g., Borkovec and Fowles, 1973) failed to find differences among progressive relaxation, self-hypnosis, and placebo subjects. Only subjects in the active treatment groups improved in the counter-demand condition while placebo subjects improved only under positive demand condition (cf. Steinmark and Borkovec, 1974).

These studies begin to attest to the potential efficacy of behavioral strategies in treating insomnia and form the empirical foundation for much of what we present in this book. It should be noted, however, that these current empirical results represent only a beginning, at best. The optimism provided by these studies needs to be balanced with a careful examination of some critical but heretofore unexamined research and clinical issues.

METHODOLOGICAL ISSUES IN BEHAVIORAL TREATMENTS FOR INSOMNIA

Research in behavioral strategies for treating insomnia have been marked by increasing use of methodological controls. Obtaining significant results when placebo, expectancy, and demand factors are controlled represents an important advance over the early research in this area. But two important methodological problems remain to be addressed before the clinical utility of these procedures can be established more firmly: (1) the need to augment self-report data; and (2) the prevalent use of analogue studies involving college students with "moderate insomnia."

SELF-REPORT (EXPERIENTIAL) DATA

Evaluations of behavioral treatments for insomnia have relied primarily on self-reports of sleeping patterns to evaluate treatment efficacy (cf. Table A-1). While perceptions of sleeping patterns form one component of the complaint of insomnia, it must be recognized that self-reports and actual sleep behavior are often divergent. *People in general, and insomniacs in particular, tend to err systematically in estimating sleep behavior.* When experiential and all-night polygraphic data (EEG, EMG, and EOG) are compared, insomniacs consistently: (1) underestimate total sleep time and frequency of nocturnal arousals; (2) overestimate time required to fall asleep (latency to sleep onset); and (3) overestimate the length of time awake after sleep onset (WASO) (Carskadon, Dement, Mitler, Guilleminault, Zarcone and Spiegel, 1976; Dement, Smythe, Hoddes, Guilleminault, Carskadon, Wilson, and Zarcone, 1974; Bixler, Kales, Leo, and Slye, 1974; Hoddes, Carskadon, Phillips, Zarcone, and Dement, 1972; Zung, 1970; Kleitman, 1963). Dement, Carskadon, Milter, Guilleminault, and Zarcone, (1976), in a comprehensive study of 122 drug-free insomniacs, found that the mean underestimation of total sleep time was 45 minutes, and sleep latency tended to be overestimated by an average of 30 minutes (the usual criterion for determining sleep disturbance in behavioral studies). These results are not unexpected. Sleep is defined commonly as the moment when normal perceptual processes cease to function and when the person no longer responds to the environment (Dement and Mitler, 1976; Kleitman, 1963). As sleep onset approaches, time perception distortions usually result in overestimations of elapsed time (Anliker, 1963). Behavioral treatment studies using only self-report data should be interpreted conservatively, and future research in this area should employ all-night polygraphic measures to supplement self- reports of sleep behavior. It is especially imperative that we explore methods for increasing the reliability and validity of the data employed to evaluate treatment strategies.

Of special concern are those studies using moderate insomniac college students (e.g., Borkovec, et al., 1973, 1975; Kellogg and Baron, 1975; Tokarz and Lawrence, 1974). Inclusion in subject pools typically requires a complaint of poor sleep combined with a reported 30 minutes latency to sleep onset (e.g., Pendleton and Tasto, 1976; Woolfolk, et al., 1976). These criteria provide the operational definition for insomnia employed in these studies. It is not clear if the complaint of poor sleep is reflected in sleep behavior measured physiologically, if these persons are among those deficient in estimating sleep behavior, or if the subjects are "pseudoinsomniacs" complaining of poor sleep without any polygraphic evidence of sleep disturbance (cf. Dement, 1972b; Hoddes, et al., 1972).

Tokarz and Lawrence (1974) enlisted the observations of spouses or roommates in the subjects' environments. But even under highly controlled conditions, ratings by others tend to be biased in directions similar to self-reports (Weiss, McPartland, and Kupfer, 1973). Self- and significant other reports of many waking behaviors suffer from similar reliability and validity problems (cf. Kazdin, 1974; Thoresen and Mahoney, 1974). It is a truism to say that adequate evaluation of any treatment strategy rests upon the reliability and the validity of the supporting data (Cronbach, 1975). If behavioral treatments of sleep disorders are to be improved, we need to spend more effort in obtaining maximally reliable and valid data. Because exclusive use of self-reports of sleep behavior are of questionable reliability and validity, it is difficult to know what is contributing to variance in pre- and post-treatment evaluations. Rather than relying on one method (questionnaire or diary) and one behavior (self-report of sleep onset) to study change, it would be a more helpful strategy to use multi-methods and multi-behaviors to evaluate changes in sleep variables over time (cf. Coates and Thoresen, 1976; Cone, 1976).

When all-night polygraphic recordings have been used to evaluate behavioral strategies, effects have been mixed. Traub, Jencks, and Bliss (1973) treated 7 chronically severe insomniacs using autogenic training using both polygraphic and experiential measures. All subjects unanimously reported overall sleep improvement but only 3 showed significant reductions in latency to sleep onset as measured by all-night EEG recordings. Two of these same 3 subjects also showed increases in delta sleep, while 4 subjects showed no changes on any EEG sleep variables. Hauri and Good (1975) found that EMG feedback training with 10 chronic severe insomniacs reduced frontalis muscle tension but had minimal effects in reducing latency to sleep onset across all subjects as measrued by EEG recordings. Again, all subjects *reported* dramatic improvements on this variable. Feinstein, Sterman, and MacDonald (1974) used EEG biofeedback training to teach subjects to produce rhythmic 12-16 cycles per second centro-frontal cortex activity. Subjects receiving this training, in contrast to control subjects, showed reductions in latency to sleep onset and body movements during sleep, along with improvements in sleep-stage cycles.

Borkovec and Werts (1976) found modest treatment effects using college students reporting greater than 30 minutes latency to sleep onset. Subjects in all groups reduced in latency to Stage 1 sleep, as measured by all-night EEG recordings. The progressive relaxation subjects, however, showed significantly superior improvements to the no-treatment subjects, and significantly less variance than the no-treatment controls and placebo subjects at posttreatment assessments. But these results are compromised by the fact that subjects were admitted to the study solely on the basis of self-reported latencies. All-night recordings revealed that some subjects reported normal latencies even before the study began. Thus it is difficult to interpret what the statistically significant posttreatment data mean. Interestingly, no differences among the groups were found in self-reported (sleep diary) latency to sleep onset.

Perceived improvement may or may not correlate with physiological changes in sleep behavior (cf. Borkovec and Werts, 1976). It is not clear at present if behavioral strategies for treating insomnia are capable of modifying physiological parameters of sleep behavior, self-reported experiences of sleep behavior, or both. Behavioral researchers need to make use of established laboratory techniques for evaluating sleep (cf. Rechtschaffen and Kales, 1968) because precise treatment effects cannot be pinpointed in the absence of all-night polysomnographic data.

Hypnotic-drug studies clearly attest to the value of physiological measures; until hypnotics were evaluated using these mearsures, the deleterious effects of drugs were not known and they were dispensed in a cavalier fashion. Replacing hypnotics with behavioral procedures will also require careful scrutiny. The five studies employing behavioral treatments and using physiological as well as experiential data suggest that more than relaxation procedures may be needed to improve the sleep of chronic insomniacs (cf. Feinstein, et al., 1974; Hauri and Good, 1974; Truab, et al., 1973).

In adopting this position, we do not discount the importance of perceived sleep both in defining the problem of insomnia and in evaluating alternative treatment procedures. *We believe that research advances require comprehensive assessment systems.* Self-reports of sleep are important in indicating experienced changes, while reports from other persons with whom the client interacts frequently can indicate the visibility of changes to others in the clients' environment. Data relative to the client's daytime behavior (e.g., fatigue, depression, stress, and tension) can be useful in determining associated problem areas and expected correlated changes. All-night polygraphic recordings are invaluable in providing evidence of physiological sleep disturbance and in documenting precise changes in sleep behavior patterns.

Comprehensive evaluations are more expensive, time consuming, and difficult to obtain than retrospective self-report measures. Carefully controlled and extensively evaluated intensive or small-scale group studies with relatively few selected subjects are needed at present to advance the research in *clinically significant ways* (cf. Glass, Willson, and Gottman, 1975; Hersen and Barlow, 1976; Thoresen, in press).

ANALOGUE RESEARCH

"Moderate insomniac" college students participating in order to fulfill specific course requirements have commonly been used in the studies reported. The length and extent of the college students' sleeping problems, and the degree to which self-reported moderate sleeping difficulty represents a clinically meaningful problem, in terms of chronicity and impaired functioning, have typically not been assessed. This point is critical because people vary widely in sleep behavior and the degree to which experienced sleep difficulty interferes with daytime functioning (cf. Dement and Guilleminault, 1973). Indeed, most sleep investigators agree that notable daytime problems (e.g., fatigue) are essential to the diagnosis of insomnia (cf. Dement and Mitler, 1976; Webb, 1975). Many of the studies have ignored this dimension in screening subjects for study (e.g., Borkovec and Werts, 1976). Needed is a broadened conceptualization of the problem to guide researchers in the selection of meaningful operational criteria.

Analogue studies can serve an important function in the total cycle of scientific inquiry (cf. Lackenmeyer, 1970; Paul, 1969). They are useful in narrowing parameters of influence in behavior change and in determining possible mechanisms of change; they can provide a more economical means of developing clinical techniques and generating explanatory principles (cf. Bernstein and Paul, 1971). College students' problems are usually less intense and can be treated in a short period of time. Other life difficulties are less likely to interfere with treatment evaluation. But generalizations from college students to clinical populations require considerable caution. As Marks (1975) noted in discussing treatments for phobias:

> . . . the differences between patient and volunteer populations outweight the overlap so much that analogue results cannot be assumed to apply automatically to patients. *Progress in treating severe pathology would accelerate if more workers dealt with the sobering realities of clinical settings.* [p. 76; italics added].

Almost any treatment may be effective in reducing the self-reported sleep disturbances of moderate insomniacs (e.g. Borkovec and Werts, 1976). Nicolis and Silvestri (1976) found that a drug placebo and an active hypnotic drug (phenobarbital) were equally effective in reducing the complaints of moderate insomniacs. Differences between the effects of the two medications appeared only with severe insomniacs. Differences in results between progressive muscle relaxation and placebo treatments have been difficult to demonstrate when moderate insomniac college students have been used as subjects (cf. Borkovec and Fowles, 1973; Borkovec et al., 1973). Hypothesizing that these failures to distinguish active and control treatments were due to demand and placebo effects, Steinmark and Borkovec (1974) introduced a counter-demand procedure (i.e., subjects were informed *not* to expect improvement until after the fourth treatment session). Any reports of improvement prior to this fourth session might be interpreted as conservative estimates of actual subjective improvement. The active-treatment groups (progressive relaxation and single-item desensitization) reported improvements by the third therapy session despite the fact that improvement was not expected until the fourth session. The placebo group improved only after the fourth session, when they were told that improvement was to be expected. Borkovec and Werts (1976), however, found no differences in *reported* improvement among treatment and control subjects. Moreover, differences in improvements among active, placebo, and no-treatment control subjects in latency to Stage 1 as measured by sleep EEG were non-significant at week 3 (when subjects were instructed not to expect improvement) and marginally significant at week 4 (when subjects were instructed to expect improvement).

While the counter-demand procedure was useful in demonstrating differences between active and placebo treatment in earlier studies, two important issues remain. First, in the absence of polygraphic data, it is not clear that the demand manipulation is effective in controlling the biases inherent in self-reported data. Does the demand manipulation increase the accuracy with which sleep behavior is reported, or does it merely delay the perception of improvement? Second, now that various strategies have been shown to impact self-reported changes in sleep behavior among moderately sleep-disturbed college students, it becomes incumbent upon us to determine the power of these techniques in improving sleep among severe insomniacs. As Rosen (1975) points out, using analogue subjects may be unnecessary when clinically disturbed subjects are readily available.

CLINICAL ISSUES IN THE TREATMENT OF INSOMNIA

This section of the Appendix is devoted to three issues that we have selected to discuss because of their special relevance to the clinician. They also have important implications for the clinician-researcher pursuing or about to begin empirical work in this area. Because we believe that insomnia is a heterogeneous and complex disorder, we take the position that treatment and research strategies need to be multifaceted and flexible, proceeding only on the basis of careful individual assessment.

ASSESSMENT AND DIFFERENTIAL DIAGNOSIS

Insomnia is not a unitary medical or behavioral disorder. It is a *complaint denoting multiple sleep disorders*: difficulty in falling asleep initially; frequent and/or extended nighttime awakenings; and premature final awakening. Further, insomnia is potentially related to a variety of physical and psychological factors:

> If the psychiatrist is concerned about the complaint of insomnia on a routine basis, he should have some notion of the evolving *differential diagnosis* in the area; he should also have some developing list of the causes and of the techniques of evaluation, as well as of treatment.
>
> The situation is analogous to the complaint of a chronic headache: if the psychiatrist is confronted with such a patient, he will want to ascertain, either on his own or by checking the appropriate referral procedures, that certain well known organic causes, such as brain tumor or hypertension, are not implicated. By the same token, it is very important to recognize that insomnia requires similar evaluation [Dement and Mitler, 1976, italics added].

At present, there is no one best treatment for all insomniacs. Without considering various etiological factors for each person, it is not possible to design treatment procedures tailored to the needs of the individual patient. Moreover, useful treatments may be judged ineffective when evaluated for subjects whose disorders they were not designed to treat.

The first task must involve eliminating subjects for whom behavioral treatments might be inappropriate. Table A-2 lists a variety of disorders that can result in the complaint of insomnia. Dement and co-workers (1976) have estimated that *identifiable* physiological disorders may account for as much as 50 per cent of the reported cases of insomnia.

Treatments such as relaxation training may be ineffective if insomnia is associated with a physiological disorder. The behavioral researcher or therapist needs to be aware of the possibility of these physiological disorders, should attempt to find out if they may be contributing to a subject's complaint, and refer the subject to a competent sleep specialist if the disorder is suspected. Failure to perform these primary discriminations can confound evaluation of behavioral strategies and, further, can represent a serious ethical problem in terms of misdiagnosis and inappropriate treatments.*

*We do not mean to imply that treatments based on social learning theory are always inappropriate for persons with major physiological problems such as apnea or narcolepsy (Table A-2). At present we simply do not know how much such treatments might aid people with these problems.

TABLE A-2

Differential Diagnosis of Insomnia

Category	*Disturbance*	*Diagnosis*
Drug Dependence (Kales and Kales, 1974; Dement and Mitler, 1974)	Insomnia associated with chronic hypnotic or alcohol ingestion; also associated with abrupt withdrawal.	Chronic use of hypnotic drugs and/or alcohol.
Insomnia Associated with Neurologic Dysfunction		
Nocturnal Myoclonus (Lugaresi, Coccagna, and Cerini, 1968)	Sudden contractions and twitching of leg muscles every 30 to 60 sec during sleep.	Patient and/or spouse reports leg twitches and kicks repeatedly during sleep.
Sleep Apnea (Guilleminault, Eldridge, and Dement, 1973)	Periods longer than 10 sec during which no air exchange occurs at nostril and/or mouth; breathing stops, followed by a deep and sudden gasp for air; minimum 30 episodes during 7 hours of nocturnal sleep.	Difficult to assess without all-night polygraph recording; excessive and chronic snoring often is a clue.
Restless-Leg Syndrome (Frankel, Patton, and Gillin, 1974)	"Crawling" or aching sensation in legs; symptoms removed only when person gets up and moves around.	Complaint of crawling or aching sensations alleviated by movement.
Alpha-delta sleep (Phillips, Mitler, and Dement, 1974)	5–20 percent delta waves combined with relatively large alpha-like rhythms.	Requires all-night polygraphic evaluation.

TABLE A–2 Continued
Differential Diagnosis of Insomnia

Category	*Disturbance*	*Diagnosis*
Insomnia Associated with Neurologic Dysfunction		
Narcolepsy (Zarcone, 1975)	Periodic cataplexy (paralysis while awake), followed by irresistible sleep attacks accompanied by hallucinations and loss of muscle tone.	Sudden and frequent cataplexy followed by short sleep "attacks" during daytime; daytime fatigue, sleepiness.
Insomnia Associated with Other Disturbances (cf. Williams, Karacan, and Hursch, 1974; Kales and Kales, 1974)		
Psychosis	Schizophrenia manic-depressive psychosis	Psychiatric examination
Pregnancy ana Post-Partum Disturbance		Physical/psychiatric examination
Organic Dysfunction	Uremic syndrome, nutritional disorders, thyroid disorders, brain tumor, liver dysfunction, diabetes, epilepsy, cardiovascular disease.	Physical examination

Behavioral treatments might be considered appropriate for subjects whose insomnia is not identified primarily as a physiological dysfunction. But this does not imply that the remainder of the insomniac population is homogeneous, that the hyperarousal hypothesis is adequate for explaining all forms of inadequate sleep, or that various relaxation strategies are sufficient for treating all or even most cases of insomnia. The call for multicomponent and flexible treatment and research strategies rests upon our current knowledge of the processes of sleep and our sketchy understanding of the nature of insomnia. Sleep research is clearly in its infancy (we were not exaggerating in Chapter 2). We have attempted, based on this incomplete knowledge, to chart some potentially useful directions based on the integration of behavioral strategies with basic sleep research.

WHAT IS INSOMNIA?

Deriving an adequate understanding of insomnia rests upon the assumption that we sleep for some very specific reasons and that interference with this process is harmful. While it seems so clearly apparent that we must sleep in order to rest and recuperate, closer inspection indicates that this may not be true. We still do not understand the basic "hows and whys" of sleep. Dement (1972a) summarized the state of the art very simply: "At the present time, hard facts about the role of the sleep state, if any, in both the adult and the developing organism are in short supply [p. 351]. "Many theories have been suggested. Sleep: (1) permits the restoration of energy deficits; (2) allows physical or psychological regenerative functions; (3) compensates oxygen debt; (4) cleanses body and central nervous system of toxins; (5) allows discharge of repressed material from the unconscious; (6) facilitates memory consolidation; and (7) permits the synthesis of critical biochemical substances" (cf. Bremer, 1974; Freemon, 1972; Hartmann, 1973). These theories have been seriously questioned on several grounds: (1) that complete vulnerability to the environment experienced during sleep is a heavy price to pay for completing such functions (Moruzzi, 1974); (2) that sleep deprivation per se is not necessarily deleterious to the organism (Dement, 1972a); and (3) that some individuals can sleep extraordinarily short amounts of time with no ill effects. There are persons in perfectly good health who have led very productive lives on less than one hour of sleep per day (Jones and Oswald, 1968; Meddis, Pearson, and Langford, 1973).

In reviewing the sleep deprivation literature (the methodology commonly used to test these theories), Dement (1972a) concluded that the research has not yielded substantial information regarding the basic purpose or functions of sleep. He hypothesized that sleep may represent an optimal situation for the occurrence of certain activities, but that these activities can occur at other times. Therefore, it really is quite unclear why the minor interruptions in sleep experienced by the insomniac should result in such severe subjective complaints and the chronic use of hypnotic drugs.

Dement and Mitler (1976) have offered what they term "the process view of sleep," which suggests that sleep must be viewed in the context of the total waking/REM sleep/non-REM sleep cycle. Many bodily functions (e.g., heart rate, or body temperature) oscillate on an internally generated daily schedule, the circadian rhythm. Sleep disturbances may represent the *desynchronization* of some of these processes. Schizophrenia, for example, may involve the intrusion of dreams into the waking state and insomnia may be characterized by one or several of these biological functions being out of phase with the others. "Alpha–delta sleep" may represent the intrusion of alpha waves into the slow-wave sleep state (Phillips, et al., 1974). Monroe's (1968) data regarding differences between good and poor sleepers may characterize desynchronization problems rather than support the popular hyperarousal theory. What has been termed "pseudoinsomnia" by some sleep researchers may have a genuine physiological basis not found in EEG records, as they are currently scored. Behavioral treatments may need to be designed to synchronize biological processes rather than to reduce arousal (cf. Feinstein, et al., 1974).

Because we currently lack evidence sufficient to substantiate any specific conceptualization of insomnia, it should also be obvious that a broad variety of treatment and assessment tools are clearly needed. Adherence to a single-modality approach or hypothetical framework is premature. The hyperarousal hypothesis has been useful but the therapeutic implications derived from the process view of sleep can suggest interesting treatment possibilities as well. In addition, heterogeneous approaches seem warranted by investigations of differences among insomniacs and normal sleepers.

INSOMNIACS VERSUS NORMAL SLEEPERS

Studies investigating differences between insomniacs and controls have compared both the sleep behavior and personality characteristics of these two groups. Both areas of research present confusing data.

SLEEP BEHAVIOR

Dement and Guilleminault (1973) attempted to use the following objective criteria to define insomnia: less that 6.5 hours total sleep time; greater than 30 minutes latency to sleep onset; greater than 30 minutes wake time after sleep onset; and evidence of impaired daytime functioning. But these definitions have proven unsuitable in that a majority of the patients with the complaint of insomnia fail to meet the criteria and have shown wide variability on these variables. In the Dement sample (1976), only 56 per cent of the subjects met the total wake-time-after-sleep-onset criteria. Only 11 of 122 subjects fulfilled all 3 criteria. It seems unreasonable to discount chronic complaints on the basis of these general criteria.

Dement et al. (1976) further compared their subjects with data from age-matched normal controls (Williams, Karacan, and Hursch, 1974) and found considerable overlap in these 2 supposedly distinct populations. Statistically significant differences in total sleep time were demonstrated only for 30–39-year-old and 50–59-year-old females. Sleep-latency differences were demonstrated only for 50–59-year-old females, and wake-time-after-sleep-onset differences were shown only for females aged 30–49, and males aged 30–39 and 50–59. These data, combined with research indicating that persons can tolerate long-term and seemingly extreme reductions in total sleep (to 5.5 hours per night) make it difficult to determine why the insomniac should complain about reduced sleep (cf. Johnson and McLeod, 1973; Webb, 1974).

Insomniacs did tend to: (1) experience a greater number of nocturnal arousals; (2) demonstrate considerable night-to-night variability; (3) experience less delta sleep than normals; and (4) show considerable *heterogeneity* in both polygraphically recorded and experienced sleep disturbance. It may be that unpredictable arousals during sleep are critical in establishing the complaint of insomnia (cf. Johnson, 1973).

The major implications of these data is that (1) selecting subjects on the basis of a complaint of 30 minutes or greater latency to sleep onset maybe a marginally useful criterion; and (2) we may need to do more than merely reduce latencies to sleep onset in or do to eliminate the complaint. Reducing sleep latency by 20 minutes may be irrelevant; more subtle changes may need to occur if a person is to consider himself a good sleeper.

PERSONALITY CHARACTERISTICS

A second line of research has been devoted to studying personality characteristic differences between insomniacs and controls (cf. Kales and Cary, 1971; Kales, 1972; Monroe, 1967; Roth et al., 1974). Some researchers, following traditional analytic formulations, have suggested that insomnia is a symptom secondary to an underlying personality psychopathology (Kales and Kales, 1974). Coursey, Buchsbaum, and Frankel (1975) generally found conflicting results among comparative personality studies. attributed to several factors: variability in subject-selection criteria (good vs. poor sleepers; insomniacs vs. controls), use of different personality inventories, and failure to use normal-sleeper control groups for comparative purposes. Using a variety of psychometric instruments (e.g., MMPI and CPI) and an evoked potentials task (EEG reactions to visual and auditory stimuli of varying intensities), they found that insomniacs tended to be more depressed, show more anxious worrying, and were "sensory reducers"* in comparison to normal controls. It is not clear if these differences are related to causes or effects of reduced sleep; if their presence merely exacerbates the subjective complaint; if depression and anxiety will be reduced if sleep is improved; or if improved sleep might take place with reductions in depression and anxiety.

*Sensory reducers, in this context, tend to respond to stimulation of minimal intensity more strongly than normals. Thus, the insomniac, in responding to small incoming stimuli, must be more aroused and upset by minor environmental noises.

BEHAVIORAL DIFFERENCES

A related and potentially fruitful line of research might involve investigations of behavioral differences between subjects who complain of insomnia and normal sleepers in terms of daytime and nighttime actions. Haynes, Follingstad, and McGowan (1974) attempted to determine if insomniacs could be differentiated from normal sleepers interms of actions performed in a sleeping environment, especially those possibly incompatible with good sleep (e.g., reading in bed). No differences were found. A college analogue population was employed. Using a similar research strategy with a clinical sample might be more informative. Other variables of interest might include activities just prior to bedtime (cf. Baekeland, Koulack, and Lasky, 1968; Cohen and Cox, 1975), mental activity at bedtime (cf. Foulkes and Vogel, 1965; Rechtaschaffen, 1968, Hanley, 1965), and nutrition and eating habits (cf. Crisp, Stonehill, and Fenton, 1971; Crisp and Stonehill, 1976; Stonehill and Crisp, 1973). What seems very clear at this point is that we know almost nothing about insomniacs' various *daytime behaviors.* Ethological-type naturalistic studies using intensive design strategies could provide a data base from which theoretical proposals could be developed and tested empirically (Thoresen, in press).

THE PROBLEM OF INSOMNIA

Insomnia is considerably more complex than is represented in the behavioral literature. While the current picture is confusing and few clear guidelines can be drawn, we will offer a few tentative generalizations cautiously.

Approximately 15 to 20 million Americans label themselves insomniacs; many use the varieties of prescription and over-the-counter medications and/or alcohol in the attempt to sleep better. Equally important is that the evaluations of behavioral strategies for treating insomnia will have to progress beyond the use of moderate insomniac college students whose complaints appear qualitatively and quantitatively different from clinical populations. When working with clinical populations, the behavioral researcher or therapist needs to be alert to the possibility of physiological disorders. Of utmost importance is the recognition that self-reports of sleep behavior, while important, represent the subjective experience alone. Behavioral treatments may be effective in modifying the perception of poor sleep, but the potential of these procedures in modifying physiologically recorded sleep behavior awaits controlled study.

In summarizing basic research on the problem of insomnia, one major conclusion predominates: *persons complaining of inadequate sleep belong to an heterogenous group.* In the absence of neurological dysfunctions (e.g., sleep apnea or nocturnal myoclonus), sleep disturbances can be related to a variety of antecedents, and no one treatment should necessarily be expected to work with all or even most cases. At the very least, differential diagnosis and treatment, using a variety of indices, will be required to develop and assess the efficacy of various treatment protocols.

Both assessment and treatment procedures need to be *multifaceted* and *comprehensive.* Assessment procedures should include physiological and experiential (self-report) measures of sleep behavior; evaluations of the subjective complaint of insomnia; reports regarding impairment of daytime functioning; and evaluation of other relevant daytime and nighttime behaviors. Self-reports, ratings by significant others, psychometric evaluations, direct obsevations, and sleep recordings might all be employed.

THE COMPLAINT AND THE TREATMENT

People with inadequate sleep might be expected to fall within one of three categories using three data sources: sleep behavior measured polygraphically, experienced (self-reported) sleep patterns, and measures of daytime functioning. This conceptualization of the problem is intended to lead to more meaningful operational definitions for use in research studies.

First are those whose sleep behavior, as measured by all-night sleep recordings, is statistically rare but who experience no discomfort as a result of sleeping short amounts of time. These people do not require therapeutic attention and probably will not come to a doctor's attention unless specifically recruited for basic research purposes.

TABLE A-3

Some Tentative Generalizations About Insomnia

Fifteen to 20 million Americans label themselves as insomniacs:
- Many use prescriptions and over-the-counter drugs to obtain better sleep.
- Significant proportions may use alcohol and/or alcohol plus drugs together.
- Most drugs generate a cycle of tolerance and dependence and actually worsen rather than improve sleep.

Persons complaining of disturbed sleep belong to a heterogenous group:
- The behavioral researcher or clinician needs to be aware of and diagnose signs pointing to the possibility of sleep disturbance secondary to neurologic dysfunction.
- Strategies effective with college students experiencing moderate and possibly transitory sleep disturbance may or may not be effective with clinical populations.

Self-reports and all-night polygraphic recordings may yield divergent information regarding sleep behavior:
- Assessment procedures need to include all-night recordings, self-perceptions of sleep, and measures of daytime functioning.
- People complaining of disturbed sleep may show impairment in self-reports, but all-night recordings may show normal sleep.
- Treatments need to be tailored to these different populations and also to contributing conditions experienced by individual patients.

The nature and causes of the complaint of poor or disturbed sleep remain to be identified, conceptualized, and studied empirically.

Second are those who complain of inadequate sleep and impaired daytime functioning but whose sleep behavior, as analyzed using current polygraphic procedures, appears normal. These people may fall asleep immediately and sleep for long periods of time without significant interruptions. Concerted basic and applied research is needed to discern the nature of their complaint and appropriate treatment procedures. Causes of the complaint, for example, may reside in close examination of various physiological measures (such as those employed by Monroe, 1967), in dysfunctions in the perceptions of sleep, or in the use of the complaint when the problem is depression, stress and tension, or daytime fatigue. Modifications in specific daytime activities may lessen depression or fatigue, and concomitantly the perception that sleep is less than adequate. Likewise, examination and modifications of cognitive factors such as beliefs about sleep, attributions about sleep problems, mythical norms of sleep behavior (e.g., every person must sleep eight hours), and the potential harm of occasional deprivation may reduce the problem by changing self-evaluations of sleep behavior (cf. Hanley, 1965; Webb, 1975). For example, awareness of the tremendous range of sleeping behavior experienced by humans may help many people in reducing their concern and excess worry about their suspected problems.

The third group of individuals comprises those who complain of poor sleep and impaired daytime functioning and whose complaints are corroborated by all-night sleep recordings. If the person is dependent on hypnotic drugs, the first order of business necessarily involves a withdrawal program. Once freed from the use of drugs, subsequent steps should be taken to diagnose the insomnia. Finding out that the cause of poor sleep is not clearly physiological would be the next step (cf. Table A-2). If no physical dysfunction can be found, a third diagnostic step should involve discriminating between acute and chronic cases of insomnia. Acute cases might be associated with transient life situations (e.g., final exams or an impending divorce). Teaching the client to modify stressors (rearranging the environment) and/or respond differently to them (e.g., relaxing at bedtime) could represent effective treatment strategies. Again, the preferred strategy to use would depend upon the intensive study of the individual case.

Finally, for those whose insomnia is both chronic and debilitating, it would be necessary to try to identify the specific nature of the sleep disorder, assess possible contributing factors, and develop treatment approaches based on these assessments (cf. Thoresen and Coates, 1976). A variety of personal actions and environmental stimuli may contribute to inadequate sleep. Excessive worry about sleep, cognitive and physiological arousal at bedtime, daytime stress and tension, depression, or disharmonized oscillating bodily functions may *all* comprise antecedent factors. If tension is an important antecedent, progressive muscle relaxation, training in cognitive focusing (self-hypnosis), physical exercise programs, or meditation may be appropriate. Combinations of these may be needed. Additional self-control strategies might be employed to help persons manage worry about sleep or daytime actions that seem to set the stage for poor sleep. Completely different strategies might be needed when the com-

TABLE A-4
Varieties of Sleep Experiences

Category	*All-Night Polygraphic Data*	*Self-Reports of Sleep*	*Daytime Functioning*
No sleep problem	Normal	Normal	Normal
Statistically rare sleep	Rare	Rare	No reported problems
Complaint of poor sleep	Normal	Abnormal/ poor	Sleepy, fatigued/ depressed
Complaint of poor sleep	Abnormal/ poor	Abnormal/ poor	Sleepy, Fatigued/ Depressed

plaint is latency to sleep onset as opposed to extended or frequent nighttime awakenings or early final awakening in the morning.

RESEARCH STRATEGIES

Research strategies also need to reflect the heterogeneity of insomnia. Experiments with individual subjects (or a few subjects) using intensive designs are useful in accommodating the individual differences and idiosyncratic patterns characteristic of insomnia (Hersen and Barlow, 1976; Thoresen, in press). These research strategies are extremely valuable in studying several measures simultaneously over time with each subject serving as his own "self-control." Intensive designs also allow for *replication* of effects across subjects suffering from similar complaints and contributing causes.

When factorial group designs are used, every effort must be made to screen and select homogeneous groups of subjects, even though somewhat arbitrary criteria may need to be employed. Continued failure to recognize and systematically accommodate various kinds of insomnia will lead to a morass of conflicting results and unexplainable variability. It may be discovered that various kinds of insomnia related to different antecedent factors can be treated using similar procedures. But this determination should be based on evaluations with homogeneous subjects to insure better experimental control.

TABLE A–5

Diagnostic Procedures and Treatment Alternatives for Managing "Insomnia"

Step 1: Person Complains of Poor Sleep and Daytime Fatigue		
Step 2: Assess Medication Use		
If person is dependent on hypnotic medication or alcohol to obtain sleep	→	Begin drug withdrawal: Stabilize sleep using safer drug and withdraw at a rate of one therapeutic dose per week.
Step 3: Physical Examination/All-Night Sleep Recording		
If insomnia secondary to physical or neurological disorder (e.g. sleep apnea) as indicated by medical examination and/or allnight recording	→	Treat by medical procedures appropriate to disorder.
Step 4: Psychological Evaluation/Behavioral Analysis		
Pseudo-Insomnia: If complaint is not verified by all-night sleep recording	→	Assist client in assessing possible cause of complaint (e.g. excessive depression, daytime tension) and provide treatment based on assessment.
Transient: If insomnia is a result of some transient problem.	→	Teach client strategies for managing and resolving problems causing poor sleep.
Chronic: If insomnia is longstanding and chronic	→	Assist client in assessing possible contributing conditions; teach clients to change, modify, or cope with conditions and behaviors antecedent to poor sleep.

IN SUMMARY

Insomnia represents a major health problem; its effects are even more deleterious when the hazards of current hypnotic drugs are taken into account. Behavioral procedures offer promise in providing alternatives to help people obtain more adequate sleep in ways not likely to cause further physical or psychological harm. The beginnings of a useful research foundation in this area are being laid. The development of clinically useful procedures await controlled and rigorous study at the theoretical as well as empirical level. Some promising beginnings have been made but we are still a long way from asserting with confidence that nondrug alternatives are available for sleeping problems.

REFERENCES

ANLIKER, J., Variation in alpha voltage of the EEG and time perception. *Science*, 1963, *140*, 1307–1309.

BAEKELAND, F., D. KOULACK, and R. LASKY, Effects of a stressful presleep experience on electroencephalograph-recorded sleep. *Psychophysiology,* 1968, *4*.

BALTER, M., and LEVINE, J. Character and extent of psychotherapeutic drug usage in the United States. *Proceedings of the Fifth World Congress on Psychiatry, Mexico City, 1971.*

BAYH, B., *Barbiturate abuse in the United States.* Report of the Subcommittee to Investigate Juvenile Delinquency to the Committee in the Judiciary, United States Senate, 1972. Washington, D.C.: Government Printing Office, 1972.

BERNSTEIN, D. A., and G. L. PAUL, Some comments on therapy analogue research with small animal "Phobias." *Journal of Behavior Therapy and Experimental Psychiatry,* 1971, *2*, 225–237.

Binns, E., *The anatomy of sleep; or the art of procuring sound and refreshing slumber at will.* London: John Churchill, 1842.

Bixler, E. O., A. Kales, L. A. Leo, and T. Slye, A comparison of subjective estimates and objective sleep laboratory findings in insomniac patients. *Sleep Research,* 1974, *4,* 143.

Bootzin, R. R., Stimulus control treatment for insomnia. Paper presented at the meeting of the American Psychological Association, Honolulu, 1972.

Bootzin, R. R., Stimulus control of insomnia. Paper presented at the meeting of the American Psychological Association, Montreal, 1973.

Borkovec, T. D., and D. C. Fowles, A controlled investigation of the effects of progressive and hypnotic relaxation on insomnia. *Journal of Abnormal Psychology,* 1973, *82,* 124–133.

Borkovec, T. D., S. W. Steinmark, and S. D. Nau, Relaxation training and single-item desensitization in the group treatment of insomnia. *Journal of Behavior Therapy and Experimental Psychology,* 1973, *4,* 401–403.

Borkovec, T. O., D. G. Kaloupek, and K. M. Slama, The facilitative effect of muscle tension release in the relaxation treatment of sleep disturbance. *Behavior Therapy,* 1975, *6,* 301–309.

Borkovec, T. D., and Werts, T. E. Effects of progressive relaxation on sleep disturbance: An electroencephalographic evaluation. *Psychosomatic Medicine,* 1976, *38,* 173–180.

Bremer, F., Historical development of ideas on sleep. In O. Petre-Quadens and J. D. Schlag, eds., *Basic sleep mechanisms.* New York: Academic Press, 1974. Pp. 3–12.

Carskadon, M. A., W. E. Dement, M. M., Mitler, C. Guilleminault, V. P. Zarcone, and R. Spiegel. Self-reports versus sleep laboratory findings in 122 drug-free subjects with complaints of chronic insomnia. *American Journal of Psychiatry,* 1976, *133,* 1382–1388.

Coates, T. J., and C. E. Thoresen. Using generalizability theory in behavioral observations. Unpublished manuscript, Stanford University, 1976.

Cohen, D. B., and C. Cox, Neuroticism in the sleep laboratory: Implications for representational and adaptive properties of dreaming. *Journal of Abnormal Psychology,* 1975, *84,* 91–108.

Cone, J. D. Multitrait-multimethod matrices in behavioral assessment. Paper presented at the meetings of the American Psychological Association, Washington, September, 1976.

Coursey, R. D., R. Buchsbaum, and G. L. Frankel, Personality measures and evoked responses in chronic insomniacs. *Journal of Abnormal Psychology,* 1975, *84,* 239–249.

Crisp, A. N., and E. Stonehill. *Sleep, nutrition, and mood.* New York: Wiley, 1976.

Crisp, A. H. E. Stonehill, and G. W. Fenton, The relationship between sleep, nutrition, and mood: A study of patients with anorexia nervosa. *Postgraduate Medical Journal,* 1971, *47,* 207–213.

Cronback, L. J., Beyond the Two Disciplines of scientific psychology. *American Psychologist,* 1975, *30,* 116–127.

Davison, G. C., N. Tsujimoto, and A. G. Glaros, Attribution and the maintenance of behavior change in falling asleep. *Journal of Abnormal Psychology,* 1973, *82,* 124–133.

Dement, W. C., Sleep deprivation and the organization of the behavioral states. In C. Clemente, D. Purpura, and F. Mayer, eds., *Sleep and the maturing nervous system.* New York: Academic Press, 1972. pp. 319–361. (a)

Dement, W. C., *Some must watch while some must sleep.* Stanford, Ca.: Stanford Alumni Association, 1972. (b)

Dement, W. C., M. A. Carskadon, M. M. Mitler, C. Guilleminault, and V. P. Zarcone, A description of sleep in 122 drug-free insomniacs. Unpublished manuscript, Stanford University, 1976.

Dement, W. C., C. Guilleminault, Sleep disorders: The state of the art. *Hospital Practice,* 1973, *8,* 57–71.

Dement, W. C., and M. M. Mitler, New developments in the basic mechanisms of sleep. In G. Usdin, ed., *Sleep research and clinical practice.* New York: Bruner/Mazel, 1972, pp. 3–22.

Dement, W. C., and M. M. Mitler, An introduction to sleep. In O. Petre-Quadens, and J. D. Schlag, ed., *Basic sleep mechanisms.* New York: Academic Press, 1974.

Dement, W. C., and M. M. Mitler, An overview of sleep research: Past, present, and future. In D. Hamburg and K. Brodie, eds., *American Handbook of Psychiatry,* Vol. 6. New York: Basic Books, 1976.

DEMENT, W. C., H. SMYTHE, E. HODDES, C. GUILLEMINAULT, M. CARSKADON, R. WILSON, and V. ZARCONE, Need all-night EEG. *Electroencephalography and Clinical Neurophysiology,* 1974, *36,* 210.

EVANS, G., Insomnia. *St. Bartholomew Hospital Journal,* 1935, *43,* 55–58.

EVANS, D.R., and I. K. BOND, Reciprocal inhibition therapy and classical conditioning in the treatment of insomnia. *Behavior Research and Therapy,* 1965, *7,* 323–325.

FARROW, E. P., A psychoanalytical method of getting to sleep. *Journal of Neurology Psychopathology,* 1925, *6,* 123–125.

FEINSTEIN, B., M. B. STERMAN, and R. MACDONALD, Effects of sensorimotor rhythm biofeedback training on sleep. *Sleep Research,* 1974, *3,* 134.

FOULKES, W., and G. VOGEL, Mental activity at sleep onset. *Journal of Abnormal Psychology,* 1965, *70,* 231–243.

FRANKEL, G. L., B. M. PATTEN, and J. C. GILLIN, Restless legs syndrome. *Journal of the American Medical Association.* 1974, *230,* 1302–1303.

FREEDMAN, R. R. Biofeedback and progressive relaxation treatment of sleep-onset insomnia: A controlled all-night investigation. (Doctoral dissertation, University of Michigan). *Dissertation Amtracts International,* 1976, *36 (3),* 3037

FREEMON, G. L., *Sleep research: A critical review.* Springfield, In.: Thomas, 1972.

FRY, A., Hypnosis in the treatment of insomnia. *British Journal of Clinical Hypnosis,* 1963, *4,* 23–28.

GEER, J. H., and E. S. KATKIN, Treatment of insomnia using a variant of systematic desensitization: A case report. *Journal of Abnormal Psychology,* 1966, *71,* 161–164.

GERSHMAN, L., and R. A. CLOUSER, Treating insomnia with relaxation and desensitization in a group setting by an automated approach. *Journal of Behavior Therapy and Experimental Psychiatry,* 1974, *5,* 31–35.

GLASS, G. V., V. L. WILLSON, and J. M. GOTTMAN, *Design and analysis of time-series experiments.* Boulder, Co.: Colorado Associated Universities Press, 1975.

GLAZIER, W. W., The task of medicine. *Scientific American,* 1973, *228,* 13-17.

GUILLEMINAULT, C., F. L. ELDRIDGE, and W. C. DEMENT, Insomnia with sleep apnea: A new syndrome. *Science,* 1973, *31,* 856-858.

HAMMOND, E. C., Some preliminary findings on physical complaints from a prospective study of 1,064,004 men and women. *American Journal of Public Health,* 1974, *54,* 11-22.

HANLEY, F. W., Modern hypnotherapy. *Applied Therapeutics,* 1965, *7,* 625-628.

HARTMANN, E. L., *The function of sleep.* New Haven: Yale University Press, 1973.

HAURI, P., and R. GOOD. Frontalis muscle tension and sleep onset. Unpublished manuscript, Dartmouth Medical School, 1974.

HAYNES, S. N., D. R. FOLLINGSTEAD, and W. T. MCGOWAN, Insomnia: Sleep patterns and anxiety level. *Journal of Psychosomatic Research,* 1974, *18,* 69-74.

HAYNES, S. N., S. WOODWARD, R. MORAN, and D. ALEXANDER, Relaxation treatment of insomnia. *Behavior Therapy,* 1974, *5,* 555-558.

HAYNES, S. N., M. G. PRICE, and J. B. SIMONS, Stimulus control treatment of insomnia. *Journal of Behavior Therapy and Experimental Psychiatry,* 1975, *6,* 279-282.

HAYNES, S.N., H. SIDES, and G. LOCKWOOD, Relaxation instructions and electromagnetic biofeedback intervention with insomnia. *Behavior Therapy,* in press.

HERSEN, M., and D. BARLOW, *Single care experimental studies: Strategies for studying behavior change.* New York: Pergamon, 1976.

HINKLE, J. E., and E. R. LUTHER, Insomnia: A new approach. *Psychotherapy: Theory, Research, and Practice,* 1972, *9,* 236-237.

HODDES, E., M. CARSKADON, R. PHILLIPS, V. ZARCONE, and W. DEMENT, Total sleep time in insomniacs. *Sleep Research,* 1972, *2,* 152.

JACOBSON, E., *You can sleep well. The ABC's of restful sleep for the average person.* New York: McGraw-Hill, 1938.

JOHNSON, L., Are stages of sleep related to waking behavior? *American Scientist,* 1973, *61,* 326–338.

JOHNSON, L., and W. McLEOD, Sleep and awake behavior during gradual sleep reduction. *Perceptual and Motor Skills,* 1973, *36,* 87–97.

JONES, H. S., and I. OSWALD, Two cases of healthy insomnia. *Electroencephalography and Clinical Neurophysiology,* 1968, *24,* 378–380.

KAHN, M., B. L. BAKER, and J. M. WEISS, Treatment of insomnia by relaxation training. *Journal of Abnormal Psychology,* 1968, *73,* 556–558.

KALES, A., The evaluation and treatment of sleep disorders: Pharmacological and psychological studies. In M. H. Chase, ed., *The sleeping brain: Perspective in the brain sciences,* Vol. 1. University of California at Los Angeles: Brain Research Institute, 1972. Pp. 447–491.

KALES, A., E. O. BIXLER, I. A. LEO, S. HEALY, and E. SLYE, Incidence of insomnia in the Los Angeles metropolitan area. *Sleep Research,* 1974, *4,* 139.

KALES, A., and G. CARY, Insomnia, evaluation and treatment. *Medical World News,* 1971, *11* (Annual Psychiatry Supplement), 85–86.

KALES, A., and J. D. KALES, Sleep Disorders: Recent findings in the diagnosis and treatment of disturbed sleep. *New England Journal of Medicine,* 1974, *299,* 487–497.

KARACAN, I., R. L. WILLIAMS, P. J. SALIS, and C. J. HIRSCH, New approaches to the evaluation and treatment of insomnia: Preliminary results. *Psychosomatics,* 1971, *12,* 81–88.

KAZDIN, A. E., Self-monitoring and behavior change. In M. J. Mahoney and C. E. Thoresen, *Self-control: Power to the person.* Monterey, Cal.: Brooks-Cole, 1974. Pp. 218–246

KELLOGG, R., and R. S. BARON, Attribution theory, insomnia, and the reverse placebo effect: A reversal of Storms and Nisbett's findings. *Journal of Personality and Social Psychology,* 1975, *32,* 231–236.

KLEITMAN, N., *Sleep and wakefulness.* Chicago: University of Chicago Press, 1963.

KNAPP, T. J., D. L. DOWNS, and J. R. ALPERSON, Behavior therapy for insomnia: A review and critique. *Behavior Therapy,* 1976, *7,* 614–625.

Lackenmeyer, C. W., Experimentation—misunderstood methodology in psychological and social psychological research research. *American Psychologist,* 1970, *25,* 617–624.

Lugaresi, E., G. Coccagna, and G. B. Cerni, Restless legs syndrome and nocturnal myoclonus. In W. Gastaut, ed., *The abnormalities of sleep in man.* Bologna, Italy: Aulo Gaggi, 1968. Pp. 285–294.

Marks, I. M., Behavioral treatments of phobias and obsessive-compulsive disorders. In M. Hersen, P. M. Miller, and R. M. Eisler, eds., *Progress in behavior modification,* Vol. 1. New York: Academic, 1975.

McGhie, A., and S. M. Russell, The subjective assessment of normal sleep patterns. *Journal of Mental Science,* 1962, *108,* 642–650.

Meddis, R., A. J. D. Pearson, and G. Langford, An extreme case of healthy insomnia. *Electroencephalography and Clinical Neurophysiology,* 1973, *35,* 213–214.

Mitchell, K. R., and White, R. G., Self-management of severe predormitional insomnia. *Journal of Behavior Therapy and Experimental Psychiatry,* in press.

Monroe, L. J. Psychological and physiological differences between good and poor sleepers. *Journal of Abnormal Psychology,* 1968, *72,* 255–264.

Monroe, L. J. Inter-rates reliability and the role of experience in scoring EEG records. *Psychophysiology,* 1969, *5,* 376–384.

Montgomery, I., G. Perkins, and D. Wise, A review of behavioral treatment for insomnia. *Journal of Behavior Therapy and Experimental Psychiatry,* 1975, *6,* 93–100.

Moruzzi, G. Find remarks. In O. Petre-Quaden and J. D. Schlag, eds., *Basic sleep mechanisms.* New York: Academic, 1974.

Nicassio, P., and R. Bootzin, A comparison of progressive relaxation and autogenic training as treatments for insomnia. *Journal of Abnormal Psychology,* 1974, *83,* 253–260.

Nicolis, P., and L. G. Silvestri. Hypnotic activity of placebo in relation to serenity of insomnia: A quantitative evaluation. *Clinical Pharmacology and Therapeutics,* 1967, *8,* 841–848.

Paul, G. L., Inhibition of physiological response to stressful imagery by relaxation training and hypnotically suggested relaxation. *Behavior Research and Therapy,* 1969, *7,* 249–256.

PENDLETON, L. R., and D. L TASTO, Effects of metronome-conditioned relaxation, metronome-induced relaxation, and progressive muscle relaxation in insomnia. *Behavior Research and Therapy,* 1976, *14,* 165–166.

PHILLIPS, R. L., M. M. MITLER, and W. C. DEMENT, Alpha sleep in chronic insomniacs. *Sleep Research,* 1974, *4,* 143.

POSER, E. G., G. W. FENTON, and L. SCOTTON, The classical conditioning of sleep and wakefulness. *Behavior Research and Therapy,* 1965, *3,* 259–264.

RASKIN, M., G. JOHNSON, and J. W. RONDESTVELDT, Chronic anxiety corrected by feedback-induced muscle relaxation. *Archives of General Psychiatry,* 1973, *28,* 263–267.

RECHSTSCHAFFEN, A., Polygraphic aspects of insomnia. In W. Gastaut, ed., *The abnormalities of sleep in man.* Bolognia, Italy: Aulo Gaggi, 1968

RECHTSCHAFFEN, A., and A. KALES, eds., *A manual of standardized terminology, techniques, and scoring system for sleep stages of human subjects.* Washington, D.C.: Public Health Service, U.S. Government Printing Office, 1968.

RIBORDY, S. C. The behavioral treatment of insomnia. (Doctoral dissertation, University of Kansas). *Dissertation Abstracts International,* 1976, *36*(B), 477.

ROSEN, G. R., Is it really necessary to use mildly phobic analogue subjects? *Behavior Therapy,* 1975, *6,* 68–71.

ROTH, T., M. DRAMER, and J. SCHWARTZ, Some preliminary observations on the nature of insomniac patients. *Sleep Research,* 1974, *4,* 145.

SPIEGEL, R., A survey of insomnia in the San Francisco Bay Area. Unpublished manuscript, Stanford University Sleep Disorders Clinic, 1973.

STEINMARK, S. W., and T. D. BORKOVEC, The effects of active and placebo treatment effects on insomnia under counterdemand and positive demand instructions. *Journal of Abnormal Psychology,* 1974, *83,* 157–163.

STONEHILL, E., and A. H. CRISP, Aspects of the relationship between sleep, weight and mood. *Psychosomatics,* 1973, *22,* 148–158.

STORMS, M. D., and R. E. NISBETT, Insomnia and the attribution process. *Journal of Personality and Social Psychology,* 1970, *16,* 319–328.

STUNKARD, A. J., From explanation to action in psychosomatic medicine: The case of obesity. *Psychosomatic Medicine,* 1975, *37,* 195–236.

THORESEN, C. E., *Let's get intensive: Single-case research.* Englewood Cliffs, N.J.: Prentice-Hall, in press.

THORESEN, C. E., and T. J. COATES, Behavioral self-control: Some clinical concerns. In M. Hersen, R. M. Eisler, and P. M. Miller, eds., *Progress in behavior modification.* Vol. 2. New York: Academic, 1976.

THORESEN, C. E., and M. J. MAHONEY, *Behavioral self-control.* New York: Holt, Rinehart and Winston, 1974.

TOKARZ, T. P., and P. S. LAWRENCE, An analysis of temporal and stimulus factors in the treatment of insomnia. Paper presented at the meeting of the Association for the Advancement of Behavior Therapy, Chicago, 1974.

TRAUB, A. C., B. JENCKS, and E. L. BLISS, Effects of relaxation training on chronic insomnia. *Sleep Research,* 1973, *3,* 164.

WEBB, W. B., Sleep as an adaptive response. *Perceptual and Motor Skills,* 1974, *38,* 1023–1027.

______________, *Sleep: The gentle tyrant.* Englewood Cliffs, N.J.: Prentice-Hall, 1975.

WEIL, G., and M. R. GOLDFRIED, Treatment of insomnia in an eleven-year-old child through self-relaxation. *Behavior Therapy,* 1973, *4,* 282–294.

WEISS, B. L., R. J. MCPARTLAND, and D. J. KUPFER, Once more: The inaccuracy of non-EEG estimations of sleep. *American Journal of Psychiatry,* 1973, *130,* 1282–1285.

WILLIAMS, R. L., I. KARACAN, and C. J. HURSCH, *EEG of human sleep: Clinical applications.* New York: Wiley, 1974.

WOOLFOLK, R. L., C. CARR-KAFFASNAN, T. F. MCNULTY, and P. M. LEHRER, Meditation training as treatment for insomnia. *Behavior Therapy,* 1976, *7,* 359–365.

ZARCONE, V., Narcolepsy. *New England Journal of Medicine,* 1975, *280.* 1156–1166.

ZUNG, W., Insomnia and disordered sleep. *International Psychiatric Clinics,* 1970, *7,* 123–146.

Appendix B

For Further Reading

BEHAVIORAL SELF—MANAGEMENT

Social learning approaches to counseling and therapy have come a long way since their inception in the early 1950s. Therapeutic techniques, once limited to the applications of reinforcers and punishers or the use of systematic desensitization, have expanded considerably. Therapies derived from a social-learning rationale now include a wide range of procedures and involve attempts to help people change thoughts and feelings, as well as visible actions. Importantly, the theoretical basis of these therapies has grown. Thoughts and emotions are conceptualized as integral to understanding behavior and a person's behavior is no longer viewed as determined solely by an unyielding environment. Rather, we are in a reciprocal relationship with our surroundings: the environment influences our behavior, but our behavior, in turn, also partially determines the makeup of our environment. The important implication of this point of view is that people can learn to modify their personal environments—cognitive, social, and physical—to change their behaviors in personally meaningful directions.

It is this approach to change, termed behavioral self-management, that we have adopted and presented here. The readings listed offer basic information regarding social-learning approaches to therapy in general, behavioral self-management in particular, and research in some of the techniques presented in this text.

IF YOU ARE NEW TO BEHAVIORAL SELF-MANAGEMENT

Several excellent texts have recently become available, designed to acquaint the mental health practitioner or interested nonprofessional with behavior therapy techniques. If you are relatively unfamiliar with this field but want to learn more about it or gain some expertise in the area, some of the texts listed might be helpful.

BERNSTEIN, D. D., and T. D. BORKOVEC, *Progressive relaxation training.* Champaign, Ill.: Research, 1973. A well done manual for the practitioner of progressive relaxation.

CORMIER, W. W., and L. S. CORMIER, *Behavioral counseling.* Boston: Houghton Mifflin, 1975. A practical introduction to the purposes, principles, and procedures of behavioral counseling and therapy. A useful place for the novice in this area to begin reading.

GOLDFRIED, M., and G. C. DAVISON, *Clinical behavior therapy.* New York: Holt, Rinehart and Winston, 1976. Presents behavior therapy as it is practiced, and attempts to describe the way therapists move from general social-learning principles to clinical applications.

GOTTMAN, J. M., and D. R. LIEBLUM, *How to do psychotherapy and how to evaluate it.* New York: Holt, Rinehart and Winston: 1974. A pragmatic introduction to the flow and practice of behavioral counseling and therapy. Helpful for the beginner or the counselor who wants to integrate behavioral approaches into daily counseling practice.

KRUMBOLTZ, J. D., and C. E. THORESEN, *Behavioral counseling.* New York: Holt, Rinehart and Winston, 1969, and KRUMBOLTZ, J. D., and C. E. THORESEN, *Counseling methods.* New York: Holt, Rinehart and Winston, 1976. These two texts present a series of case studies demonstrating the applications of a variety of behavior-therapy techniques to diverse problem behaviors. The case studies are designed to help the reader understand and learn the processes of behavior therapy as well as its outcomes. The second volume updates with new cases, but does not replace, the first text.

MAHONEY, M. J., and C. E. THORESEN, *Self-control: Power to the person.* Monterey, Cal.: Brooks-Cole, 1974. The first five chapters present a lively and easy-to-read introduction to behavioral self-management. Thirteen readings of varying difficulty follow.

TECHNICAL BOOKS

Social Learning Theory and Behavior Therapy. The following texts provide reviews and formulations of the theoretical and empirical foundations of social learning approaches to counseling and therapy.

BANDURA, A., *Principles of behavior modification.* New York: Hold, Rinehart and Winston, 1969, and BANDURA, A., *Social learning theory.* Englewood Cliffs, N.J.: Prentice-Hall, 1977. Both texts present complete reviews of the theory of and research in social learning theory. These books presume some background in the area. Even the psychologist not conversant in social learning approaches might begin with other texts before attempting to read these comprehensive volumes.

CRAIGHEAD, W. E., A. E. KAZDIN, and M. J. MAHONEY, *Behavior modification: Principles, issues, and applications.* Boston: Houghton Mifflin, 1976. A text designed to familiarize the reader with the basic principles, major assumptions and issues in behavior therapy. Ten introductory chapters are followed by chapters by experts reviewing and demonstrating the applications of behavior modification to diverse problem areas.

HERSEN, M., R. M. EISLER, and P. MILLER, *Progress in behavior modification.* New York: Academic, 1975 (Vol. 1); 1976 (Vol. 2);

1977 (Vol. 3). This is a series of yearly updates in the general field of behavior therapy. Each volume contains invited reviews by prominent researchers and covers a range of topics including research methods, ethical considerations, treatment techniques, and related problem areas.

HILGARD, E. W., and G. W. BOWER, *Theories of learning.* (4th Ed.) Englewood Cliffs, N.J.: Prentice-Hall, 1975. A comprehensive review of modern learning theory as it has developed during the twentieth century. The final chapters offer interesting predictions of future directions.

KATZ, R. C., and S. ZLUTNICK, *Behavioral therapy and health care: Principles and applications.* New York: Pergamon, 1974. Overview of procedures and problems in the application of behavioral strategies to problems traditionally considered "medical."

MAHONEY, M. J., *Cognition and behavior modification.* Boston: Ballinger, 1974. This book offers a good overview of cognitive psychology and shows how it might be integrated theoretically and clinically with behavior therapy approaches.

SKINNER, B. F., *Science and human behavior.* New York: Macmillan, 1953. This is must reading for the person interested in looking at the roots of modern behavior therapy. An interesting view of self-control.

Behavioral Self-Management. This area represents a relatively new development within the behavior therapy arena. Although much work remains to be done in conceptualizing basic self-management processes and in explaining their therapeutic utility, a few texts have emerged to describe the progress of research to date.

GOLDFRIED, M. R., and M. MERBAUM, (eds.), *Behavior change through self-control.* New York: Holt, Rinehart and Winston, 1973.

KANFER, F. A., and A. P. GOLDSTEIN (eds.), *Helping people change.* New York: Pergamon, 1975.

THORESEN, C. E., and M. J. MAHONEY, *Behavioral self-control.* New York: Holt, Rinehart and Winston, 1974.

Related Techniques. Behavioral self-management can include any procedure designed to help persons gain greater personal control over psychological, social, or physical functioning. Several of the procedures presented in this text are drawn from diverse fields and persuasions. Included here are some basic references to these procedures and their scientific and clinical foundations.

BARBER, T. X. *Hypnosis: A scientific approach.* New York: Van Nostrand, Reinhold, 1969. A theory of hypnosis from an outstanding researcher in the field.

BARBER, T. X., L. V. DICARA, J. KAMIYA, N. E. MILLER, D. SHAPIRO, and J. STOYVA, *Biofeedback and self-control.* Chicago: Aldine, 1973–76. Published annually since 1973, these volumes present a generous selection of original research reports in the area of biofeedback and related techniques (meditation, yoga, autogenic training, and self-hypnosis).

HILGARD, E. R., *Hypnotic susceptibility.* New York: Harcourt, Brace, Jovanovich, 1965. A review of hypnosis research, a theoretical exploration of hypnotic phenomena, and a discussion of its therapeutic potential.

JACOBSON, E., *Progressive relaxation.* Chicago: University of Chicago Press, 1929, and JACOBSON, E., *You can sleep well: The ABC's of restful sleep for the average person.* New York: McGraw-Hill, 1938. These two texts explain progressive relaxation and explore its potential in helping people with various problems. Like many scientific advances, its acceptance and widespread use has taken time.

LE CRON, L., *Self-hypnosis.* Englewood Cliffs, N.J.: Prentice-Hall, 1964. A readable presentation, for the lay person, of self-hypnosis.

SCHULTZ, J. H., and W. LUTHE, *Autogenic training.* New York: Grune and Stratton, 1959. A series of volumes which offers an alternative relaxation strategy, similar to self-hypnosis. Useful in learning to relax physically and mentally; some clients prefer this to progressive relaxation.

PROFESSIONAL JOURNALS

With the rising interest in social-learning approaches to therapy has also come an increasing number of professional journals designed specifically to report work in this area.

Behavior Therapy (Cyril M. Franks, Editor, Graduate School of Professional Psychology, Rutgers University, New Brunswick, N.J. 08903) is an interdisciplinary journal that publishes research results contributing to the theory or practice of behavior therapy. Problem applications and settings are quite diverse; book reviews, case studies, and methodological notes are also included.

The *Journal of Behavior Therapy and Experimental Psychiatry* (Dr. Joseph Wolpe, Editor, Eastern Pennsylvania Institute, 3300 Henry Avenue, Philadelphia, Pa. 19129) is designed to bring behavior therapy into the domain of the psychiatrist. Research studies and case reports in a wide variety of problem behaviors and settings are presented.

The *Journal of Applied Behavior Analysis* (K. Daniel O'Leary, Editor, Department of Psychology, State University of New York at Stony Brook, Stony Brook, New York) publishes reports of experimental research demonstrating the utility of the experimental analysis of behavior with human problems. Single-subject research designs prevail, and problem areas and treatment procedures reported tend to be less diverse than the other behavior therapy journals.

Behavior Research and Therapy (H. J. Eysenck, Editor, Institute of Psychiatry, Department of Psychology, De Crespigny Park Road, Denmark Hall, London, England SE5 8A2), the oldest of the behavior therapy journals, presents reports from a variety of disciplines in the application of the principles of learning theory and the experimental method with (in some cases) neurotic and psychotic problems.

Finally, the journals of the American Psychological Association (1200 Seventeenth St., N.W., Washington, D.C. 20036) are devoting an increasing number of pages to social learning issues and evaluations of behavior therapy. *The Journal of Consulting and Clinical Psychology* deals with approaches to the diagnosis and treatment of disordered behavior and *The Journal of Counseling Psychology* describes applications of therapies in academic, home, and industrial settings. *The Journal of Abnormal Behavior* publishes articles dealing with the etiology or descriptive pathology of abnormal behavior.*

THE STUDY OF SLEEP

Sleep, of course, has fascinated man for centuries, but only recently has the scientific study of sleep and its disorders become more widespread. If you are interested in pursuing research or clinical work in the area of sleep disorders, we believe it essential that you have a basic familiarity with the procedures and findings of modern sleep research. Or, you may just be curious about sleep and want to explore it just to satisfy your intellectual interests. Finding your way into and through new literature can be difficult. Our road map can help.

These seven books provide coverage of contemporary sleep research, its methods of procedure, and some of its important findings.

DEMENT, W. C., *Some must watch while some must sleep.* San Francisco: Freeman, 1976. Professor Dement, Director of the Stanford University Sleep Disorders Clinic, provides an illuminating and entertaining overview of sleep, described mostly in terms of his research in the area. Stressed are the pathologies of sleep and dreams and REM sleep; these have been Dr. Dement's continuing research interests.

KLEITMAN, N., *Sleep and wakefulness.* Chicago: University of Chicago Press, 1963. This is a 1963 edition was originally published in 1939. An encyclopedic compilation of sleep research prior to 1963, this text documents foundations of contemporary research by a famous and influential sleep researcher.

*Two new journals are *Behavior Modification* (Mischel Hersen, Editor, Western Psychiatric Institute and Clinic, School of Medicine, University of Pittsburgh, Pittsburgh, Penn. 15261, and *Cognitive Therapy and Research* (Michael J. Mahoney, Editor, Department of Psychology, Pennsylvania State University, State College, Penn.

LUCE, G. G., *Body time: Physiological rhythms and social stress*. New York: Pantheon, 1971. A well-written and understandable exposition of circadian rhythms for the lay reader.

_____, *Insomnia: The guide for troubled sleepers*. Garden City, N.Y.: Doubleday, 1969.

LUCE, G. G., and J. SEGAL, *Sleep*. New York: Coward-McCann, 1966. This book, originally written to describe sleep research programs supported by the National Institutes of Health, describes the world of sleep research in the 1960s.

WEBB, W. B., *Sleep: The gentle tyrant*. Englewood Cliffs, N.J.: Prentice-Hall, 1975. W.B. Webb, a professor of psychology at the University of Florida, has studied the reasons why we sleep, the implications of shortening sleep, and sleeping at various times of the day. He provides an interesting nontechnical overview of basic knowledge about sleep from this perspective.

_____, *Sleep: An active process*. Glenview, Ill.: Foresman, 1973. This excellent book presents seven seminal articles about the physiology of sleep with a commentary on each by the original author. While somewhat advanced, the format permits the student to see the "process" of research.

WEBB, W., and H. AGNEW, *Sleep and dreams*. Dubuque, Iowa: Brown. A brief introduction to the characteristics of sleep and its major variations such as age, time, and pathology.

Dreams. Dreams stimulate professional and general curiosity. Their biological and psychological significance remain a source of controversy and research.

FARADAY, A., *Dream power*. New York: Coward-McCann, 1972. This book, divided into three parts, reviews the "new research" on REM sleep and dream content, the methods of dreams interpretation and the author's synthesis, and the applications of dream interpretations. Both a provocative and interesting book.

FOULKES, W. D., *The psychology of sleep*. New York: Scribner, 1966. A comprehensive account of dream activity, integrating laboratory findings and psychological approaches to the topic.

FREUD, S., *The interpretation of dreams*. London: Allen and Irwin, 1954.

JUNG, C. G., *Modern man in search of a soul.* London: Trubner, 1933. Two interesting expositions of the psychoanalytic approach to dreams, their significance, and their interpretation.

HALL, C., *The meaning of dreams.* New York: Dell, 1959.

HALL, C., and R. VAN de CASTLE, *The content analysis of dreams.* New York: Appleton-Century-Crofts, 1966. Two books relating the techniques and findings from content analysis of dreams.

WOODS, R., and W. GREENHOUSE, *The new world of dreams.* New York: Macmillan, 1974. This is a very excellent anthology of writings on sleep and dreams from the beginning to the present.

Literary Resources. The importance of sleep is reflected in the diversity of persons writing about it. No list of readings would be complete without some literary references. After all, the poets may see more than anyone!

CAMDEN, C., *Shakespeare on sleep and dreams.* Houston, Tex.: Rice Institute, 1936. The bard had many penetrating insights.

RUBENSTEIN, H., *Insomniacs of the world, goodnight.* New York: Random House, 1974. This is an interesting and fun account of famous insomniacs and their personal reflections.

TECHNICAL BOOKS

Several books have been published in recent years that attempt to summarize and review findings to date. Several are listed here, and these volumes are usually appropriate for the person who has a fundamental understanding of basic terminology and methods in sleep research. Additionally, many edited volumes, containing symposium papers from experts in diverse branches of sleep research, have been published in recent years. These are excellent resources for updating your knowledge in an area of special interest to you.

SYMPOSIA AND CONFERENCE PROCEEDINGS.

CHASE, M., *The sleeping brain.* Los Angeles: Brain Research Institute, 1971. A series of symposia held at the first International Congress of the Association for the Psychophysiological Study of Sleep.

GASTAUT, H., E. LUGARESI, G. B. CERINI, and G. COCCAGNA, *The abnormalities of sleep in man.* Bologna: Aulo Gaggi, 1968. A selection of scholarly papers on the etiology, diagnosis and treatment of sleep disorders. Attempts are made to integrate applied and basic research, and to discuss findings in terms of clinical implications.

KALES, A., *Sleep: Physiology and pathology.* Philadelphia: Lippincott, 1969. A UCLA symposium covering the characteristics, etiologies, and treatments of disordered sleep.

LAIRY, G. C., *Experimental study of human sleep: Methodological problems.* New York: Elvesier, 1975. Proceedings of an international symposium held at Bardolino, Italy in 1974. Contains papers on integrations of data from animal and human subjects in basic sleep processes, studies of dreams and their significance, the implications of theoretical propositions for sleep research, and methodological problems in sleep research.

LEVIN, P., and W. P. KOELLA, *Sleep 1974: Instinct, neurophysiology, endocrinology, episodes, dreams, epilepsy, and intracranial pathology.* Basel, Switzerland: Karger, 1975. Proceedings of the Second European Congress in Sleep Research. The six symposia presented cover the range of topics presented in the title.

PETRE-QUADENS, O., and J. D. SCHLAG, eds., *Basic sleep mechanisms.* New York: Academic, 1974. A collection of papers from the NATO Advanced Study Institute devoted to basic sleep processes. Contributions are wide ranging, from basic physiological studies and developmental aspects of sleep to discussions of clinical sleep disorders.

USDIN, G., *Sleep research and clinical practice.* New York: Bruner/Mazel, 1973. Three papers originally presented at the meetings of the American College of Psychiatrists in 1972; excellent introduction for the beginner. Dement and Mitler review basic sleep mechanisms, Williams and Karacan discuss the clinical disorders of sleep, and Kales and Kales discuss recent advances in the treatment of sleep disorders.

WEITZMAN, E., ed., *Advances in sleep research.* New York: Spectrum, 1974 (Vol. 1), 1975 (Vol. 2), 1976 (Vol. 3). These volumes are designed to supply thoughtful critical reviews of the field of sleep research from a multidisciplinary perspective. Volumes 1 and 2 cover a range of basic and applied studies of sleep and its disorders; Volume 3 is devoted to studies of and clinical treatments for narcolepsy.

LITERATURE REVIEWS AND THEORETICAL EXPOSITIONS

FREEMAN, F. R., *Sleep research: A critical review.* Springfield, Ill.: Thomas, 1972. This book, written for the nonspecialist, attempts to review and integrate sleep research findings from the variety of disciplines (psychology, physiology, biochemistry, psychoanalysis) involved in the study of the phenomenon.

HARTMANN, E., *The functions of sleep.* New Haven: Yale University Press, 1973. This a well-written but ambitious attempt to "account" for the existence of sleep, particularly REM and non-REM separately. The author, using animal research, clinical observation, drug studies, and biochemical concerns shows the range of sleep research. He provides an excellent analysis of the psychology of tiredness, a subject greatly ignored.

WILLIAMS, R. L., I. KARACAN, and C. J. HURSCH, *Electroencephalography (EEG) of human sleep: Clinical applications.* New York: Wiley, 1974. Presented are data from all-night sleep recordings regarding "normal" sleep. The data are presented by sex and age groupings. Comprehensive discussions and bibliographies of the sleep disorders are also provided. A very useful resource.

Circadian Rhythms. In this book, we have adopted the view that sleep can be understood best in the context of a daily circadian rhythm cycle. The basic characteristics, significance, and clinical implications of this cycle remain little understood, but current research is fascinating and promises to shed some light on this important phenomenon. Listed are four texts which discuss this research and chart needed experimental directions.

BROWN, F. A., *The biological clock: Two views.* New York: Academic, 1970.

BUENNING, E., *The physiological clock: Circadian rhythms and biological chronometry.* New York: Springer-Verlag, 1973.

CALQUHOUN, W. P., *Biological rhythms and human performance.* New York: Academic, 1971.

CALQUHOUN, W. P., *Aspects of human efficiency: Diurnal rhythms and loss of sleep.* London: English Universities Press, 1972.

Drugs. Hypnotic medications, of course, have remained the standard treatment for insomnia. Understanding their actions is important in treating both drug-free and drug-dependent insomniacs.

The Physicians' Desk Reference. Medical Economics Co., Litton Industries, Oradell, N.J. 07649. This volume, published annually, is an indispensable resource in retrieving up-to-date information on prescription drugs. Each of 25,000 drug products are listed by brand name, generic name, category, and company. Product identification is enhanced by color and size charts. Most important, the composition, action, dosage, effects, and precautions of each drug are presented.

ABEL, E. I., *Drugs and behavior: A primer in neuropsychopharmacology.* New York: Wiley, 1974. A discussion of the basic principles of pharmacology and the factors that affect drug action.

CLIFT, A. D., ed., *Sleep disturbance and hypnotic drug dependence.* Amsterdam: Excerpta Medica, 1975. A collection of papers discussing the various insomnias and their pharmacological treatment. The authors attempt to discuss the problems of the practicing physician in treating insomnia and yet avoid the problem associated with drug dependence.

KAGAN, F., *Hypnotics: Methods of development and evaluation.* New York: Spectrum, 1975.

Sleep Recordings. All-night sleep-recording technology remains the mainstay of modern sleep research. These two manuals provide an introduction to these measurement operations and present accepted criteria for scoring these recordings.

ANDERS, T., T. R. EMDE, and A. PARMELEE, *A manual of standardized terminology, techniques, and criteria for scoring of states of sleep and wakefulness in newborn infants.* Los Angeles: UCLA Brain Information Service, 1971.

RECHTSCHAFFEN, A., and A. KALES, *Manual of standardized terminology, techniques, and scoring system for sleep stages in human subjects.* Bethesda, Md.: U.S. National Institute of Neurological Diseases and Blindness, 1968.

PROFESSIONAL JOURNALS

Sleep research is, of necessity, an interdisciplinary endeavor; understanding its basic processes precludes a unidimensional view. Keeping up with biological, sociological, biochemical, neurological, and psychological developments can tax any professional's resources. Fortunately, a service exists which assembles, categorizes, and abstracts sleep research from the varieties of professional journals in which it is published. *Sleep Reviews* and *Sleep Bulletin* are published monthly by the Brain Information Service/Brain Research Institute, University of California, Los Angeles. *Sleep Reviews* publishes abstracts of significant studies and reviews by prominent researchers. *Sleep Bulletin* provides a bibliographic listing of all articles published since the previous edition.

Sleep Research is an annual which contains the contents of the *Sleep Reviews* and *Sleep Bulletin* and abstracts of papers presented at the meetings of the Association for the Psychophysiological Study of Sleep.

OTHER HELPFUL BOOKS FOR THE PERSON WITH DISTURBED SLEEP

Sleep problems, of course, can be related to a variety of causes. For that reason, we included Chapter 9: "Looking Closely and Planning Wisely." An encyclopedia would be required to include solutions to each and every condition contributing to everyone's sleep problems. More important, it is probably more productive for you to learn problem-solving skills. The essence of behavioral self-management is that you learn to analyze and solve your own life problems so that you take charge of problems that formerly victimized you.

Listed here are some additional resource materials you may find useful in finding solutions to factors contributing to your sleep problem. Remember, it's only by experimenting and refining that enduring solutions will be found.

ADDITIONAL RELAXATION METHODS

Benson, H., *The relaxation response.* New York: Morrow, 1975. Provides a comprehensive discussion of the importance of relaxing and gives instructions in meditation and yoga.

Friedman, M. A., and R. Rosenmenn, *Type A behavior and your heart.* New York: Knopf, 1974. (Fawcett paperback). Discusses the general problem of a stressful life style and its effects on your cardiovascular disease, the top-ranked cause of death.

Rosen, G. R., *Don't be afraid.* Englewood Cliffs, N.J.: Prentice-Hall, 1976. In the context of teaching the reader to overcome fears and phobias, Rosen gives detailed instructions in Progressive Relaxation.

Walker, C. E., *Learn to relax: 13 ways to reduce tension.* Englewood Cliffs, N.J.: Prentice-Hall, 1975. A potpourri of tension-reduction strategies.

TALKING TO YOURSELF IN MORE POSITIVE WAYS

ELLIS, A., *Reason and emotion in psychotherapy.* New York: Stuart, 1962, and ELLIS, A., *A guide to rational living.* Hollywood: Wilshire, 1962. Two basic texts from a therapist who originated Rational-Emotive Therapy, designed to help people by teaching them to examine their thought processes and think in healthier ways.

LAZARUS, A., and A. FAY, *I can if I want to.* New York: Morrow, 1975. Helps the reader to identify self-defeating beliefs and suggests specific actions for challenging and changing these beliefs.

WHEELIS, A., *How people change.* New York: Harper and Row, 1973. A practising psychologist discusses how to rearrange one's life style and to think along more positive lines.

EXPANDING YOUR IMAGINATION

These books are delightful presentations of ways to increase your imaginative powers and enjoy your fantasies. These skills are important both in problem-solving and in learning mental relaxation.

DEMILLE, R., *Put your mother on the ceiling: Children's imagination games.* New York: Waker, 1967.

LEWIS, W. R., and H. S. STREITFELD, *Growth games.* New York: Harcourt, Brace, Jovanovitch, 1971. Suggestions on meditation, concentration, fantasy trips, dreams, and the like.

MCKIM, R. N., *Experiences in visual thinking.* Monterey, Cal.: Brooks-Cole, 1972.

EXERCISE

In addition to improving your general health, exercise is also useful to help people relax and to meditate. The Coopers provide a sound program of exercise for the person who is starting out cold. We recommend that you be patient with yourself and increase your exercise gradually.

COOPER, K. N., *Aerobics.* New York: Evans, 1968. (Bantam paperback)

COOPER, M. N., and K. H. COOPER, *Aerobics for Women.* New York: Evans, 1972. (Bantam paperback)

TIME MANAGEMENT

LAKEIN, A., *How to get control of your time and your life.* New York: Wyden, 1973. (Signet paperback) Improper time management can also increase stress. Conversely, learning to plan and use your time well will not only reduce stress but also give you time to do those enjoyable and pleasant activities.

ALCOHOL

MILLER, W. R., and R. F. MUÑOZ, *How to control your drinking.* Englewood Cliffs, N.J.: Prentice-Hall, 1976. If, as a result of your sleep problem, you feel that you may be drinking too much, this book (also part of the *Self-Management in Psychology* series) will help you to examine your drinking problem and to manage it without stopping completely.

EATING AND NUTRITION

Food may influence our sleep in some important ways. Keyes and Kirschmann provide comprehensive overviews of recent findings in nutrition and health, methods for determining personal nutritional intake, and suggestions for achieving a balanced diet. Changing food patterns, of course, often requires more than information. Jeffrey and Katz present a self-management approach to personal regulation of eating habits.

Crisp, A.N., and E. Stonehill, *Sleep, nutrition, and mood.* New York: Wiley, 1976. A technical overview of studies on the relationship among these three important parts of our lives.

Jeffrey, D. B., and R. Katz, *Take it off and keep it off: A behavioral program for weight loss and healthy living.* Englewood Cliffs, N.J.: Prentice-Hall, 1977.

Keyes, K., *Loving your body.* Berkeley, Cal.: Living Love Center, 1974.

Kirschmann, J. D., *Nutrition almanac.* New York: McGraw-Hill, 1975.

SOCIAL SKILLS

The inability to act assertively may be causing stress; learning good social skills can take you a long way in reducing tension and in removing sources of tension.

Alberti, R. E., and M. L. Emmons, *Your perfect right.* San Luis Obispo, Cal.: Impact, 1974.

Bower, S. A., and G. H. Bower, *Asserting yourself.* Menlo Park, Cal.: Addison-Wesley, 1976.

Informal Listing of Sleep Disorders Centers

Sleep Disorders Center
Baylor College of Medicine
Houston, Texas 77025
Director: Ismet Karacan, M.D.

Sleep-Wake Disorders Unit
Montefiore Hospital and Medical Center
111 E. 210th Street
Bronx, New York 10467
Director: Elliot Weitzman, M.D.

Sleep Clinic
Dartmouth Medical School
Hanover, New Hampshire 03755
Director: Peter Hauri, Ph.D.

Sleep Disorders Evaluation Center
Ohio State University College of Medicine
473 West 12th Avenue
Columbus, Ohio 43210
Director: Helmut Schmidt, M.D.

Southern California Center for Sleep Disorders
1260 Fifteenth Street, Suite 1402
Santa Monica, CA 90404
Director: John Beck, M.D.

Sleep Disorders Center
Stanford University Medical Center
Stanford, CA 94305
Director: William C. Dement, M.D. Ph.D

Sleep Physiology Laboratory
Veterans Administration Hospital
921 N. E. 13th Street
Oklahoma City, Oklahoma 73104
Director: William R. Orr, Ph.D.

Sleep Disorders Center
University of Arkansas
4301 W. Markham
Little Rock, Arkansas 72201
Director: Edgar Lucas, Ph.D.

Sleep Laboratory
Veterans Administration Hospital
3200 Vine Street
Cincinnati, Ohio 45220
Director: Milton Kramer, M.D.

Sleep Evaluation Center
University of Pittsburgh
Pittsburgh, Pennsylvania .5621
Director: David Kupfer, M.D.

Sleep Disorders Center
Hôpital du Sacre-Coeur
5400 ouest, Boul. Gouin
Montreal, Quebec, Canada H4J 1C5
Director: Jacques Montplaisir, M.D.

Sleep Disorders Center
Baptist Memorial Hospital
899 Madison Avenue
Memphis, Tennessee 38146
Director: Helio Lemmi, M.D.

Sleep Disorders Clinic
Department of Psychiatry
Veterans Administration Hospital
3350 La Jolla Village Drive
San Diego, CA 92161
Director: Daniel F. Kripke, M.D.

Sleep Clinic
Peter Bent Brigham Hospital and New Center of Psychotherapies
721 Huntington Avenue
Boston, Massachusetts 02115
Director: Quentin Regestein, M.D.

OTHER CONTACTS THAT MAY BE HELPFUL

Michael Anch, Ph.D.
John Remmers, M.D.
Department of Medicine
Pulmonary Section
University of Texas Medical Branch
Galveston, Texas 77550

Vincenzo Castaldo, M.D.
Department of Psychiatry
Albany Medical College of Union University
Albany, New York 12208

Augustin de la Fena, Ph.D.
Sleep Facility
Clinical Psychophysiology Lab
Audie Murphy Memorial Veterans Administration Hospital and
University of Texas Medical School
San Antonio, Texas 78284

John W. Goethe, M.D.
Department of Psychiatry
Tulane University
School of Medicine
New Orleans, Louisiana 70112

James Minard, Ph.D.
Department of Psychiatry and Mental Health Science
Department of Pediatrics
College of Medicine & Dentistry of New Jersey
100 Bergen Street
Newark, New Jersey 01703

Harvey Moldofsky, M.D.
Clarke Institute of Psychiatry
250 College Street
Toronto 2B, Ontario
Canada

Vernon Pegram, Ph.D.
Neurosciences, Box 190
University of Alabama
University Station
Birmingham, Alabama 35294

Marvin A. Sackner, M.D.
Martin Cohen, M.D.
Mount Sinai Medical Center
4300 Alton Road
Miami Beach, Florida 33140

This list was supplied courtesy of the American Association of Sleep Disorders Centers.

Give Us Your Reactions

We approached this book with two objectives in mind. We wanted to provide a self-help book for persons bothered by troubled sleep and a manual for clinicians to use in working with clients bothered by insomnia. We believe in the procedures presented. They have been evaluated experimentally in our own research. We also felt it important to ask persons with sleeping problems to read this book, try the procedures, and give us feedback about its utility. Each time we have tested the procedures or the book, we have learned more and developed our procedures further.

But our work, in many ways, is unfinished. It's important to us to continue learning and perfecting the procedures presented so that more and more persons can be helped. *Your reactions are especially important to us.* We want to know what you think about the book and the strategies. We would deeply appreciate it if you could take a few minutes, jot down some reactions to the questions, and mail the questionnaire to us. You may not want to tear a page out of this book; feel free to use another form or simply record your reactions in a letter and also to respond anonymously if you prefer. Most important, don't hesitate to give us your negative as well as your positive reactions. We often learn quite a bit from our mistakes. Write to us also if you have specific questions or are wanting more specific referral information.

Thomas J. Coates, Ph.D.
Carl E. Thoresen, Ph.D.
Center for Educational Research
at Stanford
Stanford University
Stanford, California 94305

I read this book ____ to help me with a personal sleep problem
____ to learn more about using these procedures in my professional practice

I am ____

(occupation)

Age ________ Sex ______

Description of personal (or clients') sleep problem (include type of insomnia, duration of the problem, how often the problem is experienced).

Regarding the procedures for learning to sleep better without drugs:

1. I found the following strategies most helpful in improving my (or my client's) sleep:

2. I found the following strategies least helpful in improving my (or my client's) sleep:

3. I have noticed the following changes in my (or my client's) sleep:

Regarding the presentation and format of the book:

1. The features I liked best about *How to Sleep Better* are:

2. The features I liked least about *How to Sleep Better* are:

3. I would make the following specific reccomendations for changing the book:

Thank you for your time.

Subject Index

Name Index